Twelve things which have been hidden

Vitamin

D1386277

a temple of trivia lists
and curious words

Vitamin

by
Roddy Lumsden

CHAMBERS

CHAMBERS

An imprint of Chambers Harrap Publishers Ltd
7 Hopetoun Crescent
Edinburgh
EH7 4AY

www.chambers.co.uk

First published by Chambers Harrap Publishers Ltd 2004

© Roddy Lumsden 2004

All rights reserved. No part of this publication may be reproduced, stored in a
retrieval system or transmitted by any means, electronic, mechanical, photocopying
or otherwise, without the prior permission of the publisher.

We have made every effort to mark as such all words which we believe to be
trademarks. We should also like to make it clear that the presence of a word in this
book, whether marked or unmarked, in no way affects its legal status as a
trademark.

A CIP catalogue record for this book is available from the British Library.

ISBN 0550 10145 4

.

Editor: Hazel Norris
Managing Editor: Una McGovern
Prepress Controller: Kirsteen Wright
Prepress Manager: Sharon McTeir
Publishing Manager: Patrick White

Designed and typeset by Chambers Harrap Publishers Ltd, Edinburgh
Printed and bound in Great Britain by Clays Ltd, St Ives plc

for Mark Reed, good friend

ACKNOWLEDGEMENTS

I would like to thank the following people who have supplied ideas or content for lists used in *Vitamin Q*: Joanna Quinn, Andrew Jackson, Tim Wells, Paul May, John Stammers, Eric Lumsden, Marco Rossi, Hamish and Betty Lumsden, May and Dave McGregor. I wish to express my gratitude to all those who have written to me via the website, www.vitaminq.blogspot.com, with suggestions for minor additions to the project so far.

Many websites have proved invaluable, notably the All Music Guide (www.allmusic.com) which is an excellent resource, and, of course, the incomparable Google. Thanks to everyone who kindly gave their permission to reproduce material in this book, especially Teppo Pihlajamäki of www.teppo.tv/names. I would also like to thank all those sites and individuals who helped popularize the website, including Neil Gaiman, metafilter, *USA Today*, *The Guardian*, Web User, popbitch and Yahoo!

The book version of *Vitamin Q* has been hugely aided by the good-natured and extremely thorough editing of Hazel Norris at Chambers Harrap, to whom great thanks are due. Lastly, my sincere apologies to anyone I have bored with trivia or talk of *Vitamin Q* over the years. The boy can't help it.

INTRODUCTION

I started *Vitamin Q* as a website on a dull afternoon in August 2002. I recalled that the marriage of Elvis and Priscilla and the Battle of Culloden both lasted exactly eight minutes. I doubt either is true, but those facts clashed in my mind. I had thought of having a weblog for months; bored between the poetry readings from which I make a living, I wanted somewhere I could express myself on the web. Yet, I sensed trouble: as someone prone to splurging, and needing that element in my poems, I worried that my blog might be full of true confessions, and the poetry might dry up.

So it was lists. Puzzles, quizzes, lists, trivia, strange words. These have always been around me, from family quiz sessions, to teenage grappling with advanced cryptic crosswords, to quiz machine playing to fund my bohemian twenties, to hosting pub quiz nights, to puzzle writing for newspapers. At first, a handful of friends read the site each week as I added entries. Over time this grew and grew, thanks to the recommendations of those who had chanced on my little temple. *You should do a book version*, someone suggested.

There is much in this collection which does not appear on the site, and vice versa. The site is more personal, a touch more flippant, less concerned with facts. Here, we tried to get it right, ending up in bizarre conversations about giraffe spittle and the invention of Y-fronts.

I had long admired popular reference books of various sorts: lists books, 'strange but true' and statistical trivia. But I wanted a new approach, something which had a hip edge, a personal slant, a stab at offbeat humour, but which could also dip its toe into the shallows of lexicography. The result is *Vitamin Q* – 'stuff, but in a good way' as someone put it so succinctly.

Roddy Lumsden
London, May 2004

www.vitaminq.blogspot.com

AND AS FOR ME ...

Ten things you don't need to know about the author

1   He was born in St Andrews, Scotland, in May 1966 and now lives in Stoke Newington in North London; he has also lived in Edinburgh, Aberdeen and Bristol.

2   He is a puzzle writer and is one of Britain's leading younger poets; *Mischief Night: New & Selected Poems* is published by Bloodaxe Books.

3   He has given poetry readings all over the UK and also in Canada, the USA, Ireland, Sweden and the Philippines.

4   His happiest moment occurred while alone in a New York hotel room in January 2002.

5   His favourite musical artists include Wim Mertens, Kate Rusby, Michael Nyman, Stina Nordenstam, Microdisney, Robin Holcomb and the Durutti Column.

6   He is good at pinball, kissing, cooking, talking nonsense and not much else.

7   Both his parents have the uncommon surname Lumsden – that's how they met.

8   He has a triple crown, double-jointed fingers, eleven fingernails and he sleepwalks.

9   His favourite things are: *food*: Chinese • *colour*: dark green • *piece of music*: 'Children on the Hill' by Harold Budd • *drink*: Arctic Red beer • *place*: Fargo, ND

10   He has been described as 'childlike', doomed', 'seeing', 'magnetic', 'gentle', 'eccentric', 'brooding', 'hyperchromatic', 'likely to die young' and as looking like a 'camp bricklayer'.

CONTENTS

DIVINE INVENTION

Twenty-four things supposedly invented or developed by clergymen

1. the barocyclonometer
2. the written form of the Inuktitut language
3. the reaping machine
4. the percussion cap detonator for rifles
5. the rickshaw
6. bourbon
7. the pantograph
8. the knitting machine
9. Bayesian algorithms
10. the rain gauge
11. the Stirling engine
12. the corkscrew
13. the slide rule
14. the tobacco boat
15. the gutta percha golf ball
16. Father John's lung and throat tonic
17. the Gamble Radiated Telegraph
18. the induction coil
19. the Oliver Standard Visible Writer (an early typewriter)
20. the Eclipse windmill
21. the pyramidon organ stop
22. the stocking frame
23. Tweedledum and Tweedledee
24. the pedal radio

I HAVE NO GUN BUT I CAN SPIT

Ten bad-mannered creatures which spit

1 Some **walruses** spit jets of water into the sandy seabed in order to loosen clams and other shellfish.

2 **Spitting cobras** don't wait to bite. Instead, they send a spray of strong venom at their enemy.

3 **Llamas** spit at each other to enforce territorial boundaries.

4 **Dromedaries** and other camels do this too, but mostly to claim rights on food.

5 The tropical **velvet worm** (or walking worm) traps its insect or slug prey by spitting streams of a gluey substance – from a distance of up to 50cm/20in – which hardens, spreading over the victim like a net.

6 Many **cats** will spit as part of their limited but generally successful arsenal to frighten dogs and other predators. Animals such as ferrets will also act in this way.

7 The **archer fish** overcomes the mathematics of perspective and shoots a stream of water at insects above the surface.

8 The **spitting spider** coats its prey with poisonous spittle to overpower it.

9 **Flamingos** eat by supping mouthfuls of water, combing out the food and spitting out the residue.

10 The **swiftlet** uses its own saliva to help hold its nests together. These are the highly prized nests used in authentic bird's-nest soup.

MELONS, MANGOS, MORRIS MARINAS!

Sixteen strange spokes of the Aroma Wheel

1 Horsey
2 Artichoke
3 Dusty
4 Concrete
5 Tar
6 Skunk
7 Burnt Match
8 Wet Dog
9 Filter Pad
10 Wet Cardboard
11 Fishy
12 Soapy
13 Soy Sauce
14 Butterscotch
15 Burnt Toast
16 Sweaty

The Aroma Wheel, of which several variations exist, is used by wine experts to describe the smell of wine. The Wheel is divided into ten or twelve categories (fruity, woody, etc), each of which is sub-divided (eg citrus, berry) and sub-divided again into around 100 scents. These are some of the less likely ones.

WHEN HARE GOT SILLY

Alternatives to the Hare Krishna chant 'Call out Gouranga, be happy!'

Call out gooseberry, be pippy!
Call out goulash, be nippy!
Call out Good Hope, be capey!
Call out gourmet, be crêpey!
Call out Guggenheim, be preppy!
Call out Gutenberg, be typey!
Call out goosander, be flappy!
Call out goodnight, be sleepy!
Call out Goonhilly, be slopey!
Call out googly, be dippy!
Call out Goolagong, be Skippy!
Call out goosebumps, be creepy!
Call out Goombay, be weepy!
Call out guru, be hippy!
Call out Goodyear, be non-slippy!
Call out goujon, be strippy!
Call out gouache, be drippy!
Call out goo-goo, be nappy!
Call out Goodwood, be snappy!
Call out goudale, be sippy!
Call out Goodge Street, be shoppy!
Call out Gudmundsdottir, be stroppy!
Call out Goodman, be boppy!
Call out goober nut, be croppy!
Call out gourami, be guppy!
Call out ghoul, be duppy!
Call out Goofy, be puppy!
Call out Good Vibrations, be poppy!
Call out Goon Show, be loopy!
Call out Gujarat, be rupee!

FACE FURNITURE

A dozen nicknames for a moustache

1 lip tickler
2 soup strainer
3 'stache
4 lip spinach
5 cookie duster
6 muzzy
7 upper lip plumage
8 misplaced eyebrow
9 dot and dash
10 mouser
11 tash
12 face fungus

And a dozen types

1 the bandit
2 the Hitler
3 the Scouser
4 the handlebar
5 the Chaplin
6 the horseshoe
7 the Zapata
8 the Selleck
9 the pencil
10 the toothbrush
11 the bumfluff
12 the walrus

FISH OF AMERICA

Some unusually-named fish found in the seas, rivers and lakes of North America

sarcastic fringehead • burrito grunt

chilipepper • spiny lumpsucker

frecklebelly madtom • warmouth

quillback carpsucker • unicorn filefish

johnny darter • convict tang

fat snook • tinsel squirrelfish

saucereye porgy • white crappie

high-hat • ballyhoo • smooth dreamer

hornyhead chub • puddingwife

river redhorse • lovely hatchetfish

northern hog sucker • pugjaw wormfish

horned whiff • butter hamlet • mimic shiner

pumpkinseed • brown Irish lord

chocolatestriped squeaker • penpoint gunnel

slippery dick • javelin spookfish

decorated warbonnet • Simony's frostfish

windowpane • fluffy sculpin • spinycheek sleeper

hogchoker • shovelnose guitarfish

California sheephead • tiger musky

sailor's choice • monkeyface prickleback

My favourite 25 My Little Pony® names

1. Seawinkle
2. Trickles
3. Backstroke
4. Baby Gusty
5. Crumpet
6. Quackers
7. Skippety Doo
8. Slugger
9. Tipsy Tulip
10. Bonnie Bonnets
11. Tossles
12. Barnacle
13. Baby Graffiti
14. Puddles
15. Bunkie
16. Shovels
17. Baby Countdown
18. Shaggy
19. Dangles
20. Squirmy
21. Pinkie Pie
22. Pretty Beat
23. Bubblefish
24. Love Petal
25. Lucky, the Stallion

LOAD OF PONY

ONE MAN'S MEAT

Twenty foods I
hope never to taste

One man's meat is another man's muck. Strange foreign foods are not strange to those whose ancestors came up with the idea. I consider this as I knock back a plateful of the much maligned and misunderstood Scottish haggis (which, apparently, over 40% of Americans believe is a real creature.) OK, so it's a mulch of spiced innards and oats loaded into a sheep's stomach and boiled, but it's wonderful (and an aphrodisiac, probably!). Here, though, is a rundown of some dishes I won't be choosing from the world's great menu ...

20 Although nowadays usually made from chicken, ham and thin noodles, proper **bird's nest soup** uses the nests of cave swiftlets and is said to be an aphrodisiac and to lead to long life – the usual excuses for eating something disgustingly exotic. The seaweed nests are held together with a mushy substance made from a mix of super-thick bird saliva, fish spawn and plankton, which effectively becomes the soup stock.

19 Enjoyed in various cuisines, the **soft shell crab** is, to my mind, an abomination of a culinary idea. Hmm, this crab has a soft shell, so why don't we chow down on its stinking carapace as well? I don't think so. At least it doesn't have a tongue, though: in Newfoundland, deep-fried cod tongues are a common snack. And you thought Mars® bars were an odd thing to deep-fry? Mind you, my niece Mhairidh recently spotted a girl in a Scottish chip shop ordering a deep-fried Milkybar® (the sickly white chocolate) with chips and salt and brown sauce.

18 Though the Thais prefer their fish-flavoured condiment in bottled liquid form ('nam pla'), Malay cooking tends to use a product named **belachan** – blocks of dough made from salted shrimps. Though it adds great flavour to food, the blocks smell so pungent that they can clear a room in seconds and have to be kept in airtight containers. Salty condiments made from crustaceans and fish such as anchovies have been used since ancient times: anyone jetting off in a time machine to a Roman banquet would find many dishes over-laced with **liquamen**, a pungent fish sauce. These sauces are nutritionally very good for you – it has been suggested that a daily drink of a vitamin-enriched version might contain all the ingredients required to keep you healthy. Expect the nam pla diet book to hit the shops soon.

17 The eccentric English father and son scientists William and Frank Buckland both experimented with eating exotic dishes in an attempt to find new foods which could aid Victorian food shortages. Although they found kangaroo and hedgehog palatable, William declared that the only thing worse than mole meat was cooked **bluebottles**. It is claimed that he also ate the embalmed heart of King Louis XIV of France.

16 Ever wondered what that musky tang is in the air at markets in your local Chinatown? That's the **durian** – the fruit that 'tastes like Heaven and smells like Hell'. Banned on public transport in some parts of the Far East, the delicious fruit unfortunately smells like a sewer. Eating some is said to give you bowel breath for hours.

15 Take one **cuy**, defur and skin it, leaving on the head and legs. Remember, however, to remove from its skull the tiny earbone so admired by gamblers as a gaming token, or which may instead be swallowed with alcohol after the meal for good luck. Then split it, grill or deep-fry it and devour (soft, small bones and all.) Cuyes are known in English as guinea pigs. Meep meep.

14 I know! Why don't we take large amounts of fish egg gunk, turn it into a paste flavoured with lemon and garlic, make it look like strawberry ice cream and call it **taramasalata**!

13 Maybe tales of serial killers have put me off the idea even more, but any soup or stew made by long-term boiling of a whole head seems a debatable idea. In Scotland, we used to do 'powsowdie' (literally 'scalp-broth'), a sheep-brain stew. In the West Indies, **goat's head soup** is still popular and goes by the wonderful name of 'mannish water'.

12 **Akutuq**, sometimes called 'Eskimo ice cream', is a treat enjoyed by the Native American peoples of Alaska. It takes a long time to prepare and is made from caribou fat and marrow, seal oil, snow and berries. It is whipped (women used to hold singing parties while doing so) for an hour or more until it is light and creamy.

11 In Tibet and Mongolia, a tea is sometimes drunk that's made from heavily salted, rancid mare or **yak's milk**. Yak's milk is pink, of course, due to a taint of blood. Except it isn't pink – that's just a rancid old myth.

10 They taste a bit like chicken (what doesn't?). They taste like sweet fresh cream. They taste a bit like prawns. They taste like scrambled eggs. Mmm, what are they and can I have some now? They're the larvae of the ghost moth, also known as **witchetty grubs**. Actually, I'll take a lifelong raincheck on these Aussie overgrown maggots.

9 What to do with a honking great half-fish/half-monster full of bones and tasting of silt? How about **jellied eels** – a speciality of London's East End. Anything that has to be masked with a layer of slime perhaps made from calves' hooves, and served with various pungent sauces, is probably fairly rank to begin with.

8 'L'Enfer, c'est les Autres', they say. But Hell is also other people's offal. I'll happily tuck into liver and onions, but watching Turks sup up a plateful of kidneys or south-east Asians tucking into blood and entrails stew – well, no thanks. And may I never have to nibble on the humble **andouillette**, a French sausage reputedly smelling strongly of faeces, which is made from pig intestines.

7 As with the oyster, the food of the poor often, in time, becomes that of the rich. A rustic Italian stew called **cibreo** is another good example. Using those bits of a chicken most of us don't want to sample, namely the testicles and combs of the cockerel, it has become an unlikely delicacy. And while we're on the subject of testicle eating (orchiophagy, to give it a posh name), why all the coy euphemisms – 'calf fry', 'lamb stones' and 'mountain oysters'?

6 You may have heard of **kopi luwak**, the world's most expensive coffee. Gourmet delicacy or money-stripping con, you decide. The luwak is an Indonesian palm civet, a mammal which feeds on the fruit surrounding the coffee bean. The half-fermented beans are harvested from their droppings and are sold for up to £1,000 per kilo. Just a cup of Maxwell House® for me please, Mrs Miggins.

5 Though a fabulous cuisine blending south-east Asian and Spanish recipes, some Filipino food can seem odd to the Westerner. Everything is sweeter – a lasagne sauce will taste pretty much like custard, bread like cake. But the 'scare the tourist' food in Manila is the **balut** – an incubated duck egg containing a half-formed chick, which is boiled and eaten with salt. The true balut experience is not complete unless you feel the beak catch momentarily in your throat!

4 **Casu marzu** is a Sardinian pecorino cheese which has now been banned by the Italian authorities. It is livid with maggots. Farmers claim these are just oversized bacteria, but the cheese has been ripened outdoors uncovered and, in truth, flies have been laying their eggs all over it. Inevitably, it is considered an aphrodisiac. Some slightly squeamish cheese lovers wrap the casu in an airtight bag and wait for the noise of wriggling, hatching and attempts at flight to stop, then enjoy the foul curd.

3 The proper way of preparing **escargots** (snails) for cooking is to starve them for a week, or perhaps feed them only herbs to give them flavour. They should be kept in wooden boxes to help dry them out. They are then covered in salt, at which point they begin disgorging and foaming as all their inner juices leak out. They are then cleaned, their pancreases are removed and they are scalded and boiled.

2 Fancy some cucumber? Not if it's the brown, cone-like **sea cucumber**, known also as 'bêche de mer' or 'trepang'. A relation of the sea urchin, it is said to have a bitter taste and a rubbery, gelatinous consistency. Sour, slimy starfish with fries and a shake, anyone?

1 A common street food in Cambodia, **deep-fried tarantulas** must be the dish I most hope I never have to try. The legs are crunchy and fibrous, the head contains soft white meat and the abdomen is filled with a cooked brown mush consisting of innards and excrement. Bon appetit!

FAR FETCHED

Non-existent things which people who are 'new to the job' are sent to fetch in a so-called 'fool's errand'

1 sky hooks

2 a 'long stand'

3 a bucket of steam

4 pigeon's milk

5 sparks for the fire

6 the bubble for a spirit level

7 a glass hammer

8 tartan paint

9 a Second Aid kit

10 a beeline

11 a left-handed spoon

12 a hard punch

13 snake oil

14 a compass wrench

15 white ink

16 a length of shoreline

17 dehydrated water

18 a packet of 10mm holes

19 an inflatable dart board

20 elbow grease

MOVING IN MYSTERIOUS WAYS

The Bristol Stool Form Scale

Type 1 separate hard lumps, like nuts

Type 2 sausage-shaped but lumpy

Type 3 like a sausage or snake, but with cracks on the surface

Type 4 like a sausage or snake, smooth and soft

Type 5 soft blobs with clear-cut edges

Type 6 fluffy pieces with ragged edges, a mushy stool

Type 7 watery, no solid pieces

This scale describing the various genres of human faeces was developed in the 90s at Bristol Royal Infirmary to aid diagnosis in patients with bowel problems.

Twelve professions in which numbers are believed to be steadily declining in the USA

1 typists

2 railroad workers

3 fishermen

4 telephone operators

5 farm workers

6 oil drillers

7 milkmen

8 elevator operators

9 millwrights

10 textile workers

11 proofreaders

12 dressmakers

LAST ORDERS

FEATHERS FLYING

Some old Scots names for birds (according to Alexander Warrack's *The Scots Dialect Dictionary* of 1911)

ailsa-cock (puffin)
allanhawk (Richardson's skua) • bagaty (sea owl)
basket-hinger (gold-crested wren) • birritie (willow warbler)
bitterbank (sand martin) • bog-bumper (bittern)
bonnivochil (Great Northern diver) • bubbly-jock (turkey)
buttermilk-gled (falcon) • cheepart (meadow pipit)
corny-skraugh (landrail) • feltie (mistle-thrush)
fuffit (long-tailed titmouse) • gekgo (jackdaw) • goyler (Arctic gull)
guck (cuckoo) • gutter-teetan (rock pipit)
half-web (red-necked phalarope) • heather-peep (sandpiper)
heaven's hen (lark) • hell-jay (razorbill) • hill-linty (twite)
horse-cock (snipe) • huddy (carrion crow)
imber (Great Northern diver) • jenny-cut-throat (whitethroat)
joctibeet (wheatear) • killieleepsie (common sandpiper)
kitty-needy (sandpiper) • lair-igigh (green woodpecker)
little-pickle (little tern) • luggie (horned owl)
mither-o'-the-mawkins (little grebe) • monthly bird (fieldfare)
muffie wren (willow warbler) • Norawa'-wifie (little auk)
oat-fowl (snow bunting) • oven-builder (willow warbler)
pickie-burnet (black-headed gull)
potterton-hen (black-headed gull) • pyardie (magpie)
ruddock (robin) • sand-back (martin) • scarf (cormorant)
scouti-aulin (Arctic gull) • sea-pie (oystercatcher)
sinnie-fynnie (black guillemot) • skatie-goo (skua) • sleeper (dunlin)
sod (rock dove) • stane-gall (kestrel) • steenie-pouter (sandpiper)
strok-annet (sheldrake) • tammie-cheekie (puffin)
tom-thumb (willow warbler) • trumpie (skua) • waeg (kittiwake)
wallap (lapwing) • water-peggie (dipper) • whaap (curlew)
willie-whip-the-wind (kestrel) • witch-hag (swallow)
witherty-weep (plover)

IT COMES WITH THE JOB

Twenty-five nicknames for certain professions

1	psychiatrist	shrink
2	author	scribbler
3	electrician	sparky
4	police officer	cop
5	office worker	pen-pusher
6	carpenter	chippy
7	dancer	hoofer
8	flight attendant	trolley dolly
9	doctor	quack
10	boxer	pug
11	sailor	tar
12	journalist	hack
13	pharmacist	pill-pusher
14	detective	gumshoe
15	artist	dauber
16	judge	wig
17	actor	luvvie
18	prison officer	screw
19	taxi driver	cabbie
20	doorman	bouncer
21	scientist	boffin
22	bus conductor	clippie
23	soldier	squaddie
24	magistrate	beak
25	photographer	snapper

THE NIGHT BEFORE

Fifty of the many acts who have covered the Beatles' song 'Yesterday'

P P Arnold

Chet Atkins

Florence Ballard

The Band of the Irish Guards

The Bar-Kays

Count Basie

Dame Shirley Bassey

Acker Bilk

Cilla Black

Michael Bolton

Pat Boone

Boyz II Men

Ray Charles

Perry Como

Vic Damone

Placido Domingo

Val Doonican

En Vogue

Percy Faith

Marianne Faithfull

Jose Feliciano

Marvin Gaye

Mikey General

Bobby Goldsboro

Jan and Dean

Tom Jones

Howard Keel

Patti LaBelle

James Last

Liberace

Dame Vera Lynn

Matt Monro

Nana Mouskouri

Willie Nelson

Lou Rawls

Marty Robbins

Smokey Robinson

Royal Philharmonic Orchestra

The Seekers

Frank Sinatra

Spirit

The Supremes

Carla Thomas

Sarah Vaughan

The Ventures

Wet Wet Wet

Andy Williams

Nancy Wilson

Klaus Wunderlich

Tammy Wynette

Since it was written by Paul McCartney in the mid 60s, 'Yesterday' has become one of the most covered songs ever. The song, at its early, guide vocal stage, was famously called 'Scrambled Eggs'.

EVER DECREASING CIRCLES

Twenty-nine clichés and common sayings used as sitcom and television comedy titles

1. only fools and horses
2. king of the hill
3. never mind the quality, feel the width
4. absolutely fabulous
5. not in front of the children
6. dream on
7. keeping up appearances
8. some mothers do 'ave 'em
9. happy days
10. love thy neighbour
11. diff'rent strokes
12. it ain't half hot, Mum
13. to the manor born
14. all in the family
15. last of the summer wine
16. Father knows best
17. are you being served?
18. one foot in the grave
19. in sickness and in health
20. open all hours
21. man about the house
22. bless this house
23. till death us do part
24. the good life
25. don't wait up
26. going straight
27. just good friends
28. mind your language
29. the thin blue line

FROM WHERE?

Some unusual US place names ✓

Intercourse, Alabama
Chicken, Alaska ✓
Surprise, Arizona ✓
Umpire, Arkansas
Bivalve, California
Parachute, Colorado ✓
Giants Neck, Connecticut
Hourglass, Delaware
Frostproof, Florida ✓
Thunderbolt, Georgia
Haiku, Hawaii
Fruitland, Idaho
Oblong, Illinois
Fickle, Indiana
Gravity, Iowa ✓
Buttermilk, Kansas ✓
Typo, Kentucky
Waterproof, Louisiana ✓
Bingo, Maine ✓
Boring, Maryland ✓
Marblehead, Massachusetts
Pigeon, Michigan ✓
Savage, Minnesota
Chunky, Mississippi
Enough, Missouri ✓
Divide, Montana
Valentine, Nebraska

Jackpot, Nevada
Bungy, New Hampshire
Cheesequake, New Jersey ✓
Tingle, New Mexico
Neversink, New York ✓
Toast, North Carolina ✓
Concrete, North Dakota ✓
Fly, Ohio
Bowlegs, Oklahoma ✓
Zigzag, Oregon
Panic, Pennsylvania ✓
Woonsocket, Rhode Island
Coward, South Carolina
Porcupine, South Dakota
Difficult, Tennessee
Oatmeal, Texas ✓
Mexican Hat, Utah
Bread Loaf, Vermont
Pocket, Virginia
Humptulips, Washington
Quick, West Virginia
Embarrass, Wisconsin ✓
Camel Hump, Wyoming ✓

That 'hubble bubble' recipe in full*

poison'd entrails
toad's swelt'red venom
fillet of a fenny snake
eye of newt
toe of frog
wool of bat
tongue of dog
adder's fork
blind-worm's sting
lizard's leg
owlet's wing
scale of dragon
tooth of wolf
witches' mummy
maw and gulf of the ravin'd salt-sea shark
root of hemlock
liver of blaspheming Jew
gall of goat
slips of yew
nose of Turk
Tartar's lips
finger of birth-strangled babe
     tiger's chaudron
       baboon's blood (for cooling)

WEIRD SISTERS CAFÉ

* When Hecate and three more witches arrive, they go on to add the blood of a bat, leopard's bane, the juice of a toad, the oil of an adder and three ounces of a red-haired wench. Later they also add the blood of a sow that had eaten her nine piglets and grease from a murderer's gibbet.

Source: *Macbeth* by Shakespeare (some ingredients only available in larger branches)

FOREVER ENGLAND
Some quaint and unusual English village names

Ainderby Quernhow	1	London Apprentice	19
Allerton Mauleverer	2	Lydiard Millicent	20
Appleby Parva	3	Maggots End	21
Ashford Carbonel	4	Mappowder	22
Askham Bryan	5	Martyr Worthy	23
Barton in the Beans	6	Melbury Osmond	24
Belchamp Walter	7	Nempnett Thrubwell	25
Blubberhouses	8	Nether Wallop	26
Bradfield Combust	9	New Invention	27
Compton Pauncefoot	10	Ottery St Mary	28
Cow Honeybourne	11	Queen Camel	29
Frisby on the Wreake	12	Ryme Intrinseca	30
Fulmodeston	13	St Giles in the Wood	31
Great Weeke	14	Upper Slaughter*	32
Gussage All Saints	15	Weston-under-Lizard	33
Haselbury Plucknett	16	Westward Ho!	34
Huish Champflower	17	Worth Matravers	35
Little Snoring	18	Zeal Monachorum	36

* Upper Slaughter, despite its name, was one of about 30 so-called 'Thankful Villages' – those from which a group of young men left to fight in World War I and to which all returned alive.

GROSERS

Odd character types from Captain Francis Grose's *Dictionary of the Vulgar Tongue*, compiled in the 1780s and specializing in the underground and criminal slang of London

amuser	a mugger who carried snuff to throw into a victim's eyes
ape leader	an 'old maid', a woman who had never had children; it was thought their punishment would be 'leading apes in Hell'
bed-maker	a woman who attended to the rooms of students at Cambridge University; it was said that they generally had pretty daughters 'who unmake the beds, as fast as they are made by their mothers'
bitch booby	a soldier's term for a country wench
bob tail	a lewd woman 'that plays with her tail' (still common in the phrase 'rag, tag and bobtail')
Bristol man	'the son of an Irish thief and a Welch whore'
buck fitch	a 'lecherous old fellow'
bull chin	a fat child
catch fart	a young footman who followed close behind his master
chaunter culls	those who were employed to write the popular ballads of the day
dark cully	a married man who visits his mistress at night
Durham man	a knock-kneed person said to grind mustard between his knees, Durham having been famed for its mustard
fire ship	a woman suffering from venereal disease
flaybottomist	a flogging schoolmaster (a pun on 'phlebotomist')

fly-by-night	a reproachful term for an old woman, hinting at witchcraft (the phrase now refers to someone who is unreliable)
frig pig	a man of little worth or importance
fubsey	a plump, healthy wench
fusty luggs	a bad-tempered and loose-moralled woman
hop-o-my-thumb	a person so small in stature that it was said that 'a pigeon, sitting on her shoulder, might pick a pea' from her backside
hot stomach	one who is always pawning their clothes for drink money
jingle brains	a 'wild, thoughtless, rattling fellow'
lank sleeve	a one-armed man
melting moment	one of a pair of overweight lovers 'in the amorous congress'
mutton monger	a man addicted to womanizing and sex
nightingale	a serviceman who shamefully 'sang' (cried out) while being whipped as a punishment; to prevent this further humiliation, the flogee would chew on a bullet
prigstar	a love-rival
queer rooster	an informer who feigns sleep in order to hear the confessions of criminals in prison cells
rantallion	a man whose scrotum is longer than his flaccid member
slamkin	a slovenly woman 'whose clothes seem hung on with a pitch-fork'
slush bucket	one overly-fond of greasy food

sneaking budge	a night burglar who steals clothes
sparrow mumbler	a participant in the rather cruel game played at fairs and wakes, whereby (with hands tied behind the back) you attempted to bite the head off a wing-clipped sparrow placed in an upturned hat
spoil pudding	a parson prone to very long sermons which lasted until the waiting lunch was spoiled
three-penny upright	a 'retailer of love', who for this sum would entertain a man while standing against a wall
Wigsby	a nickname given to a man sporting a wig
word grubber	one who is prone to using unusual or difficult words in everyday speech

FAIR TRADE

The seven who borrowed Tom Pearce's grey mare and went to Widecombe Fair in the famous song

Bill Brewer

Jan Stewer

Peter Gurney

Peter Davy

Daniel Whiddon

Harry Hawk

Old Uncle Tom Cobbleigh

OOH ER

The German prefix _er-_ can change a verb's meaning in interesting ways denoting, broadly, excess; the effect is somewhat poetic

brechen	to burst	erbrechen	to vomit
denken	to think	erdenken	to think up
drosseln	to reduce speed	erdrosseln	to choke to death
drücken	to squeeze	erdrücken	to crush to death
fahren	to travel	erfahren	to discover
finden	to find	erfinden	to invent
fassen	to grasp	erfassen	to overcome
forschen	to search	erforschen	to explore
hängen	to hang	erhängen	to hang until death
nennen	to name	ernennen	to nominate
schlagen	to hit	erschlagen	to smite
pressen	to press	erpressen	to blackmail
sticken	to embroider	ersticken	to smother
trinken	to drink	ertrinken	to drown
wecken	to wake	erwecken	to arouse or raise from the dead
weisen	to show	erweisen	to prove

WOULD LIKE TO MEET

What those terms used in dating ads really mean

youthful	bitter at the world
blue-eyed	self-obsessed
semi-retired	arch meddler
cheerful	small talk only
amicable	whistling misfit
confident	hellbound
affectionate	needy, grasping
genuine	in deep despair
sincere	tea towel dull
self-employed	church mouse, shorn of style
many interests	but none that come to mind
loves socializing	loud, booze-guzzling
enjoys adventures	career fantasist
down-to-earth	owner of a dishwater soul
vivacious	psychotic
no ties	has criminal record
bubbly	must be centre of attention
likes nights in	spoiling for an argument
shy	personality missing in action

sultry	wrath-nursing
gentle	bovine
easy-going	passive-aggressive
positive	stuck in the vicious circle
caring	domineering
loves salsa dancing	sheepishly faddish
loving	broody
outgoing	unfathomable lusts
sporty	lacking a sense of self
own home	neighbours say he was a loner
sophisticated	dreary and middle-class
for good times	for an extramarital affair
must be tall	hi, I'm superficial
solvent	misanthropic workaholic
curvy	egglike
impulsive	mercurial, weepy
likes cinema	easily bored, escapist
slim/fit	gangly/balding
home-loving	couch potato
charming	predatory
witty	can parrot comedy catchphrases
literate	wannabe know-all
distinguished	ancient and bonkers

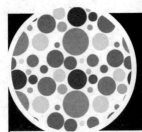

APPLE HAMS

Sixty actors born in New York City

Alan Alda	Ben Gazzara
Woody Allen	Sarah Michelle Gellar
June Allyson	Whoopi Goldberg
Rosanna Arquette	Melanie Griffith
Lauren Bacall	Fred Gwynne
Anne Bancroft	Rita Hayworth
Ellen Barkin	Danny Kaye
Angela Bassett	Harvey Keitel
Bonnie Bedelia	Burt Lancaster
Humphrey Bogart	Jennifer Lopez
Clara Bow	Lee Marvin
Matthew Broderick	Walter Matthau
Adrien Brody	Andrew McCarthy
Mel Brooks	Viggo Mortensen
Steve Buscemi	Carroll O'Connor
James Caan	Al Pacino
James Cagney	Anthony Perkins
John Carradine	Christopher Reeve
John Cassavetes	Mickey Rooney
Lee J Cobb	Susan Sarandon
Tony Curtis	George Segal
Robert De Niro	Brooke Shields
Vin Diesel	Christian Slater
Robert Downey, Jnr	Sylvester Stallone
Richard Dreyfuss	Barbara Stanwyck
David Duchovny	Barbra Streisand
Emilio Estevez	Gene Tierney
Douglas Fairbanks, Jnr	Sigourney Weaver
Peter Falk	Tuesday Weld
Jane Fonda	Mae West

BEDSIDE MANNERS

Thirty-two medical names for various ailments and body parts

1. epistaxis (nosebleed)
2. niphablepsia (snow blindness)
3. syncope (fainting)
4. paronychia (whitlow)
5. candidiasis (thrush)
6. hallux (the big toe)
7. allergic rhinitis (hay fever)
8. cholelithiasis (gallstones)
9. pityriasis capitis (dandruff)
10. genu valgum (knock knees)
11. genu varum (bow legs)
12. mammary ptosis (breast sag)
13. tympanum (eardrum)
14. comedo (blackhead)
15. paroniria (morbid dreaming)
16. epidemic parotitis (mumps)
17. external humeral epicondylitis (tennis elbow)
18. nocturnal enuresis (bed wetting)
19. encopresis (involuntary soiling)
20. naevus (birthmark or mole)
21. prepatellar bursitis (housemaid's knee)
22. talipes (club foot)
23. dyspepsia (indigestion)
24. lentigo (freckles or liver spots)
25. varicella (chicken pox)
26. amblyopia (lazy eye)
27. urticaria (nettle rash)
28. tinea pedis (athlete's foot)
29. pertussis (whooping cough)
30. ptosis (eyelid droop)
31. onchocerciasis (river blindness)
32. striae atrophica (stretch marks)

BEASTLY BUSINESS

In 1607, the heyday of Shakespeare and Galileo, a clergyman named Edward Topsell published his natural history tome *The Historie of Foure-Footed Beasts*. This curious and fascinating book shows us the vague knowledge of the animal world in the early 17th century.

Topsell was not a naturalist – much of his information and illustrations came from the work of a 16th-century Swiss writer, Konrad von Gessner – and was over-reliant on classical sources. There is little distinction between fabulous animals and real, exotic ones from far-off lands, while even familiar creatures are described as having some outlandish characteristics. Here is a small selection of highlights ...

Topsell shows us a picture of a **Gorgon** ('a strange Lybian Beast'). It appears to be an armour-plated pig with a bovine face and a long mane. When threatened, we are told, the Gorgon blows up its mane and, having ingested poisonous plants, it spews forth a venomous breath which endangers all in its path.

Of the **Manticore**, Topsell seems unsure, calling it a 'beast or rather monster' which lives among the Indians. He depicts it as a lithe, spiny-tailed lion with a man's head and several rows of teeth. Its voice is like that of a small trumpet. The only way to tame one is to catch it as a youngster and bruise its back end so badly as to stop the deadly scorpion tail developing.

Topsell's eerie drawing of the **Lamia** shows it to be like a plated big cat with a woman's head and breasts, lion's front paws, hooves at the back and male genitals. He tells us that the Lamia could remove and replace its eyes.

Topsell shared Gessner's view that **dragons** might be real. With large lizards and komodo dragons in mind, they may have been right. But they still believed in the dragon of myth, though both reported that dragons and man did in some places live in harmony. Topsell tells us that dragons are particularly fond of eating lettuce, but avoid apples. If this makes them all seem meek, it should be added that he believed some were prone to fire-starting and that another of their ruses was to hide in trees and to leap down on and strangle elephants. A century later, since no one had discovered a specimen despite the great rewards offered, the belief in dragons died out among naturalists.

Of the **Cockatrice** (or Basilisk), we are told that this fearsome serpent (which 'goeth halfe upright') is born when, towards the end of its life, a cockerel lays a sort of egg, composed from putrefied seed. This egg is nursed by a snake or toad and from it emerges the Cockatrice, with its distinctive crowned head and deadly venom. The only way to repel this beast is to carry with you a crowing cockerel. The only way to catch it is to set after it a weasel which has been amply fed with the herb rue as an antidote.

Among Topsell's odd beliefs about real creatures were that apes are scared of snails, that the **hippopotamus** was a breed of horse which feeds on crocodiles (in fact, a hippo is more likely to be eaten by one) and that elephants were sun-worshippers and would turn meek in the presence of a beautiful girl. **Panthers** had such sweet breath when they belched that it would attract prey to them. Cats were a danger to the human body and soul as they were often witches' familiars, although the powdered ashes of a black cat's head could, he noted, cure blindness. **Weasels**, he told us, gave birth through their ears, squirrels' hearts were packed with excrement, and lemmings tended to graze in the clouds. He suggested that when **reindeer** walked, their legs made a sound quite like 'cracking nuts'. He thought that foxes would cover themselves in red mud and lay still on their backs until a foolish bird landed on them. In classical belief, it was thought that life could be spontaneously generated from dirt, and Topsell believed mice were often born this way, as well as by normal breeding methods.

BIG BIRD

A list of some of the world's albatrosses

1   Gibson's albatross
2   Antipodean albatross
3   waved albatross
4   Salvin's albatross
5   northern royal albatross
6   Chatham albatross
7   Campbell albatross
8   black-footed albatross
9   Buller's albatross
10 short-tailed albatross
11 southern royal albatross
12 light-mantled albatross
13 Atlantic yellow-nosed albatross
14 wandering (or snowy) albatross
15 Laysan albatross
16 black-browed albatross
17 grey-headed albatross
18 shy albatross
19 Amsterdam albatross
20 Indian yellow-nosed albatross
21 sooty albatross
22 Tristan albatross
23 white-capped albatross
24 Pacific albatross

Twenty-five proverbs changed by one letter, but still true

1. A rolling scone gathers no moss
2. Bed news travels fast
3. Actions speak louder than worms
4. Love is bling
5. Flood is thicker than water
6. A biro in the hand is worth two in the bush
7. Better Sade than sorry
8. Don't wash your dirty liner in public
9. The Devil finds work for idle bands
10. Great minks think alike
11. A stitch in time saves Nina
12. If at first you don't succeed, cry again
13. A cat has nine lices
14. Death is the great reveller
15. Don't put all your eggs in one basset
16. A miss is as good as a male
17. History repents itself
18. Everything comes to he who wails
19. Honesty is the best police
20. It's no use crying over spilt milt
21. There's no place like Hove
22. Too many Coors® spoil the broth
23. A watched pet never boils
24. Where there's a will, there's a war
25. Look before you leak

MIME — THE GREAT HEALER

MID-LIFE CRISIS

Twenty-five reasons why I know I am getting older

1 It's been a decade since I read a novel

2 I own some wonderful, Chinese leather slip-on shoes, my first ever laceless pair

3 A near-extinct interest in the pop singles charts

4 Increasing intolerance to noise

5 Growing interest in the natural world and a faint, frightening notion that gardening might be fun

6 The age difference between myself and my girlfriends seems to be expanding into double figures

7 Number of pets – 0; number of pet hates – 100

8 I now eat things (eg carrots, olives) which I hated when I was a young thing

9 A notable lack of knowledge about current showbiz celebrities

10 My clothes no longer always smell of bars

11 My age has crept above my waist size

12 Only a glimpsing memory of my first kiss

13 I can't recall when I last wore training shoes

14 My parents now do some of the things which annoyed them about their parents when I was a child

15 I no longer own T-shirts with band names on them

16 My heroes are grey

17 The men who girls fancy look like children to me

18 A girlfriend recently called me 'Mum' by mistake

19 Aches and pains, and knowledge of their cures

20 A taste for good real ales

21	A growing cache of recipes of my own devising
22	Swelling pride for those fewer portions of my body I am still content with
23	Wearing a beard unless I have a good reason not to
24	A diminishing list of possible bedtime antics I am still curious to try
25	A sneaking suspicion that life isn't what it used to be

In 2002, against Bury in football's Worthington Cup, Fulham fielded a team of players from eleven different countries

England
Scotland
Wales
Northern Ireland
Latvia
Republic of Ireland
Japan
Jamaica
Cameroon
Morocco
Denmark

Only the English player was not a full internationally-capped player.

Fulham also had players from Portugal, France and Argentina on the bench.

WORLD CUP MATCH

DOUGH RE MI

The Best Songs About Pasta Album in the World ... Ever!

1	'Speedy Linguini'	Viv Cionetti
2	'Squeeze Me Macaroni'	Mr Bungle
3	'Spaghetti'	Tanya Donelly
4	'Lasagne'	Stockton's Wing
5	'Farfalle'	Domenico Modugno
6	'Ravioli'	Peter Pan's Pixie Players
7	'Oodles of Noodles'	Jimmy and Tommy Dorsey
8	'Macaroni Man'	The Three Degrees
9	'On Top of Spaghetti'	Little Richard
10	'Ska Tagliatelle'	L'ensemble Rayé
11	'Cottage Cheese and Noodles Polka'	The Casuals
12	'Eating Spaghetti at Pam's'	Peter Clemens
13	'Surrounded by Lasagne'	C H
14	'Fusilli'	Michael Prime
15	'Love and Nuts and Noodles'	Rosemary Clooney
16	'Spaghetti Betty'	Barron Knights
17	'Fettucini Manfredo'	Manfredo Fest
18	'Chianti, Spaghetti, Ravioli'	Frank Zander

All genuine, but I can't say I can hum many of these tunes. Best not to try to hum number 14, since it consists of a recording of a pot of pasta boiling on a gas cooker.

Some cloths and garments which take their names from places

SOFT CENTRES

astrakhan lamb's-wool cloth, originally from the Caspian port of that name

balaclava woollen head covering, presumably worn to keep out the chill in Balaklava in the Crimea

balmoral man's bonnet, after the royal palace in Scotland

basque this name has been used for various garments; originally, a pleated jacket worn by women of the Basque region of Spain

breton white brimmed hat, as worn by women in Bretagne (Brittany) in northern France

buckram the name of this stiff fabric may be connected to the Tartar city of Bukhara

cashmere fine goat's-wool cloth, from the Kashmir region of India/Pakistan

cravat neck-scarf, commonly worn by Croat soldiers and merchants

denim 'de Nîmes', from the town in France where the cloth supposedly originated

derby US name for the bowler hat, named after the city in middle England

dunstable straw hat, from the town in Bedfordshire, England

galligaskins baggy trews of yesteryear, which derive their name from a corruption of an old French word for 'Greek-style'

glengarry ribboned Scottish cap, named after the northern town

guernsey tight woollen jumper, after the Channel island

Homburg	felt hat, originally from the German town
Inverness	a long coat with a cape, suitable for the weather around the northern Scottish city
jean	a cotton named after the French word for Genoa in Italy (Gênes), giving its name to jeans
jersey	fine wool, or the garment made from it, from the Channel island more commonly associated with cows
jodhpurs	tight, thick trousers for horse-riding, taking their name from the Indian city of Jodhpur
kolinski	mink fur, from the Kola peninsula in northern Russia
madras	patterned silk fabric, from the Indian city (now called Chennai)
melton	thick cloth, originally made in Melton Mowbray, England
nankeen	dark cotton material, once a speciality of the Chinese city of Nanking
oxford	light cotton cloth, named after the English city
paisley	patterned fabric, based on designs from the rainy Scottish town
panama	hot-weather headwear, named after the Central American state despite the hats actually being from nearby Ecuador
polonaise	woman's frock and underskirt in the rustic Polish style, from the French word for 'Polish'
satin	this cloth's name may derive from the Chinese city of Zaitun
tuxedo	the American jacket for evening wear takes its name from Tuxedo Park, a resort in New York state popular with wealthy socialites in the early 20th century
ulster	long style of overcoat, first made in Northern Ireland

Some near misses ...

acton   stuffed military jacket, named from the Arabic for cotton, not the London suburb

cardigan   named after a lord of that name, not the place

nubia   woolly headscarf for women, from the Latin for cloud; nothing to do with the African area

nylon   the man-made fibre was said to be named after New York and London but this is probably not true, although its origin is disputed

raglan   this overcoat is named after a lord, rather than the Welsh village

tweed   from 'twilled' meaning woven, probably not from the Scottish river

The five rivers of Hell

STEAMY

Acheron

Cocytus

Lethe

Phlegethon

Styx

NECK AND NECK

Fifteen things you need to know about throats

1 *Genghis Blues* is a 1999 film about throat-singing in the small Russian province of Tuva. Throat-singing is also popular among Finns and the Inuit.

2 The throat chakra, in alternative medicine, is properly called the 'visuddha'.

3 Both Linda Lovelace and her former husband Chuck Traynor, best known for the controversial porn film *Deep Throat*, died in mid 2002.

4 Prayers for the health of your throat should be addressed principally to St Blaise, but can also be offered to the following saints: Andrew the Apostle, Ignatius of Antioch, Etheldreda, Godelieve, Lucy of Syracuse, Ludmilla or Swithbert.

5 Fierce Throat is an experimental choir from Melbourne, Australia.

6 Cut-Throat Jake was a bad pirate in TV's *Captain Pugwash*.

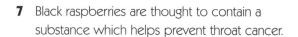

7 Black raspberries are thought to contain a substance which helps prevent throat cancer.

8 Only three people (plus the man himself, if still alive) are supposed to know the identity of 'Deep Throat', the informer in the Watergate scandal, though investigators now have it down to just a handful of possible suspects.

9 'Woman With Her Throat Cut' is one of Giacometti's most famous sculptures.

10 Operation RubyThroat is an attempt to promote the well-being of hummingbird species.

11 Both the word 'gules' (red in heraldry) and 'gargoyle' come from old words for 'throat'.

12 A Deep Throat cocktail usually contains vodka, Tia Maria® or Kahlúa® and whipped cream. Feech!

13 'Cut throat pinochle' is a card game.

14 The Anglo-Saxon name for the thistle meant 'boar's throat' due to the bristles.

15 Throat Coat® Tea is a herbal brand aimed at curing sore throats, including 'Teacher's Voice', a throat condition.

Ninety-eight ways of talking nonsense

apple-sauce
babble
balderdash
balls
baloney
bilge
blabber
blah
blarney
blather
blethers
bollocks
bombast
bop
bosh
bullshit
bunkum
cant
claptrap
cobblers
cock
codswallop
crap
crock
drivel
drool
eyewash
fiddle-faddle
flannel

flapdoodle
flimflam
fluff
flummery
folderol
froth
fudge
fustian
gabble
gammon
garbage
gas
gibberish
goop
guff
havers
hocus-pocus
hogwash
hokum
hooey

hoo-hah
horsefeathers
humbug
jaberwocky
jargon
jaw
jazz
jive
junk
keech
kidstakes
malarkey
mince
moonshine
mumbo-jumbo
mummery
nonsense
palaver
pants
piffle

pishery-pashery
pishogue
poppycock
prattle
punk
rhubarb
rigmarole
rot
rubbish
scat
skimble-skamble
slipslop
spew
strumming
stuff
taradiddle
tomfoolery
tommyrot
tosh
toss
trash
tripe
trumpery
twaddle
waffle
wind
windbaggery
wishwash
yackety-yack

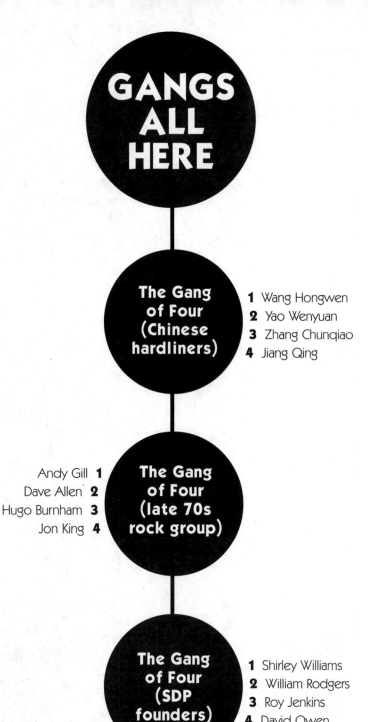

GANGS ALL HERE

The Gang of Four (Chinese hardliners)
1 Wang Hongwen
2 Yao Wenyuan
3 Zhang Chunqiao
4 Jiang Qing

Andy Gill 1
Dave Allen 2
Hugo Burnham 3
Jon King 4
The Gang of Four (late 70s rock group)

The Gang of Four (SDP founders)
1 Shirley Williams
2 William Rodgers
3 Roy Jenkins
4 David Owen

BARD OF CURD

Ten titles of poems by the 'Cheese Poet'

1
'Ode on the Mammoth Cheese'

2
'Oxford Cheese Ode'

3
'Fertile Lands and Mammoth Cheese'

4
'Ensilage'

5
'Prophecy of a Ten Ton Cheese'

6
'Dairy Ode'

7
'Father Ranney, the Cheese Pioneer'

8
'Lines Read at a Dairymen's Supper'

9
'Hints to Cheese Makers'

10
'Lines Read at a Dairymaids' Social, 1877'

The 'Cheese Poet' was one James McIntyre (1827–1906), a rival for William McGonagall as worst-ever Scottish poet. He lived in Canada from his teens, in an area known for its dairy farming, and found cheese a fitting subject for his odes.

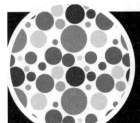

THE JAGS

Thistle — The List

1   Slender thistle

2   Musk thistle (Nodding thistle)

3   Brook thistle

4   Melancholy thistle

5   Cabbage thistle

6   Meadow Plume thistle

7   Dwarf thistle (Ground thistle)

8   Spear thistle

9   Creeping thistle (Way thistle)

10   Tuberous thistle

11   Carline thistle

12   Milk thistle (Marian thistle)

13   Woolly thistle (Scotch thistle)

14   Welted thistle (Field thistle)

15   Marsh thistle

16   Tuberous Plume thistle

17   Common Star thistle

18   Slender-Flowered thistle

19   Yellow Star thistle (St Barnaby's thistle)

20   Holy thistle (Blessed thistle)

21   Marsh Plume thistle

22   Meadow thistle

The sow thistle is a thistle in name only, and is not by any other name still a thistle.

A list of unusually-named human ailments and conditions

Epstein pearls
monkeypox
Adie's pupil
signe de Dance
croup
Gamna-Gandy nodules
beri-beri
Austin Flint's murmur
yaws
Ondine's curse
Siegrist spots
Shiraz dwarfism
ganglion cyst
Hutchinson's freckle
St Anthony's fire
pinta
Cabot ring
scabies

scrumpox
Shy-Drager syndrome
dartitis
stagnant loop syndrome
Malta fever
Milkman's fractures
shingles
silk glove sign
Bowditch staircase
infarct of Zahn
leprechaunism
farmer's skin
Howship's lacunae
scurvy
clay shoveller's fracture
gingivitis

FLAWS AND CRACKS

Terry's nails
Birbeck's granules
Hampton's hump
bamboo spine
Corrigan's pulse
Osgood-Schlatter disease
Irish's node
grocer's itch
Pancoast's tumour
cri du chat
Zumbusch's psoriasis
trench mouth
unhappy triad
Harrison's Groove
lupus
raccoon eyes
Roth's spot
Plummer's nail

Sister Mary Joseph nodule
Klumpke's palsy
impetigo
blue rubber bleb nevus syndrome
strabismus
Waldeyer's tonsillar ring
vitiligo
Blumer shelf
St Vitus's dance
valley fever
Beck's triad
vulvodynia
MacCallum's plaques
Zenker's diverticulum
stiff man syndrome
Fallot's tetralogy
cat-scratch disease

RIVER BEASTS

Twenty English rivers with creature names

1	Ant	**11**	Mite
2	Brock	**12**	Mole
3	Camel	**13**	Nanny
4	Char	**14**	Otter
5	Cocker	**15**	Ray
6	Crake	**16**	Roach
7	Crane	**17**	Sow
8	Deer	**18**	Swift
9	Dove	**19**	Tern
10	Lark	**20**	Wolf

Twelve songs that the Beatles let Ringo sing

1 'I Wanna Be Your Man'
2 'Octopus's Garden'
3 'What Goes On'
4 'Act Naturally'
5 'Yellow Submarine'
6 'With A Little Help From My Friends'
7 'If You've Got Trouble'
8 'Good Night'
9 'Honey Don't'
10 'Boys'
11 'Matchbox'
12 'Don't Pass Me By'

That's a whole album's worth! I wonder why it's never been ... no, I don't.

OLD NICKS

US presidential nicknames

George Washington
Sword of the Revolution • The Old Fox
Sage of Mount Vernon • Father of his Country

John Adams
Atlas of Independence • His Rotundity
Father of the American Navy

Thomas Jefferson
The Sage of Monticello • Long Tom

James Madison
Father of the Constitution • Jemmy

James Monroe
The Last Cocked Hat • The Era of Good Feeling President

John Quincy Adams
Old Man Eloquent • The Accidental President

Andrew Jackson
Old Hickory

Martin Van Buren
The Sage of Lindenwald • The Red Fox • Old Kinderhook
The Little Magician • King Martin the First

William Henry Harrison
Old Tippecanoe

John Tyler
His Accidency • Young Hickory

James K Polk
The People's Choice

Zachary Taylor
Old Rough and Ready

Millard Fillmore
The American Louis Philippe • His Accidency

Franklin Pierce
Handsome Frank

James Buchanan
The Sage of Wheatland • The Bachelor President • Old Buck

Abraham Lincoln
The Great Emancipator • Honest Abe • The Original Gorilla
The Tycoon • The Man of the People • Rail-splitter
The Ancient • The Illinois Baboon • Black Republican
The Sectional President • The Sage of Springfield

Andrew Johnson
The Tennessee Tailor • King Andy

Ulysses S Grant
Unconditional Surrender • United States
Hero of Appomattox • Useless

Rutherford B Hayes
Dark Horse • His Fraudulency

James A Garfield
The Preacher • The Martyr President

Chester Arthur
The Dude • His Accidency

Grover Cleveland
The Hangman of Buffalo • Uncle Jumbo • Big Steve
Grover the Good • The Pretender • Big Beefhead
The Perpetual Candidate • The Stuffed (or Dumb) Prophet

Benjamin Harrison
Little Ben • The Centennial President • Kid Gloves

William McKinley
The Napoleon of Protection • Wobbly Willie

Theodore Roosevelt
Bull Moose • Teddy • Trust Buster • The Rough Rider

William Howard Taft
Big Bill • Big Lub • Uncle Jumbo • Peaceful Bill

Woodrow Wilson
The Professor • Tommy • The Schoolmaster

Warren G Harding
Wobbly Warren

Calvin Coolidge
Silent Cal • Cautious Cal

Herbert Hoover
The Grand Old Man • The Chief

Franklin D Roosevelt
The Champ • That Man in the White House
A Traitor to his Class • The New Dealer

Harry S Truman
The New Missouri Compromise • High Tax Harry
The Man of Independence • The Haberdasher
Give 'Em Hell Harry

Dwight D Eisenhower
Ike • The Swedish Jew

John F Kennedy
Jack • JFK • John-John

Lyndon B Johnson
Landslide Lyndon • LBJ

Richard Nixon
Tricky Dick • Gloomy Gus

Gerald R Ford
Jerry • Mr Nice Guy • Jerry the Jerk

Jimmy Carter
Grits • The Grin • Hot Shot • The Peanut Farmer

Ronald Reagan
The Great Communicator • The Gipper
Dutch • The Teflon President

George Bush
Poppy

Bill Clinton
Slick Willie • The Comeback Kid • Bubba

George W Bush
Dubya • Shrub • Mini-Me • The Great
Pretender • Commander-in-Thief
Junior

THREE LAWS

Godwin's Law

'As a discussion grows longer, the probability of a comparison involving Nazis or Hitler approaches one.' This is the theory of one Mike Godwin; the 'law' originated in the jargon of the Usenet world, but is now applicable to any lengthy argument. The party dragging up the taboo subjects as a trump card automatically ends the argument on the losing side.

Murphy's Law

'If anything can go wrong, it will.' Attributed to Captain E Murphy of the Wright Field Aircraft Laboratory. Or is it engineer Ed Murphy of the Edwards Air Force Base, California? Already, a mist settles on the true derivation. Some claim the original saying was a slur on a sloppy technician: 'if there's a way to do it wrong, he'll find it', which is semantically quite different. Whatever, it is more likely that the attribution is due to that mildly pejorative sense of pithy, homespun logic which the Irish are said to treasure.

Sod's Law

There is no definite wording of Sod's Law. It is essentially a comic explanation of ironic misfortune. It maintains that a piece of bread and butter dropped will land butter side down; that the most inconvenient thing is the most likely to happen. Basically, in a moment of crisis, forces beyond your control, inanimate objects, the weather, etc, will join forces to make the crisis steeper. The difference between Murphy's Law and Sod's Law is quite subtle and can get a bit mathematical.

HEADS OF STATE

People and creatures on US state flags

California	bear
Delaware	ox, farmer, soldier
Florida	Native American Seminole woman
Idaho	elk's head, goddess, miner
Illinois	bald eagle
Iowa	another bald eagle
Kansas	horses, farmer, buffaloes, Native American hunters, oxen
Kentucky	pioneer, gentleman
Louisiana	pelican family
Maine	farmer, sailor, moose
Massachusetts	Native American man
Michigan	eagle, elk, moose, man
Missouri	three grizzly bears, bald eagle
Nebraska	blacksmith
New Jersey	two goddesses, horse's head
New York	two goddesses, bald eagle
North Dakota	bald eagle
Pennsylvania	horses, bald eagle
South Dakota	horses, cattle
Utah	bald eagle, bees in hive
Vermont	stag's head, cow
Virginia	Roman goddess Virtus, vanquished figure of Tyranny
Washington	George Washington
Wisconsin	badger, sailor, miner
Wyoming	bison, woman, farmer, miner

QUONTINENTAL

Some interesting French, German and Spanish Q words

1	quolibet	a gibe
2	quincaillière	a female ironmonger
3	quelquefois	sometimes
4	quoique	although
5	quadrillage	a grid
6	quignon	the end crust of a baguette
7	quittance	receipt
8	quatorzième	fourteenth
9	quinzaine	a fortnight (despite meaning a set of 15!)
10	quille	a bowling skittle

1	quengeln	to grizzle like a baby
2	quicklebendig	full of beans
3	Quatscherei	blethering
4	Quetschkommode	squeezebox
5	quietschvergnügt	merry, chirpy
6	Quanten	big feet or hooves
7	quieken	to squeal like a mouse
8	Quirl	an egg beater
9	Qualle	a jellyfish
10	Quaste	a tassel

1	quesera	a woman who makes or sells cheese
2	quiquiriquí	cock-a-doodle-doo
3	quemado	burnt woodland
4	quiebro	jinking
5	quitanieves	a snowplough
6	quebradura	hernia
7	quitasueño	night worries
8	quijada	jawbone
9	quebrantapiedras	saxifrage
10	quincalla	trinkets

The Wash is a large bay which separates Lincolnshire and Norfolk on the east coast of England. These are the somewhat poetically-named sands, sometimes submerged, which form part of it

Peter Black Sand **1**

Seal Sand **2**

Bulldog Sand **3**

Breast Sand **4**

Old South **5**

Mare Tail **6**

Gat Sand **7**

Toft Sand **8**

9 Roger Sand

10 Black Buoy Sand

11 Butterwick Low

12 Friskney Flats

13 Wainfleet Sand

14 Long Sand

15 The Scalp

WASHED UP

TOP SPOT TUSSLES

Long-term Number One hits, and the songs which finally knocked them off

1	'From Me to You'	'I Like It'
2	'Green Green Grass of Home'	'I'm a Believer'
3	'Hello Goodbye'	'The Ballad of Bonnie and Clyde'
4	'Sugar Sugar'	'Two Little Boys'
5	'In the Summertime'	'The Wonder of You'
6	'Bohemian Rhapsody'	'Mamma Mia'*
7	'Mull of Kintyre'	'Up Town Top Ranking'
8	'You're the One That I Want'	'Three Times a Lady'
9	'Summer Nights'	'Rat Trap'
10	'Two Tribes'	'Careless Whisper'
11	'(Everything I Do) I Do It For You'	'The Fly'
12	'Stay'	'Deeply Dippy'
13	'I Will Always Love You'	'No Limit'
14	'I'd Do Anything For Love (But I Won't Do That)'	'Mr Blobby'
15	'Love Is All Around'	'Saturday Night'
16	'Think Twice'	'Love Can Build a Bridge'
17	'Unchained Melody'	'Boom Boom Boom'
18	'Wannabe'	'Flava'
19	'Believe'	'To You I Belong'

* Thereby being replaced by a song title from its own lyric!

All these songs were at the top for seven weeks or more.

Fifteen-letter words in fairly common use

FIFTEEN TO ONE AND ALL

straightforward	**1**
appropriateness	**2**
electromagnetic	**3**
rationalization	**4**
dessertspoonful	**5**
undistinguished	**6**
entrepreneurial	**7**
decontamination	**8**
individualistic	**9**
professionalism	**10**
distinguishable	**11**
unsophisticated	**12**
notwithstanding	**13**
unsubstantiated	**14**
misapprehension	**15**
comprehensively	**16**
dissatisfaction	**17**
experimentation	**18**
gastroenteritis	**19**
unwholesomeness	**20**
confidentiality	**21**
physiotherapist	**22**
contemporaneous	**23**
condescendingly	**24**
disrespectfully	**25**
resourcefulness	**26**
heterosexuality	**27**
intellectualize	**28**

INFAMY! INFAMY!

The 'Carry On …!' films began in 1958 with the forgettable army farce *Carry On Sergeant* starring William Hartnell and a young Bob Monkhouse, and ended two decades later with the bawdy and embarrassing *Carry On Emmannuelle*. An early 90s attempt to revive the series with younger comic actors (*Carry on Columbus*) was not successful. The best of the 30 or so films – especially those made in the late 60s and early 70s – have become part of the fabric of British entertainment, with their naughty scripts, slapstick and hammy but loveable ensemble of character actors. The ten actors who starred in the most of these romping films are as follows:

1	Kenneth Williams	25	(typical character: camp and waspish zealot)
2	Joan Sims	24	(saucy, winking minx/nagging other half)
3	Charles Hawtrey	23	(bespectacled and other-worldly innocent)
4	Sid James	19	(guffawing, leather-faced, sex-mad anti-hero)
5	Kenneth Connor	17	(nervy, uptight or accident-prone Mr Average)
6	Peter Butterworth	16	(bumbling rustic/ageing comic sidekick)
7	Hattie Jacques	14	(fierce matron/silently lusting spinster)
8	Bernard Bresslaw	14	(gentle giant/randy everyman)
9	Jim Dale	11	(edgy, gauche but handsome young chappie)
10	Peter Gilmore	11	(dashing doctor/bloke next door)

Bubbling under: Patsy Rowlands (put-upon wife), Barbara Windsor (eye-rolling wench/tart with a heart) – both 9, Jack Douglas (stuttering, cowardly buffoon) – 8, Terry Scott (would-be man-about-town/blustering clown) – 7.

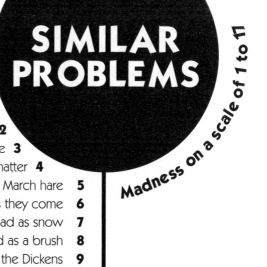

SIMILAR PROBLEMS

Madness on a scale of 1 to 11

mad as a fish **1**
mad as hops **2**
mad as a magpie **3**
mad as a hatter **4**
mad as a March hare **5**
mad as they come **6**
mad as snow **7**
mad as a brush **8**
mad as the Dickens **9**
mad as a pink balloon **10**
mad as honey **11**
mad as Napoleon **12**
mad as cheese **13**
mad as a skipload of squirrels **14**
mad as fudge **15**
mad as a wet hen **16**
mad as a box of frogs **17**

Note, this is 'mad' as in lunatic, not as in angry — the American 'mad as a hornet' or Australian 'mad as a cut snake' sense of anger.

Compare also
crazy as hell
crazy as a loon
crazy as a fox
crazy as a soup sandwich
crazy as a jaybird

SUPER TO MEET YOU

The real names of 35 comic superheroes

1	The Incredible Hulk	Bruce Banner
2	Black Canary	Dinah Lance
3	Daredevil	Matt Murdock
4	The Human Torch	Johnny Storm
5	Superman	Kal-El/Clark Kent
6	Robin/Nightwing	Dick Grayson
7	Robin (mark II)	Jason Todd
8	Robin (mark III)	Tim Drake
9	Green Lantern	Hal Jordan
10	Green Arrow	Oliver Queen
11	Batgirl/Oracle	Barbara Gordon
12	She-Hulk	Jennifer Walters
13	Son of Satan	Daimon Hellstrom
14	Mary Marvel	Mary Batson
15	The Atom	Ray Palmer
16	Captain Marvel	Billy Batson
17	Spidergirl	May Parker
18	The Ragman	Rory Regan

19	The Invisible Woman	Susan Storm-Richards
20	Captain America	Steve Rogers
21	Supergirl	Kara-El/Linda Danvers/Linda Lee
22	Gambit	Remy LeBeau
23	Isis	Andrea Thomas
24	Power Girl	Karen Starr
25	Mr Fantastic	Reed Richards
26	Spiderman	Peter Parker
27	Captain Action	Clive Arno
28	Batman	Bruce Wayne
29	Spectre	Jim Corrigan
30	Firestorm	Ronnie Raymond
31	Flash (mark I)	Jay Garrick
32	Flash (mark II)	Barry Allen
33	Swamp Thing	Dr Alec Holland
34	The Thing	Ben Grimm
35	Cyclops	Scott Summers

Ambiguity regarding Batman and Superman character names is due to multi-media versions, plot changes and birth names versus pseudonyms.

CRIME SCENES

The nine rooms on a Cluedo® board

Hall
Kitchen
Lounge
Ballroom
Conservatory
Billiard Room
Study
Library
Dining Room

SYRUP OF FIGS

Five rhyming phrases

1
Easy, peasy, lemon squeezy (meaning, I can do that, no problem)

2
Yum, yum, pig's bum (meaning, I love bacon)

3
Super dooper, Gary Cooper (meaning, that's fabulous or, conversely, you think you're fabulous, don't you?)

4
Oompah, oompah, stick it up your jumper (a long-lasting playground taunt)

5
Liar, liar, pants on fire (meaning, you're telling porkies)

THE LITTLE PEOPLE

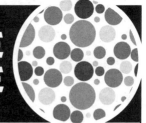

Thirty-three miniature subjects of nursery rhymes (as found in the *Oxford Dictionary of Nursery Rhymes*)

1	Little Betty Blue	18	Little King Pippin
2	Little Betty Pringle	19	Little Mary Ester
3	Little Betty Winkle	20	Little Miss Hetty Cote
4	Little Bo-peep	21	Little Miss Mopsey
5	Little Boy Blue	22	Little Miss Muffet
6	Little Brown Betty	23	Little Nancy Etticoat
7	Little Dickey Dilver	24	Little Peg a Ramsey
8	Little General Monk	25	Little Polly Flinders
9	Little Goody Tidy	26	Little Shon a Morgan
10	Little Jack Dandy-prat	27	Little Tammie Tyrie
11	Little Jack Horner	28	Little Tee-Wee
12	Little Jack Jingle	29	Little Tom Dandy
13	Little Jenny Flinders	30	Little Tom Tittlemouse
14	Little John Jiggy Jag	31	Little Tom Twig
15	Little Johnny Morgan	32	Little Tommy Tacket
16	Little Johnny Stutter	33	Little Tommy Tucker
17	Little King Boggers		

FRUITS OF THE FOREST

One hundred and eleven berries

lathberry
johnnyberry
winterberry
boysenberry
milkberry
wolfberry
hogberry
indigoberry
salmonberry
juniper berry
partridgeberry
snowberry
redberry
serendipity berry
waxberry
maleberry
dewberry
loganberry
bearberry
elderberry
guavaberry
stretchberry
peaberry
blaeberry
shadberry
Juneberry
cowberry
fenberry
wineberry
bayberry

crowberry
cheakyberry
foxberry
inkberry
silverberry
crakeberry
cloud berry
barberry
baneberry
hindberry
maidenberry
serviceberry
mangroveberry
teaberry
scaldberry
soapberry
sugarberry
crackerberry
gooseberry
youngberry
thimbleberry
pudding berry
twinberry
mooseberry
mulberry
raspberry
marlberry
hackberry
bunchberry
Rhineberry

turkey berry
roughfruit berry
punchberry
farkleberry
naseberry
goldenberry
buffaloberry
pokeberry
huckleberry
blackberry
gallberry
wonderberry
beautyberry
capberry
chokeberry
snakeberry
cockroach berry
Christmasberry
blueberry
canker berry
salal berry
limeberry
roebuck berry
seaberry
raccoon berry
globeberry
coral berry
Andes berry

tayberry
locustberry
cranberry
miracle berry
cakalaka berry
quinsyberry
flameberry
bilberry
whortleberry
deerberry
pigeonberry
pearlberry
squashberry
nannyberry
catberry
checkerberry
Worcesterberry
curlewberry
dogberry
strawberry
sheepberry
bristle berry
groundberry

**Some of these may not be
strictly botanical berries, but
all are genuine plants;
inevitably, some are names for
the same type of shrub.**

SUPPER'S READY

Twelve examples of pica (strange food cravings, especially during pregnancy)

1 ice cubes
2 large amounts of sweet or bitter fruit
3 cigarette ends and ash
4 coal
5 washing powder
6 peanut butter
7 pickles
8 clay or soil
9 strong cheese
10 gallons of ice cream
11 buckets of olives
12 wood, eg toothpicks or pencils

Pica differs from normal food cravings in that the feelings often derive from mineral deficiencies.

ALL YOU NEED

The Beatles' 'love' songs

1 'Hallelujah, I Love Her So'
2 'Love Me Do'
3 'PS I Love You'
4 'All My Loving'
5 'She Loves You'
6 'And I Love Her'
7 'Can't Buy Me Love'
8 'Words Of Love'
9 'You've Got To Hide Your Love Away'
10 'It's Only Love'
11 'Love You To'
12 'Lovely Rita'
13 'Step Inside Love'
14 'All You Need Is Love'
15 'Real Love'

FOLLYAGE

Forty-two unusual plant names

1 Paddy's river box
2 townhall clock
3 showy tidytips
4 old-fashioned baby's breath
5 Our Lady's bedstraw
6 grim-the-collier
7 hairy puccoon
8 kiss-her-in-the-buttery
9 ramping fumitory
10 divorce vine
11 naked boys
12 pony bee balm
13 cuckoo's meat
14 becky leaves
15 American wake robin
16 sauce alone
17 cuddle me
18 American beautyberry
19 woolly Dutchman's pipe
20 three-faces-under-a-hood
21 silver lace dusty miller
22 burry vervain
23 godfathers and godmothers
24 bastard toadflax
25 hooker's onion
26 water pumpy
27 beaver poison
28 smooth darling pea
29 sweet herb of Paraguay
30 Jack-go-to-bed-at-noon
31 Armenian yard-long cucumber
32 false goatsbeard
33 viper's bugloss
34 Adam's flannel
35 bachelor's buttons
36 wolf's peach
37 miltwaste
38 thorough-wax
39 cock-drunk
40 pellitory of the wall
41 cudbear
42 pigsqueak

CAREERS OF YESTERYEAR

Forty old-fashioned professions

acolyth
a minor church official

almoner
a medical adviser who aided the poor and the sick

beaver
a maker of felt or other thick cloth for hats

bosun
a ship's officer in charge of the crew and the rigging

bottom-knocker
an apprentice who helped make saggars (clay containers)

bummaree
a middleman seller at fish markets

cat's-meat man
one who roamed the streets selling pet food

caulker
a tradesman who ensured the hulls of boats were watertight

chandler
a dealer in oil and candles

cinder-wench
a scullery maid who was in charge of a house's fires

coistril
a groomer of horses

crossing sweeper
one who kept roads clean and dry for use by pedestrians

dripping-man
a dealer in solidified fat collected from roasted meat

famulus
an assistant to an expert in magic or arcane knowledge

ferreter
a manufacturer of silk ribbon and tape

jingler
a travelling horse-trader

kisser
a maker of cuisses (thigh armour)

lombard
a financier or moneylender

mercer
a merchant who specialized in fine cloth

mudlark
one who combed river edges for scrap

muggler
a farmhand who looked after pigs

muleteer
one who drove a group of mules

musketoon
an infantryman

navvy
a canal labourer

orange-girl
one who sold fruit and other refreshments in theatres

panegyrist
a bard who wrote and performed elaborate praise
poems and eulogies

pieman
a street-seller of penny pies containing mutton, beef or
apples

powder monkey
a boy carrying powder to the gunners on a warship

pure-picker
one who collected dog's excrement for use in leather tanning

scullion
a kitchen servant or odd-job boy

sempster
a needleworker

shragger
a labourer whose task was to keep trees trimmed

silentiary
an official whose job was to ensure quiet in a public place

skinker
a man who looked after the barrels of beer in a taphouse

slubber doffer
a textile worker whose job was to remove bobbins from looms

stay-stitcher
one who fashioned corsets stiffened with bone or metal strips

throwster
a yarn-maker

wailer
a coal worker who removed stones and other impurities from loads

wainwright
a manufacturer of wagons

wharfinger
the person in charge of a landing-stage for boats

A GUID WAUK SPILET

Suggested Scots names for the 18 holes of the world's nastiest golf course

1 The Brustit Byke (the burst wasp's nest)

2 Clootie's Cla' (the Devil's claw)

3 The Scunner (the disgusting or irritating thing)

4 The Besom's Snood (the bitch's ribbon)

5 Ill-willie (malicious)

6 Waefu'-Woodie (the hanging noose)

7 The Yad's Baggie (the old mare's belly)

8 Waesucks (alas)

9 Stanepilkers' Weird (stonepickers' doom)

10 The Oxter (the armpit)

11 The Hingin' Kail-Runt (the filthy cabbage stalk)

12 The Skelper's Mools (the bad golfer's grave dust)

13 Wanchancie (treacherous)

14 The Paidle (the aimless search)

15 The Libbet Tyke (the neutered dog)

16 The Daftie's Fecket (the idiot's vest)

17 The Midden Stank (the dungheap drain)

18 Plowterie Vennel (muddy alley)

LONG LIVE THE QUEEN!

Those lyrics from 'Bohemian Rhapsody' explained

Scaramouche	Originally 'Scaramuccia', one of the stock figures in Italian *commedia dell'arte* theatre; a swashbuckling beau dressed in black, who was never quite as brave as he pretended.
Figaro	The pseudonym of a prominent 19th-century Spanish writer, and also the name of a city in northern Spain. However, Figaro is best known as the witty and rebellious barber in Beaumarchais's novels *Le Barbier de Séville* and *Le Mariage de Figaro*, both later made into operas.
Silhouetto	A cod-Italian form of *silhouette*, an outline seen against a lighter background, named, for unknown reasons, after Étienne de Silhouette, an 18th-century French finance minister. The cutting of silhouette shapes and profiles became a fad.
Bismillah	An Arabic interjection meaning 'in the name of God'.
Beelzebub	Chief spirit of evil; the name means 'lord of the flies' and was first used for a Philistine god. Milton uses the name for Satan's right-hand fallen angel in *Paradise Lost*. The name is sometimes used as a synonym for Satan.
magnifico	Italian word for magnificent or, by extension, a nobleman or any high-ranking person.
fandango	A Spanish courtship dance in triple time, performed by a couple, often employing castanets.
Galileo	Galileo Galilei (1564–1642), Italian astronomer and philosopher.

THE DRINK TALKING

Some subjects which, if you sit with a group of friends in a bar for long enough, you will eventually discuss

1
your middle names

2
first crush on a famous person

3
embarrassing vomit stories

4
relationships with your siblings

5
sweets, toys and TV from the past

6
childhood nicknames

7
the one drink you can't drink anymore

8
first record bought

9
your parents' first names

10
'unbelievable' coincidences

11
loss of virginity particulars

12
prizes or competitions you have won

13
paranormal experiences

TOP OF THE SHOP

Some bingo-related trivia

1   Bingo has existed in some form since at least the early 1500s, when there were already established lottery games played in **Italy**.

2   **Bing Crosby** reportedly received his childhood nickname of Bingo from his favourite jug-eared character in a comic strip called the 'Bingville Bugle'.

3   In British slang, **bingo wings** is the name given to loose skin or flabby flesh on the undersides of the upper arms. It comes from the idea that bingo is largely played by overweight elderly women.

4   It is becoming quite popular to play bingo at **bridal showers** in the USA, with cards depicting traditional gifts which are struck off, as numbers usually are, when the bride unwraps that item.

5   Bingo became a fad in early 30s New York when introduced by one Edwin Lowe, who had seen the game played at travelling carnivals in the South. Numbers were covered with beans and winners shouted **Beano!** when all numbers were covered. Legend has it that when one of Lowe's players wrongly shouted Bingo! he adopted this as the name of the game.

6   **Cow chip bingo** (aka 'cow pie bingo' and 'bessie bingo') is a game played in Australia and the USA in which a field is marked off in squares, the squares are raffled and a cow is let into the area. The winning square is the one where the cow lays down a pat.

7   Bingo, the tubby orange monkey in the TV series **the Banana Splits** was played by Terence Winkless and voiced by Daws Butler. Since Bingo was drummer with the men-in-animal-suits pop group, and since it was partly a spoof on the Monkees, who were an attempt to create an American Beatles, it's likely that his name was a play on Ringo.

8   Numbers were given nicknames in bingo (a practice now dying out as the game tries to escape its tawdry image.) These names were a mix of rhyming slang, visual image and topical cant, eg 'Maggie's den' (10), 'legs eleven', 'key to the door' (21), 'two little ducks' (22) and 'two fat ladies' (88). The nickname for nine ('doctor's orders') came from the advertising for an early 20th-century **laxative** named 'Number 9'.

9   There have been many **songs about bingo**, including the Upsetters' 'Bingo Kid', Patrik Fitzgerald's fey punk 'The Bingo Crowd', Matt McGinn's fun-folky 'Bingo Bella', girl-band Cleopatra's 'Bingo My Love', the Fall's early effort 'Bingo-Master's Break-out' and Tom Verlaine's 'Mr Bingo'.

10   On a CD of songs by Native American women, I encountered the Six Nations Women Singers, an **Iroquois** vocal combo, and marvelled at the breadth of their subject matter. The first song was about the White Man's destruction of Mother Earth, the second about bingo (translation 'I only have two dollars, but I'm going to bingo anyway.')

11   Early **pinball** machines, especially those in the 30s, were often based on the game of bingo. These machines tended to have prize money, as opposed to being the usual 'for amusement only'. Players had to achieve runs of certain numbers by landing balls in holes.

THE ROAD TO ELEVENHAM

Some number-related British place names

Onecote	Three Sisters
Two Bridges	Threemilestone
Two Dales	Four Ashes
Two Gates	Four Cabots
Twopenny Knowe	Four Crosses
Three Bridges	Four Elms
Three Burrows	Four Forks
Three Chimneys	Four Gotes
Three Cocks	Four Lanes
Three Crosses	Four Marks
Three Cups Corner	Four Mile Bridge
Three Holes	Four Oaks
Three Leg Cross	Four Roads
Three Legged Cross	Four Throws
Three Mile Cross	Fourpenny
Three Miletown	Fourstones
Three Oaks	Five Ash Down
Three Pikes	Five Ashes

Five Bells

Five Bridges

Five Oak Green

Five Oaks

Five Penny Borve

Five Roads

Five Sisters

Five Turnings

Five Ways

Five Wents

Fivehead

Fivelanes

Six Ashes

Six Mile Bottom

Six Rues

Sixhills

Sixmile Cottages

Sixpenny Handley

Seven Ash

Seven Bridges

Seven Dials

Seven Kings

Seven Sisters

Seven Springs

Seven Stones

Seven Wells

Sevenhampton

Sevenoaks

Eight Ash Green

Nine Ashes

Nine Barrow Down

Nine Elms

Nine Mile Burn

Ninebanks

Ninemile Bar

Ten Mile Bank

Twelve Oaks

Twelveheads

Sixteen Foot Drain

Twenty

Twenty Foot River

Forty Foot

Forty Green

Forty Hill

Twelve tongue-twisters

spoiled

1 Scarlet truck, golden truck, scarlet truck, golden truck.

2 Latex fenders for infant carriages.

3 She is a vendor of bivalve casings on the beach.

4 The sixth Arab potentate's similarly numbered ovine mammal is unwell.

5 The Edinburgh port constabulary tell us we can leave.

6 The untidily dressed rogue sprinted around the jagged boulder again and again.

7 A loud sound irritates a pearl-bearing shellfish.

8 It's not usually me who defeathers game birds, it's my father. I'm only doing this until he arrives.

9 In the counties of Hertfordshire and Hampshire, and also in the city of Hereford, a whirlwind is a rare occurrence.

10 Elizabeth purchased a quantity of butter, though it turned out to be sour.

11 Mr P Piper harvested two gallons of gherkins.

12 What quantity of timber might a marmot throw into the air if such a thing were possible?

Twelve names which I reckon might do for a pony but not a fully-grown horse

NAME THAT NAG

Tarmac
Ariadne
Bawbee
The Pride of Strathmiglo
Juniper
The Corporal's Sleeve
Zydeco
Cumulus
Skipper
Amulet
Cottonsocks
Lumpy

SHH! LISTEN ...

Ten places where magical things might happen

along the pier at dawn **1**
in the dusty dark beneath a bed **2**
on a Ferris wheel **3**
on a bench by a bubbling stream **4**
in a walled orchard **5**
in the cellar of a junk shop **6**
among the sand dunes **7**
on the lip of a volcano **8**
anywhere there is a well **9**
in a cool, quiet pantry **10**

HONEY TONGUED

One hundred and one people's suggestions for 'my favourite word'

lugubrious • crepuscular • pickle • requiem • quagmire
anyway • flan • snooze • corduroy • heather
cookie • serene • monkey • flibbertigibbet • assimilate
tetchy • gnarly • plinth • imperial • frump • pilchard
diphthong • simulacrum • paradox • mollusc
ambivalence • aquifer • aardvark • petard • scabies
doily • transmogrify • calamity • onomatopoeia
threnody • swank • elephant • mint • opsimath
sphincter • molybdenum • whelk • serendipity • giblet
rainbow • cerulean • turquoise • loquacious
precarious • roadkill • juxtaposition • fuselage • lentil
bordello • smock • gargantuan • inamorata • rhubarb
lasso • purple • swizzlestick • zeitgeist • epitome
harmony • curmudgeonly • phlegm • jive • contrast
plectrum • segue • macabre • moth • vibe
synchronicity • plethora • loophole • acquiesce
catalyst • oxymoron • arcane • beeves • shampoo
delirium • nibble • squiggle • reverie • prissy
mew • liaison • moist • syzygy • glimpse • sassy
melodic • ubiquitous • malarkey • cloaca
shenanigans • cognac • ointment • wench

**Personally — oh, how can I choose — I like
nearby, pippin, spillage, behalf and cotton.**

BYGONES

horse troughs **1**
brushed nylon sheets **2**
bellows **3**
cakestands **4**
football pools coupons **5**
milk floats **6**
inkwells **7**
nightcaps **8**
three-wheeled cars **9**
Black Maria police vans **10**
savings stamps **11**
mangles and wringers **12**
pocket watches **13**
milk bottles **14**
Jew's harps **15**
carbolic soap **16**
tank tops **17**
flatirons **18**
powdered orange juice **19**
hairnets **20**
starting handles **21**
combination underwear **22**
solid toothpaste **23**
snake belts **24**
sanitary napkins **25**
half-time scoreboards **26**
leather school satchels **27**
basques **28**

Things you don't see as often any more

29 scrubbing boards
30 car running boards
31 shorthand
32 shaving strops
33 school belts for punishment
34 cassette personal stereos
35 twin tub washers
36 lace-up footballs
37 radio shops
38 toasting forks
39 shuffleboards
40 tea cosies and egg cosies
41 cotton handkerchiefs
42 nuns
43 typewriters
44 cycle clips
45 cuspidors and spittoons

KINGS OF MUSIC

Fifty musical kings

1	King of the Surf Guitar	Dick Dale
2	King of Ragtime	Scott Joplin
3	King of Ballads	Peabo Bryson
4	King of Tango	Carlos Gardel
5	King of Reggae	Bob Marley
6	King of the Kazoo	Rick Hubbard
7	King of Disco Soul	George McCrae
8	King of the Waltz	Johann Strauss, the Younger
9	King of Kora	Sidiki Diabaté
10	King of the Swamp Blues	Tabby Thomas
11	King of the Honking Tenor Sax	Big Jay McNeeley
12	King of Crock (country rock)	Teddy Glenn
13	King of Bluegrass	Jimmy Martin
14	King of the Twelve-String Guitar	Leadbelly
15	King of Calypso	Harry Belafonte
16	King of Violinists	Fritz Kreisler
17	King of the Twist	Chubby Checker
18	King of Slide Guitar	Elmore James
19	King of Western Swing	Bob Wills
20	King of Belly Dance Music	George Abdo
21	King of Salsa	Eddie Torres
22	King of Afro-Cuban Jazz	Machito
23	King of Rhumba Rock	Papa Wemba
24	King of Mountain Soul	Ralph Stanley

25	King of Mambo	Perez Prado
26	King of the Endless Boogie	John Lee Hooker
27	King of Pop	Michael Jackson
28	King of Country Music	Roy Acuff
29	King of Pipers	John Ban Mackenzie
30	King of Rai	Cheb Khaled
31	King of Soul	Otis Redding
32	King of Rock and Roll	Elvis Presley*
33	King of the Blues	B B King
34	King of Zydeco	Clifton Chenier
35	King of Jewish Reggae	Ron Wiseman
36	King of Swing	Benny Goodman
37	King of Rock 'n' Soul	Solomon Burke
38	King of Jazz	Paul Whiteman
39	King of Slow Soul	Percy Sledge
40	King of New Age	David Lanz
41	King of the Harmonica	Larry Adler
42	King of the Delta Blues	Robert Johnson
43	King of Latin Music	Tito Puente
44	King of Corn	Spike Jones
45	King of Hi-De-Ho	Cab Calloway
46	King of Gospel Music	James Cleveland
47	King of Champagne Music	Lawrence Welk
48	King of Vibes	Lionel Hampton
49	King of Disco	Sylvester
50	King of Skiffle	Lonnie Donegan

* Earlier, Elvis was known as the King of Western Bop.

IT'S A WRAP

Three names for 'sausages wrapped in bacon'

1 pigs in blankets (England)
2 weenies in scarves (North America)
3 kilted sausages (Scotland)

FROSTIES

Twelve songs about snowmen

1	'The Great Snowman'	John D Loudermilk
2	'Cat and Snowman'	Tangerine Dream
3	'My Friend the Snowman'	Bananas in Pajamas
4	'Suicide Snowman'	Marilyn Manson
5	'Snowman in the Summer'	The Lazy Eights
6	'Snow Man'	Elvis Presley
7	'Abominable Snowman'	Manfred Mann
8	'Snowman's Land'	Keith Emerson
9	'Frosty the Snowman'	Gene Autry
10	'Johnny Snowman'	Conway Twitty
11	'Jolly Jolly Snowman'	The Tumble Tots
12	'Mr and Mrs Snowman'	Hank Thompson and his Brazos Valley Boys

TOPSY-TURVY

Twenty swapwords

1	takeover	overtake
2	offset	set-off
3	gunshot	shotgun
4	long-life	lifelong
5	boathouse	houseboat
6	outlook	lookout
7	fall-back	backfall
8	takeout	outtake
9	phonecard	cardphone
10	line-out	outline
11	schoolday	day-school
12	turnover	overturn
13	layout	outlay
14	setback	backset
15	uptake	take-up
16	sleepover	oversleep
17	punch-card	cardpunch
18	breakout	outbreak
19	outwith	without
20	upset	set-up

A swapword is a compound word where the first and last parts can be swapped to make a new word. Both words must be whole or hyphenated, not phrases. I have gone along with *The Chambers Dictionary*'s definitions on whether swapword candidates are one word, two or have a hyphen. There are surprisingly few.

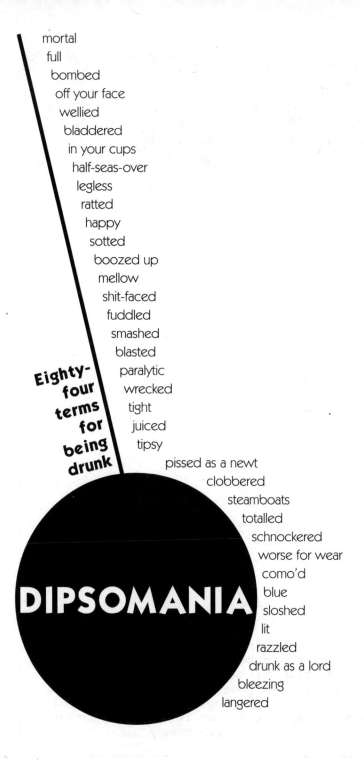

mortal
full
bombed
off your face
wellied
bladdered
in your cups
half-seas-over
legless
ratted
happy
sotted
boozed up
mellow
shit-faced
fuddled
smashed
blasted
paralytic
wrecked
tight
juiced
tipsy
pissed as a newt
clobbered
steamboats
totalled
schnockered
worse for wear
como'd
blue
sloshed
lit
razzled
drunk as a lord
bleezing
langered

Eighty-four terms for being drunk

DIPSOMANIA

tanked up
guttered
miraculous
stinko
on the sauce
hoovered
mashed
pished
Brahms and Liszt
out of your tree
three sheets to the wind
squiffy
nuggets
woozy
trolleyed
under the influence
locked
blitzed
steaming
polluted
trousered
plastered
blotto
nappy
fleein'
trashed
pickled
rat-arsed
blootered
ripe
seshed

zombied
shot
high
merry
lush
arseholed
wasted
soaked
soused
pie-eyed
hammered
sozzled
stocious
slaughtered
wazzocked
stonkered

GLOBAL KENNEL

Countries and some of their particular dog breeds

Afghanistan	Tazi (Afghan Hound)
Argentina	Dogo Argentino
Australia	Queensland Heeler (Australian Cattle Dog)
Austria	Alpine Dachsbracke
Belgium	Schipperke
Brazil	Fox Paulistinha (Brazilian Terrier)
Canada	Canadian Eskimo Dog
China	Chow Chow
Cuba	Havana Silk Dog (Havanese)
Czech Republic	Cesky Fousek
Democratic Republic of the Congo	Basenji
Denmark	Broholmer
England	Springer Spaniel
Estonia	Gontchaja Estonskaja (Estonian Hound)
Finland	Suomenpystykorva (Finnish Spitz)
France	Ariégeois
Germany	Rottweiler
Greece	Hellinikos Ichnilatis (Hellenic Hound)
Hungary	Pumi
Iceland	Islenkur Fjárhundur (Icelandic Sheepdog)
India	Mudhol Hound
Ireland	Glen of Imaal Terrier
Israel	Kelef K'naani (Canaan Dog)
Italy	Bergamasco
Japan	Akita

Latvia	Latvian Hound
Macedonia, Serbia and Montenegro	Sarplaninac
Madagascar	Coton de Tuléar
Malaysia	Telomian
Mali	Azawakh
Malta	Pharaoh Hound
Mexico	Xoloitzquintle (Mexican Hairless Dog)
Morocco	Sloughi
The Netherlands	Drentse Patrijshond (Dutch Partridge Hound)
New Zealand	Huntaway
Norway	Dunker
Peru	Peruvian Inca Orchid (Peruvian Hairless)
Papua New Guinea	New Guinea Singing Dog
Poland	Tatra Shepherd Dog
Portugal	Portuguese Podengo (Portuguese Warren Hound)
Russia	Borzoi
Scotland	Dandie Dinmont
Slovakia	Slovenský Cuvac (Slovakian Chuvach)
Slovenia	Kraski Ovcar (Karst Shepherd Dog)
South Africa, Zimbabwe	Rhodesian Ridgeback
Spain	Galgo Español
Sweden	Drever
Switzerland	Appenzeller Sennenhund
Thailand	Thai Ridgeback Dog
Tibet	Lhasa Apso
Turkey	Akbash Dog
USA	Treeing Tennessee Brindle
Wales	Cardigan Corgi

MCBANQUET

**'The Blythesome Bridal' is an uproarious Scottish song probably written around 300 years ago.
It tells of the wedding ceremony of Jock and Maggie, 'the lass wi' the gowden hair', the motley crew of guests and the food and drink consumed. Here is a guide to the wedding guests and their feast ...**

Sawney the soutar (Alexander the shoemaker)

Will wi' the meikle mou (Will with the big mouth)

Tam the blutter (Tom the dirty, clumsy chap)

Andrew the tinkler (Andrew the vagabond)

bow'd-legged Robie (bow-legged Robert)

Thumbles Katie's godman

blue-cheeked Dowbie

Lawrie the laird of the land

sowlibber Paatie (Patty the pig-spayer)

plucky-fac'd Wat i' th' mill (pimply-faced Walter from the mill)

capper-nos'd Francie (copper-nosed, or red-nosed, Francis)

Gibbie that wons in the how o' the hill (Gilbert who lives in the dell)

Alaster Sibbie wha in wi' black Bessiy did mool (who slept with dark-haired Elizabeth)

snivling Lilly

Tibby the lass that stands oft on the stool (the girl who often does penance in church)

Madge that was buckled to Stennie and cost him grey breeks to his arse, wha after was hangit for stealing (ie who spent all his money)

gleed Geordy Janners (squinting George Janners)

Kirsh wi' the lily-white leg who gade to the south for manners

Juden Mecourie

blinkin daft Barbara Macleg (very stupid)

flea-lugged sharney-fac'd Lawrie (flea-eared, dung-faced Lawrence)

shangy-mou'd halucket Mag (hare-lipped, giddy Margaret)

happer-ars'd Nansy (Nancy with the scrawny backside)

fairy-fac'd Flowrie (fairy-faced Florence)

Muck Madie

fat-hippet Grisy, the lass wi' the gowden wame (ie golden womb, probably a sexual slur) girn-again Gibby (moan-again Gilbert)

glaiket Jenny Bell (stupid Jenny Bell)

mealy-shin'd Mungo Macapin that was skipper himsel (dusty-legged Mungo McAlpine)

And the food ...

sybows (spring onions)

risarts (redcurrants)

carlings that are baith sodden and raw (boiled and uncooked peas)

langkail (unchopped cabbage)

porridge

bannocks of barley-meal (meal scones)

good sawt herring

a cogue of good ale

fadges (flat loafs)

brochen (honey porridge)

south of good gabbock of skate (best portions of skate)

powsowdie (sheep-head broth)

drammock (gruel)

crowdie (type of cheese)

caller nowtfeet (fresh calves' heels)

partens (large crabs)

buckies (whelks)

whytens (whitings)

spaldings (dried fish)

singit sheepheads (singed sheep heads)

haggies (haggis)

scadlips (hot broth)

lapper'd-milk kebbucks (cheese made with curdled milk)

sowens (gruel of fermented oat husks)

farles (savoury scones)

baps (bread rolls)

swats (beer made from sowens)

well-scraped paunches (tripe)

brandy in stoups and in caps

mealkail (a dish of mashed cabbage and oats)

castocks (cabbage stems)

skink (beef soup)

roasts to roast on a brander of flowks that were t'ken alive

scrapt haddocks

wilks (whelks)

dulse and tangles (seaweed)

Guests could also take advantage of a mill of good snishing to prie (good snuff to sample).

Source:
from the collection of Scottish songs by David Herd (a contemporary of Robert Burns).

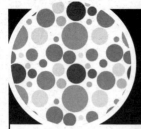

CHARMING

Thirty-one items and images worn or carried for luck

1. eye of Horus
2. coal
3. birthstones
4. lucky T-bone (from a sheep's head)
5. rabbit's paw
6. cameo brooch
7. St Christopher medal
8. rosary beads
9. ankh
10. wishbone
11. beans or seeds washed up on the seashore
12. dried piece of umbilical cord
13. four-leaved clover
14. lucky coin
15. gonk or other small furry toy
16. likeness of a saint
17. garlic
18. horseshoe
19. coral
20. dice
21. Star of David
22. unusual pebble
23. mini rice storage-bag (Japan)
24. lizard or pig amulets
25. bullet
26. lucky garment
27. white heather sprig
28. crucifix
29. henna markings
30. small figurine
31. knotted string

There are only ten body parts with three letters

1	leg	**6**	gum
2	ear	**7**	eye
3	rib	**8**	jaw
4	arm	**9**	toe
5	hip	**10**	lip

Of course, there are many slang ones too, and ones that are not really body 'parts', eg gut or fat. There are contractions (eg lid) and pedantic obscurities (eg rods in the eye), but it's more or less just the ten.

TEN BY THREE

SLIPS OF THE FINGER

The ten words I most often botch while typing

coudl	**1**
whcih	**2**
ahev	**3**
forwrad	**4**
somehting	**5**
ot	**6**
tryign	**7**
coem	**8**
thansk	**9**
eb	**10**

93

A list of celebrated women who have been regally nicknamed

VITAMIN QUEENS

1	Queen of the Music Halls	Marie Lloyd (Victorian superstar)
2	Queen of Rai	Cheikha Rimitti (Algerian musician)
3	Queen of the Cowgirls	Dale Evans (Western actress)
4	Queen of Courts	Helen Wills (tennis legend)
5	Queen of the Screamers	Evelyn Ankers (horror movie actress)
6	Queen of Trumpet and Song	Valaida Snow (30s jazz musician)
7	Queen of Romance	Dame Barbara Cartland
8	Queen of Country Music	Kitty Wells
9	Queen of Silent Serials	Pearl White (early film actress)
10	Queen of the Creeks	Mary Musgrove (US colonist)
11	Queen of Crime	Dame Agatha Christie
12	Queen of Clean	Linda Cobb (household tips expert)
13	Queen of Housewife Rock	Helen Reddy (singer)
14	Queen of Soul	Aretha Franklin
15	Queen of Burlesque	Gypsy Rose Lee
16	Queen of Gospel	Mahalia Jackson
17	Queen of Tin Pan Alley	Bernice Petkere (songwriter)
18	Queen of Disco	Donna Summer*
19	Queen of Mean	Leona Helmsley (real estate tycoon)

20	Queen of the Blues	Bessie Smith**
21	Queen of the Piano	Clara Wieck (later the wife of Schumann)
22	Queen of the Rustlers	Ann Bassett (wild west adventurer)
23	Queen of the Mods	Cathy McGowan (60s pop TV presenter)
24	Queen of the B Movies/ Comedy	Lucille Ball
25	Queen of Technicolor	Maria Montez (actress)
26	Queen of the Channel	Alison Streeter (sea swimmer)
27	Queen of the Bluestockings	Elizabeth Montagu (writer and society leader)
28	Queen of the Muckrakers	Jessica Mitford (writer)
29	Queen of Hearts	Diana, Princess of Wales
30	Queen of the Strippers	Lili St Cyr (burlesque star)
31	Queen of the Dippers	Martha Gunn (18th-century bathing magnate)
32	Queen of Hollywood	Myrna Loy
33	Queen of Boogie Woogie	Hadda Brooks (singer)
34	Queen of the Air	Amy Johnson
35	Queen of Rock and Roll	Stevie Nicks
36	Queen of the Dogsleds	Nell Shipman (early adventure film star)
37	Queen of the Confederacy	Lucy Holcombe Pickens (southern American Confederate supporter)
38	Queen of the Beatniks	Judy Henske (cult folk 'n' blues singer)

* Sometimes Gloria Gaynor.
** Sometimes Dinah Washington.

MADE FOR EACH OTHER

Twenty-one surprisingly good taste combinations

1   grilled fish & cranberry sauce

2   kale & mushrooms

3   chorizo & lentils

4   Vegemite® & Dijon mustard

5   soy sauce & butter

6   carrots & sesame oil

7   cheddar & pears

8   cassoulet & pale ale

9   venison & juniper

10 rhubarb & salmon

11 lamb & ginger

12 fish roe & spaghetti

13 wheat beer & oysters

14 feta & garlic

15 tom yam soup & rambutan juice

16 mango & spinach

17 shrimps & raspberry sauce

18 Oreos® & absinthe

19 hot dog & coffee soda

20 caviar & white chocolate

21 champagne & crab spring rolls

CLOTH EARS

Twenty-five garments celebrated in song

1	'Evening Gown'	Mick Jagger
2	'Mini Skirt'	Lightnin' Hopkins
3	'Baggy Trousers'	Madness
4	'Thong Song'	Sisqo
5	'Raspberry Beret'	Prince
6	'Famous Blue Raincoat'	Leonard Cohen
7	'Homburg'	Procol Harum
8	'Kool in the Kaftan'	B A Robertson
9	'Trouser Suit'	Betty Page
10	'Green Shirt'	Elvis Costello
11	'Undone (The Sweater Song)'	Weezer
12	'Vicar in a Tutu'	The Smiths
13	'Blouse and Skirt'	Gregory Isaacs
14	'Jumper on the Line'	R L Burnside
15	'New Dress'	Depeche Mode
16	'Jacket Hangs'	Blue Aeroplanes
17	'Kimono'	Pizzicato Five
18	'Knickers'	Chumbawamba
19	'Man's Tight Vest'	Baby Bird
20	'Hot Pants'	James Brown
21	'From Panties to Bloomers'	Jimmy Lewis
22	'Petticoat Fever'	Merle Travis
23	'Silk Pyjamas'	Thomas Dolby
24	'Velvet Pants'	Propellerheads
25	'My Blue Bonnet Girl'	Jimmie Davis

CURD L

**Twenty-five
cheeses
beginning
with L**

1	Langres
2	Lebbene
3	Leigh
4	Leder
5	Lappernas Renost
6	Lebenen
7	Leicester
8	Licki
9	Lombardo
10	Lapland
11	Liptauer
12	Latvysky Syr
13	Lisieux
14	Livarot
15	Labneh
16	Lour
17	Lescin
18	Laguiole
19	Leyden
20	Liederkranz
21	Limburger
22	Levroux
23	Liptauer
24	Lodigiano
25	Luneberg

MACLUCIFER

Some old, old names from Scots for the Devil

LIFF REVISITED
PART ONE

In the wonderful *The Meaning of Liff* (Pan 1983), **John Lloyd** and the late, lamented **Douglas Adams** used place names to give words to the 'many hundreds of common experiences, feelings, situations and even objects which we all know and recognize, but for which no words exist'. With a tip of the hat to Lloyd and Adams, here are some new Liff-style definitions.

BAGBY (*n*) a frightening and unwieldy bra which more resembles an instrument of torture

BALMULLO (*n*) an awkward sensation caused by knowing something unpleasant (someone being sacked, a boil being lanced) is happening right now in the next room

BINGHAM (*n*) an especially irritating ringtone

BOATH (*vb*) to steel oneself, eg for an injection or a washing machine repair man's estimate

CHATSWORTH (*n*) a noisy gaggle of office workers who, having spent all day detesting work, are now happily talking about it for hours in the pub

CHETTLE (*vb*) to stand there wondering why a fly flies round and round the light fitting

CLOUGH (*n*) an enormous and ostentatious shock of frizzy grey hair cultivated by women of a certain age and ilk. Also known as the 'salt-and-pepper helmet'

CLUNTON (*n*) someone you eventually meet after a lengthy email correspondence who has forgotten to inform you that they are enormously tiresome in real life

CRIEFF (*n*) a specialized type of fine, statically-charged dust which attaches itself to a television screen

DREGHORN (*n*) a seething right-wing article in the *Daily Mail* actually written to order by a left-wing twenty-something hack with dinky spectacles while eating a hoisin duck wrap

DULWICH (*n*) one who is smugly au fait with which wine goes with what food and which should be chilled, even though the protocol will be changed again by game-playing 'experts' next week

DUNFERMLINE (*n*) the embossed lettering which books must, by law, have on their covers in order to be on sale in airports

FLAXBY (*n*) a misunderstood phrase in an email which leads you to think an acquaintance hates you or is developing an unhealthy crush

FOBBING (*participial vb*) running one's thumbnail round a roll of sticky tape, searching ever more desperately for the wirral (qv)

FOOLOW (*vb*) to not know the words of a song but to mumble along to it nevertheless

FOXUP (*n*) a loud and lengthy argument about hunting between two people with exactly the same views on the subject but who don't want to let that interfere with the pleasure of arguing

GISSING (*participial vb*) being undecided as to whether the tide is coming in or going out

GREAT WITLEY (*n*) a hilarious joke which somehow isn't hilarious when you try to tell it

GRIMINISH (*n*) a rarefied and confusing form of the English language in which computer error messages are composed

GRITLEY (*adj*) of the elderly, experiencing a specific mixture of anxiety and territorial indignation brought on by having booked train seats

GUTHRIE (*adj*) descriptive of the smell in a room in which two large men have recently slept

GWESPYR (*n*) a feeling of vague satisfaction caused by watching the wind buffet a boat's sail

HIDCOTE BOYCE (*n*) the modern female social faux pas of not showing one's underwear in public

HONING (*n*) the sound made by a fridge

JOHNBY (*n*) the special wave given to one another by bus drivers

KELSO (*n*) the last piece of toilet roll which is glued to the cardboard tube

KELTY (*n*) a piece of clothing which no longer fits or suits you but which you keep due to its part in a memory of a notable bedroom encounter

KIPPAX (*vb*) to become suddenly and unexplainably aware of honing (qv)

LEUCHARS (*n pl*) the tiny, white congealed pieces which swirl in coffee when the milk has turned

LITTLE PETHERICK (*n*) a small measure. One little petherick is the tiny discrepancy between wanting to join a political protest and not wanting to be seen with the sort of people who protest, which keeps you at home listening to the radio

LUDWORTH (*n*) one who perpetrates the myth that older equals wiser

LUXULYAN (*n*) a pink, tooth-rotting chemical liquid being marketed as a 'juice drink sensation'

... continued on p202

The original version of the popular board game Monopoly® is based on the streets of Atlantic City, New Jersey. Many other cities in the USA and elsewhere now have their own versions, as do sports teams and leagues, universities, states and countries. Over 100 editions of Monopoly® are available. Here are 42 of the more unusual versions

Garfield® edition	**1**	**22**	Century of Flight aviation edition
International Euro edition	**2**	**23**	Millennium edition
Betty Boop® edition	**3**	**24**	I Love Lucy® edition
National Parks edition	**4**	**25**	Mustang® edition
US Space Program edition	**5**	**26**	Bass Fishing edition
The Simpsons® edition	**6**	**27**	Dot Com edition
The Lord of the Rings® trilogy edition	**7**	**28**	Ford 100th Anniversary edition
The Dog edition	**8**	**29**	Surfing edition
Alaska's Iditarod* edition	**9**	**30**	Golf edition
Super Bowl XXXII edition	**10**	**31**	The Power Puff Girls® edition
Corvette® 50th Anniversary edition	**11**	**32**	Mountaineering edition
NASCAR® edition	**12**	**33**	Muppets® edition
Las Vegas edition (based on nightlife and casinos)	**13**	**34**	Looney Tunes® edition
World Cup France 98 edition	**14**	**35**	Peanuts® edition
Justice League of America®** edition	**15**	**36**	Hollywood edition
Star Trek® edition	**16**	**37**	United States Navy edition
Scooby Doo® edition	**17**	**38**	Pokémon® edition
Coca-Cola® edition	**18**	**39**	Historical Harley Davidson edition
Elvis 25th Anniversary edition	**19**	**40**	Wizard of Oz® edition
Disney® edition	**20**	**41**	Dale Earnhardt®*** edition
Marvel Comics® edition	**21**	**42**	Star Wars® edition

BOARD OF LIFE

* Husky racing championship.

** Superheroes.

*** Racing driver.

PLEASE DON'T SAY THAT

Thirty phrases you do not want to hear

1 We need to talk

2 Can you spare a minute or two?

3 There's been an accident

4 And now, a few of my own songs

5 Step into the office for a moment

6 It's not you, it's me

7 I'm phoning on behalf of …

8 Maybe you should sit down

9 Close your eyes and open your mouth

10 I like you, just not in that way

11 I want to talk to you about Jesus*

12 Please don't get angry, but …

13 Just pop your clothes on that chair

14 About last night …

15 Do you mind if I join you?

16 What's that on your shoe?

17   … and you can't miss it

18   You'll have to suck the poison out

19   I'm from the *News of the World*

20   Of course he doesn't bite

21   Mum, I can't hold it in any longer

22   Go on, have a bite, it tastes a bit like chicken

23   I'm doing a sponsored walk …

24   So I think you should have a test too,
just in case

25   I had this weird dream last night

26   No, be honest, do I look fat?

27   It's all about this man who …

28   Can you watch these two for me whilst
I nip out?

29   My next poem is a long one and
was inspired by the death of my
mother/birth of my first child/
my holiday in Tuscany …

30   This is going to hurt a little bit

* Compare the even more ominous '*Jesus* told a
joke once …'

SONGBOOK

A selection of genuine titles of folk songs and old popular tunes

'About the Bush, Willy'

'Andy's Gone With Cattle'

'Blancheflour and Jellyflorice'

'Blink Over the Burn, Sweet Betty'

'Can Ye Sew Cushions?'

'Cape Cod Girls They Have No Combs'

'The Castration of the Strawberry Roan'

'Fanny Power'

'Fly Up, My Cock'

'Give Ear to a Frolicksome Ditty'

'Golden Ring Around My Susan Girl'

'Gonna Keep My Skillet Greasy'

'Hallelujah I'm a Bum'

'Have Some Madeira, M'Dear'

'He Went to Sleep – the Hogs Ate Him'

'I Catch-a da Plenty of Feesh'

'I Had a Wee Cock'

'I Wanted a Kitten to Love Me'

'I Will Bow and Be Simple'

'I'll Hae Nae Mair o' Yer Cheese'

'Into the Air, Junior Birdmen'

'The Lean and Unwashed Tiffy'

'Let Simon's Beard Alone'

'Lumps of Pudding'

'Making Babies By Steam'

'May the Bird of Paradise Fly Up Your Nose'

'Morrisey and the Russian Sailor'

'My Gal's a Corker'

'My Word, You Do Look Queer!'

'Never Throw a Lighted Lamp at Mother'

'Nine Inch Will Please a Lady'

'Risselty-Rosselty'

'Sexcamel'

'She Perished in the Snow'

'The Shearin's Nae for You, My Bonnie Lassie O'

'The Squid-Jigging Ground'

'The Sugar Notch Entombment'

'There Was a Wee Bit Mousikie'

'There's an Empty Cot in the Bunkhouse Tonight'

'Violate Me (In the Violet Time)'

'We Loop in the Purple Twilight'

'What Kind o' Pants Does the Gambler Wear?'

'When She Cam Ben, She Bobbed'

'When the Ice Worms Nest Again'

'Woman Belly Full o' Hair'

'The Wren She Lies in Care's Bed'

'Zack, the Mormon Engineer'

YOU AND YOU

A '_u_u' alphabet

auau the Maori word for 'frequent' or 'frequently'

Bubu a Malaysian resort known as the 'best sexy body beach'

Cucu a Romanian surname

DuDu® a mountain bike made by Kona

Eueu a shortened or pet form of the name Eugenia

fufu a type of extremely thick porridge eaten in Africa

gugu gugu badhun is an Aboriginal language in Queensland

huhu an edible New Zealand beetle grub found in decaying wood

iuiu *Alpinia carolinensis*, a large tropical plant

juju a West African fetish or charm, or the magic associated with these objects

kuku a large New Zealand wood pigeon

lulu any outstanding thing

mumu an earth oven in Papua New Guinea, where you will also find a …

nunu … which is an initiation house; men hide in the roof space to frighten women and boys

Ouou a Chinese girl's name and an Algerian surname

pupu the Hawaiian term for snacks or appetizers

ququ a kind of dumpling from the Xinjiang region of China

ruru a New Zealand owl, also called the mopoke or morepork from its cry

Susu a people of West Africa, living mainly in Mali, Guinea and Sierra Leone

tutu a frilly ballet skirt

uuuu a Swiss webhosting company

vuvu a Brazilian percussion instrument

wuwu the Taoist term for 'non-thingness'

Xuxu® a strong German brand name drink, made from strawberries and a dash of vodka

YuYu® an Italian-made stool available in ivory, orange, pale grey or lilac blue

Zuzu the little girl in the homely movie classic *It's A Wonderful Life*

Forty-four words for that part of us which sits

IT'S BEHIND YOU

1	botty	**23**	tush
2	peach	**24**	fanny
3	ass	**25**	patootie
4	queener	**26**	seat
5	fundament	**27**	fud
6	rump	**28**	heinie
7	beam-end	**29**	dowp
8	moon	**30**	bubble
9	hootchie	**31**	can
10	booty	**32**	BTM
11	behind	**33**	duff
12	arse	**34**	quoit
13	bahookie	**35**	derrière
14	keister	**36**	rear
15	spankit	**37**	croupon
16	buns	**38**	bahakas
17	thang	**39**	hinderlings
18	butt	**40**	backside
19	broadside	**41**	nates
20	bum	**42**	posterior
21	prat	**43**	rusty-dusty
22	tail	**44**	sit-upon

RUM PUNCH

In 'cant' (common or criminal slang) rum meant fine, remarkable or great. Here are some 18th-century slang definitions using the term *rum* from Captain Francis Grose's *Dictionary of the Vulgar Tongue* from the 1780s

rum beck	a justice of the peace
rum bite	a clever cheat
rum bleating cheat	a fat wether sheep
rum blowen	a handsome wench
rum bluffer	a jolly host
rum bob	a young apprentice
rum boozing welts	bunches of grapes
rum bubber	a dexterous fellow at stealing silver tankards from taverns
rum bugher	a valuable dog
rum bung	a full purse
rum chant	a song
rum chub	among butchers, a custom easily imposed on, as to the quality and price of meat
rum clout/wiper	a fine silk or cambric handkerchief
rum cod	a purse of gold
rum cole/ghelt	new money or medals
rum cove	a clever rogue
rum degen/tilter/tol	a fine sword

rum dell/doxy	a fine wench
rum diver/dubber/file	an expert pickpocket
rum drawers	silk stockings
rum duke	an odd eccentric fellow
rum gaggers	cheats who tell wonderful stories of their sufferings at sea, or when taken by the Algerines
rum glymmer	king of the link-boys
rum kicks	breeches of gold or silver brocade
rum mawnd	one that counterfeits a fool
rum mort	a queen or great lady
rum nab	a good hat
rum nantz	good French brandy
rum ned	a very rich silly fellow
rum pad	the highway
rum padders	highwaymen well mounted and armed
rum peepers	fine looking-glasses
rum prancer	a fine horse
rum quids	a great booty
rum ruff peck	Westphalia ham
rum snith	a smart fillip on the nose
rum squeeze	much wine, or good liquor, given among fiddlers
rum topping	a rich commode or women's head-dress
rum ville	London

SIP UP

For starters, here are 60 soups of the world

1	The Bahamas	conch chowder
2	Nigeria	egusi soup (meat broth thickened with melon seeds)
3	Romania	bors de berbec (sour mutton broth)
4	France	soupe au pistou (vegetables with garlic garnish)
5	Venezuela	chupe criollo (spiced chicken)
6	Egypt	milookhia (green herb soup)
7	Spain	gazpacho (chilled tomato)
8	Libya	shourba bil hout (haddock and tomato)
9	Slovakia	držková polievka (tripe)
10	USA	filet gumbo (spicy meat or fish and okra)
11	Thailand	tom yam goong (spicy prawn broth)
12	Trinidad	breadfruit soup
13	Ireland	yellow broth (vegetables and oatmeal)
14	Morocco	harira (lamb and lentils)
15	Chile	caldillo de congrio (eel chowder)
16	Russia	borscht (beetroot)
17	Hawaii	Portuguese bean soup
18	Indonesia	soto ayam (spicy chicken soup)
19	Italy	stracciatelle (egg broth)
20	Argentina	puchero de costilla con porotos (beef ribs and beans)
21	Cameroon	ndolé soup (bitter leaf)
22	India	mulligatawny (spicy meat soup)
23	Lithuania	saltibarsciai (cold beetroot soup)
24	Mexico	corn and poblano soup
25	Germany	Frankfurter Linsensuppe (lentil and sausage)
26	Greece	avgolemono (egg and lemon)
27	Georgia	kharcho (beef soup)

28	England	brown Windsor (beef and vegetables)
29	Jamaica	mannish water (goat head soup)
30	Czech Republic	vánocní rybí polévka (Christmas fish broth)
31	Vietnam	mang tay cua (asparagus and crabmeat)
32	Japan	tsumire-jiru (sardine ball broth)
33	Philippines	sinigang (sour broth)
34	Turkey	yayla corbasi (dill and yoghurt soup)
35	Ukraine	krupnik (barley broth)
36	Haiti	soupe joumou (squash)
37	Ghana	okra soup
38	Korea	yuk gae chang (spicy beef and vegetables)
39	Austria	Biersuppe (beer and milk)
40	Slovenia	goveja juha (beef and beef-bone broth)
41	Belgium	waterzooie (cream of chicken)
42	Brazil	sopa de piranha (piranha head soup)
43	Lebanon	shorabit addas (lamb and red lentils)
44	Finland	Hapankaalikeitto (beef and pickled cabbage)
45	Portugal	caldo verde (cabbage and potato)
46	Jordan	labenaya (spinach and yoghurt)
47	Bulgaria	tarator (chilled yoghurt and cucumber)
48	Burundi	elephant soup
49	Cambodia	khao poun (pork balls)
50	Scotland	cullen skink (cream of smoked haddock)
51	Cuba	guiso de garbanzos (chick peas)
52	Singapore	bak ku teh (pork rib tea soup)
53	Myanmar (Burma)	schwe payon hinjo (spiced pumpkin)
54	Iran	aash-e anaar (meat and pomegranate)
55	Algeria	jary (vegetables with wheat and lemon)
56	New Zealand	toheroa soup (shellfish)
57	Switzerland	Kuttelsuppe (tripe and vegetables)
58	China	tang mian (noodles)
59	Hungary	halászlé (fish and peppers)
60	Iceland	fjallagrasamjólk (moss soup)

DAVING THE LILY

Personal names which have a different meaning in old Scots

Ann   an extra salary payment made to a minister's widow
Barry   to thresh corn
Bella   a bonfire
Ben   a pile of empty coal containers
Bess   to sew together loosely
Bill   a bull
Billy   the golden warbler
Blair   to bleat like a sheep
Bob   a nosegay
Bobby   a grandfather
Bonnie of a wound, healing
Boyd   a blackberry
Brad   a derogatory word used for an old man
Buck   the sound made by something dropped into water
Carl   a clown or boor
Carly   a precocious boy
Carrie a type of wheelbarrow
Cath   to bat a ball along
Chuck   a girls' pebble game
Clair   to rake through a pile
Dale   a board for measuring a corpse
Dave   of pain, to lessen
Dee   a dairymaid
Dilly   a sandcastle
Dirk   to grope in the dark
Dolly   getting worse at poetry due to ageing

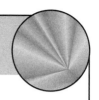

Don	an intimate acquaintance
Eve	a conger eel
Fay	near to death
Fern	gut used as violin strings
Frank	a heron
Gail	to be split by frost
Glen	a daffodil
Grant	to moan
Harry	to pilfer birds' eggs
Hope	a small bay
Jack	a leather drinking cup
Jake	to waste time
Jamie	a yokel
Jessie	a wig
Jenny	a centipede
Jilly	a pubescent girl
Jimmy	an oatmeal pudding
Jo, Joe	a sweetheart
Johnny	a half-glass of whisky
Jordan	a urinal or cesspool
Kate	of a cat, to be on heat
Kay	a jackdaw
Keith	a bar across a river to stop salmon
Ken	a whole season's worth of cheese
Kent	a pole used by shepherds to jump ditches
Kevin	a piece of refuse left after separating grain
Kim	a tub or ladle
Kyle	a bowling pin
Kylie	a little stick; a small haystack
Lawrie	a fox
Lee	the ashes of green weeds
Lily	thrush suffered in childhood

Luther a heavy blow

Maggie	the guillemot
Mark	darkness
Mattie	a young or fat herring
Maud	a shepherd's plaid
Meg	a sulky, short-tempered girl
Michael	a term applied to a girl
Miles	wild spinach
Neil	the Devil
Nell	to talk loudly or fluently
Nick	to drink heartily
Pam	a jack in cards, especially the jack of clubs
Paul	a puzzle
Penny	fancy food
Peter	to snub or irritate
Polly	a turkey
Ray	a song or poem
Rick	smoke
Rob	blackcurrant jam
Roddy	a path or trackway
Rodger	a big, ugly animal
Rory	drunk and loud
Rosie	red clay marble
Shane	to break a witch's spell
Sharon	cow's dung
Sol	a windowsill
Steve	uptight, stubborn
Tim	to empty out
Tom	a horsehair fishing line

Tommy a loaf of bread

Tyler a masonic lodge doorkeeper

Walt a crust of cheese

Walter confusion or an upset

INDIAN LINGO

The 18 official languages of India

1. Assamese
2. Bengali
3. Gujarati
4. Hindi
5. Kannada
6. Kashmiri
7. Konkani
8. Malayalam
9. Manipuri
10. Marathi
11. Nepali
12. Oriya
13. Punjabi
14. Sanskrit
15. Sindhi
16. Tamil
17. Telugu
18. Urdu

Over 200 recognized languages and dialects have been recorded in India — there are probably far more. Of the above 18, many of which have broad similarities, most are regional. Sanskrit is an ancient language no longer spoken, while Urdu is confined mainly to Muslims and Sindhi to those from an ethnic group originating in Pakistan. English does not have full official status, but is widely spoken.

ALL TOGETHER NOW

Some selections from the CD '50 Favourite Chinese Children's Songs'

1 'Children, Children, Spring of the Motherland'

2 'Labour is the Most Glorious'

3 'Being at the Side of the Teacher'

4 'Little Girl Picking Mushrooms'

5 'Child on the Cow's Back'

6 'Sitting on the Wings of the Song'

7 'We Want to be Good Children of Lei Feng Type'

8 'Happy Uncle Kuerban'

9 'My Little Chicken'

10 'How Wonderful the School Campus Is!'

11 'Let's Row Our Oars!'

12 'Little Herding Flute'

13 'Song of Selling Newspapers'

14 'Whenever I Walk Past the Teacher's Window'

15 'Cute Blue Fairy'

16 'Song of Horse Herding'

17 'Light Rain in March'

RAISE YOUR GLASSES

Twenty-five Scottish slang terms, old and new, for whisky

1 ackarity

2 ardent

3 aunty

4 barley-bree

5 barley-joice

6 barley-unction

7 blue thread

8 cratur

9 donald

10 dram

11 fusky

12 Hielan' blue

13 hooker

14 Jock Tamson

15 John Barleycorn

16 Johnny Maut

17 mountain dew

18 Norland-blue

19 oil of malt

20 peat-reek

21 royal blue

22 usquabae

23 wee-drap

24 whauky

25 Willie Arnot

CITY LIFE

Some 'city of' nicknames

1	Hyderabad (India)	the city of pearls
2	Fengdu (China)	the city of devils
3	Baltimore (USA)	the city of firsts
4	Bangalore (India)	the city of draught beer
5	Dundee (Scotland)	the city of discovery*
6	Tacoma (USA)	the city of vacant lots
7	Meissen (Germany)	the city of porcelain
8	Kansas City (USA)	the city of fountains
9	Puerto Madryn (Argentina)	the city of whales
10	Agadir (Morocco)	the city of the blue men**
11	Oxford (England)	the city of dreaming spires
12	Puebla (Mexico)	the city of tiles
13	Baguio (Philippines)	the city of pines
14	Escazú (Costa Rica)	the city of the witches
15	Chicago (USA)	the city of big shoulders
16	Porto (Portugal)	the city of work
17	Leiden (The Netherlands)	the city of refugees
18	Galway (Ireland)	the city of tribes
19	Antwerp (Belgium)	the city of the Madonnas
20	Philadelphia (USA)	the city of brotherly love
21	Prague (Czech Republic)	the city of a hundred spires
22	Austin (USA)	the city of the violet crown***

23	Auckland (New Zealand)	the city of sails
24	Moyobamba (Peru)	the city of orchids
25	Adelaide (Australia)	the city of churches
26	Ratnapura (Sri Lanka)	the city of gems
27	Kuching (Malaysia)	the city of cats
28	Guangzhou (China)	the city of five goats

* From explorer Robert Scott's famous Antarctic ship *Discovery*, made and now docked there.

** From the uniform of camel drivers.

*** From the purple haze on the surrounding mountains.

There are hundreds more of these 'city of ...' titles, often sounding suspiciously like they were made up by local officials trying to tempt people to 'the city of roses, warmth, festivals' etc (of which there are many examples). These are just some of the more interesting ones.

Five unlikely bands who had hit singles with songs about the conflict in Northern Ireland

LOOKING FOR TROUBLES

Madness ('Michael Caine')

The Police ('Invisible Sun')

Bananarama ('Rough Justice')

Spandau Ballet ('Through the Barricades')

Boney M ('Belfast')

blockhead

ignoramus

nitwit

moron

noodle

schmuck

jackass

ba'heid

clown

plonker

duffer

birdbrain

goose

twit

galoot

chipochia

dingbat

gull

clodpoll

plum

ninny

chump

dimwit

gimbo

silly-billy

pinhead

imbecile

dunderhead

booby

kook

fathead

mug

tomfool

ass

numbskull

cretin

dobird

schlep

daftie

nutjob

gumph

lummox

simpleton

airhead

buffoon

thicko

gowk

stupe

clot

doofus

bonehead

schlemiel

pudding

dullard

pranny

divvy

glaik

scatterbrain

twerp

knucklehead

goon

halfwit

THE FOOL PACK

bumpkin   lackwit

dork   goof

screwball   schmo

dolt   dumb-bell

mooncalf   beetlehead

nincompoop   mumchance

pea-brain   boofhead

oaf   fondling

dottle   woodcock

loonie   jughead

dumbo   cuddy

jobernowl   malt-horse

lunk   omadhaun

dummy   stumer

dope   dweeb

galah   Charlie

feeb   wigeon

juggins   goop

featherbrain   snipe

muttonhead   coof

Sammy   josser

dimbulb   cluck

eejit   sumph

shit-for-brains   muggins

wally   dodo

meathead   dill

dip   sawney

gomeril   gubbins

zany   nong

lamebrain   Tom-noddy

cuckoo   muppet

DOWN, FLIP-FLOP WEAZEL MULL OF KINTYRE, DOWN!

Twelve rumly-monickered Best in Show winners at Crufts Dog Show

1 Tracy Witch of Ware (1950)

2 Tzigane Affri of Nashend (1955)

3 Treetops Golden Falcon (1956)

4 Silbury Soames of Madavale (1964)

5 Oakington Puckshill Amber Sunblush (1966)

6 Hendrawen's Nibelung of Charavigne (1969)

7 Abraxas Audacity (1972)

8 Brookewire Brandy of Layven (1975)

9 Ginger Xmas Carol (1986)

10 Olac Moon Pilot (1990)

11 Ozmilion Mystification (1997)

12 Torums Scarf Michael (2000)

ON TOP

Twenty-two garnishes to add to soup

1   pastina (tiny pasta shapes)

2   dumplings (eg herb, liver or semolina)

3   kneidlach (matzo balls)

4   croutons (fried bread cubes)

5   crostini (similar to above)

6   chiffonades (ribbons of herbs and greens)

7   wasabi and daikon (Japanese horseradish and radish)

8   haystacks (deep-fried leek strips)

9   lokshen (noodles)

10 sippets (croutons or other bread pieces)

11 egg balls (pieces of cooked yolk)

12 kreplach (filled doughballs)

13 rivels (small pieces of dough)

14 mandeln (similar to above)

15 cream swirls

16 custard cut-outs (baked custard shapes)

17 crisped bacon

18 garlic crisps (deep-fried slices)

19 tofu pieces and spring onions

20 gnocchi (semolina, flour or potato doughballs)

21 printanier (snips of eg turnip and carrot)

22 smetana (high-fat sour cream)

HIDE THE GINGER BEER

The crime-solving children's gangs in the books of Enid Blyton

The Famous Five
Julian, Anne, Dick, George (properly Georgina), Timmy*

The **Adventure** books (eg *The Castle of Adventure*)
Jack, Lucy-Ann, Dinah, Philip

The Secret Seven
Barbara, Jack, Colin, Pam, George, Janet, Peter

The **Mystery** books (eg *The Ring o' Bells Mystery*)
Roger, Diana, Barney, Snubby

The Five Find-outers (*The Mystery of ____ books*)
Larry, Daisy, Pip, Fatty, Bets

The **Secret** books (eg *The Secret Mountain*)
Nora, Mike, Peggy, Jack

* Timmy was a dog. The Five Find-outers' dog was Buster, who was evidently not good enough at sniffing out crimes to be included as number six; Scamper the dog was an honorary member of the Secret Seven. The Mystery series' dog was Loony.

HOW THE POETS GOT THEIR NAMES

Three famous British poets of recent times have had very unusual first names

1 **Wystan** (AUDEN) was named after a Mercian princeling killed by his uncle Bertulph during a power struggle in 849. He was buried in Repton Abbey, Derbyshire according to de Marleberge's *Chronica Abbatiae de Evesham*.

2 **Dylan** (THOMAS) was named after a very minor figure in the *Mabinogion*, the classic collection of Welsh folklore. Dylan is a yellow-haired child born when his supposedly virginal mother Arianrhod steps over a magic wand. The child immediately heads for the sea. The name probably means 'ocean' or 'wave'. It is properly pronounced *dullan*, not *dillan*, though Thomas' family mispronounced it. It was a very rare name at the time.

3 **Rudyard** (KIPLING) was named after the place, Rudyard Lake in Staffordshire, where his parents are thought to have met. The name means either 'place where rudd are kept' or 'garden where rue is planted'.

MOVE OVER ANDROCLES

The tools on a Swiss Army Knife
(Victorinox SwissChamp XLT® model)

Large Blade • Small Blade • Pharmaceutical Spatula

Corkscrew • Can Opener • Small Screwdriver

Bottle Opener • Large Screwdriver • Wire Stripper

Electrician's Blade • Reamer, Punch & Sewing Eye

Scissors • Hook • Wood Saw

Fish Scaler, Hook Disgorger & Ruler • Pruning Blade

Wrench with 4mm & 5mm Female Hex Drive and

Phillips Pozidrive 0 & 1 • 4mm Slotted Bit

Phillips 2 Bit • 4mm Hex Bit • Torx 8 Bit

Torx 10 Bit • Torx 15 Bit • Nail File & Nail Cleaner

Metal Saw & File • Fine Screwdriver

Mini Screwdriver • Phillips Screwdriver

Magnifying Glass • Ballpoint Pen & DIP Switch Setter

Stainless Steel Pin • Chisel

Pliers & Wire Cutters • Crimpers • Wire Bender

Keyring • Tweezers • Toothpick

Twenty-three common words originally derived in some way from Arabic

MIDDLE EASTERN

1 alcohol
2 rook
3 algebra
4 sequin
5 mattress
6 giraffe
7 amber
8 crimson
9 gazelle
10 hazard
11 arsenal
12 lute
13 sofa
14 zero
15 alcove
16 safari
17 sherbet
18 alkali
19 candy
20 syrup
21 check
22 admiral
23 magazine

... and twenty-three Arabic-derived words connected with plants

24 couscous
25 lilac
26 henna
27 apricot
28 coffee
29 spinach
30 cork
31 artichoke
32 tarragon
33 cotton
34 carob
35 jasmine
36 lime
37 caraway
38 lemon
39 tamarind
40 orange
41 loofah
42 aubergine
43 alfalfa
44 hashish
45 camphor
46 saffron

THE KING IS DEAD

The strange deaths, according to popular belief, of some British monarchs

Edmund II, Ironside
(c.990–1016)   spear attack

Saxon toilets consisted of a wooden seat with a pit dug below. Edmund is said to have been killed by two thrusts up the rectum from a sword-wielding enemy soldier who was hiding in the pit.

William I, the Conqueror
(1027–87)   horse accident

William died in France in September 1087, having sustained serious injuries a few weeks before when his horse reared up and threw him.

William II
(c.1056–1100)   arrow in the heart

William Rufus, an unpopular king, was shot in the heart while hunting deer in the New Forest. It may have been an accident, but the king had so many enemies, even within his own hunting party, that murder seems more likely.

Henry I
(1133–89)   surfeit of lampreys

Henry died in his late 60s while on a hunting trip in Normandy. It appears to have been a case of greed. At a feast, Henry had partaken of a large amount of lampreys (small eels), a favourite dish of his. The resulting intestinal problems finished him off.

Richard I, the Lionheart
(1157–99)   gangrene

Having survived wars, crusades and imprisonment by the age of 35, Richard died a few years later after an arrow grazed his shoulder during a trifling battle in France in 1199. Gangrene set in and the minor wound was enough to do for him.

130

John
(1167–1216)   greed

The unpleasant King John died of natural causes in 1216 but, seeing as he was only 48 at the time, it is thought that his hugely overweight frame, caused by lifelong gluttony, was a major factor.

Alexander III
(1241–86)   drunk driving

In 1286, after a drunken feast at Edinburgh Castle, this Scottish king, hungry for his new, young wife, decided to undertake the five-hour ride back to his home in Fife, despite a freezing storm. While riding along the clifftops, lost in the darkness, his horse is thought to have panicked and thrown him over the edge to his death.

Edward II
(1284–1327)   red hot poker

Queen Isabella, tiring of her older husband who had had relationships with male courtiers, hatched a plot with her lover Mortimer to overthrow him. Mortimer had Edward murdered at Berkeley Castle. A red-hot bar of iron was thrust up his rear-end. He died screaming; the corpse was said to have borne a terrifying grimace.

Richard II
(1367–1400)   murder

Crowned at the age of ten and taking charge of England in his mid-teens, Richard started well, but by his late 20s had become a dangerous tyrant. Having been forced to abdicate in 1399, in favour of his hated relative Henry IV, he was quietly done away with in Pontefract Castle the following year.

Richard III
(1452–85)   in battle

At the age of 32, Richard led his large, experienced army against Henry Tudor's supposedly weaker forces. But great bands of men began deserting Richard for the Tudor side and he died in the thick of a battle he ought to have won.

Edward VI
(1537–53)   poison?

In 1553, still only in his mid-teens, the promising boy-king had fallen victim to tuberculosis. He may have been helped along the way with poison by the power-hungry Duke of Northumberland. The night of his death was marked by a terrible storm all over England.

William III
(1650–1702)   death by mole

The frail and grieving William was riding his horse Sorrel when it tripped on a molehill and collapsed. William fell and broke his collarbone. He died of a fever some days later, never quite recovering from the accident.

George I
(1660–1727)   seasickness

The German-born king, never comfortable with his life as British monarch, spent much of his later life back in Hanover. He was on his way there when he had a stroke which was rumoured to have been brought on by nausea from overeating melons in an attempt to soothe seasickness. He was taken to Osnabrück Castle where, by chance, he died in the same room in which he had been born.

George II
(1683–1760)   toilet trouble

George died at the ripe age of 78 in 1760. When his servant heard troubled sounds emanating from the palace lavatory, he was not too worried, since the king had notorious bowel troubles and could make a lot of noise. However, on investigation it turned out that the king had collapsed with the strain of it all, and had smashed his head open on fittings as he slumped dead.

as happy as a pig in mud **1**
as happy as can be **2**
as happy as a clam* **3**
as happy as Larry **4**
as happy as the day is long **5**
as happy as a lark **6**
as happy as kings **7**
as happy as a box of birds **8**
as happy as a dog at the beach **9**
as happy as a sandboy** **10**
as happy as a kid in a candy store **11**
as happy as a bag of wigs **12**
as happy as the cat that got the cream **13**
as happy as a bull in a spring paddock **14**
as glad as a breeze **15**
as glad as a fox in his nest **16**
as glad as a bird in May **17**
as glad as adders **18**
as glad as a newborn kitten **19**
as glad as the shamrocks **20**
as pleased as a kitten with a ball of wool **21**
as pleased as a jay with a bean **22**
as pleased as a kid with a new toy **23**
as pleased as a peach **24**
as pleased as a fox in a henhouse **25**
as pleased as a Cheshire cat **26**
as pleased as a chickadee with a sunflower seed **27**
as pleased as a peacock **28**
as pleased as a dog with a bone **29**
as pleased as a sailor on his wedding day **30**
as pleased as a little dog with two tails **31**
as pleased as pie **32**
as pleased as a penny carrot **33**
as pleased as Punch **34**
as pleased as a pig in a poke **35**
as pleased as a brass ha'penny **36**

H.A.P.P.Y.

Some cheerful similes

* In full, 'a clam at high tide', ie when it would not be picked.
** Sandboys provided sand for the floors of shops and taverns. It could be a lucrative business, with little outlay and the prospect of lost coins and valuables sifted from the dirty sand carted away.

DON'T LET NATURE KILL YOU

Ten poisonous natural substances to avoid

1

The yellow fruit called the **ackee**, common in African and West Indian cooking, is prohibited or strictly controlled in much of the USA. The problem lies in knowing just when the fruit is ripe. Too soon or late and the fruit can poison or even kill you.

2

Although a stimulant in tiny quantities, in coffee and other drinks, **caffeine** is extremely toxic if ingested in larger amounts.

3

Industrial ethanol, sometimes used as a fuel, is not good for us, though many people used to drink it as a cheap and potent booze. To combat this, manufacturers add **methanol**, which is poisonous, to make methylated spirits.

4

Though most turtles are edible and are commonly eaten in various parts of the world, a few species, including the **hawksbill** turtle, have skin and flesh which contain chemicals which are toxic.

5

In rural India, food shortages sometimes drive people to exist on 'tanku peejaw', a simple gruel made from boiled **mango** seeds. Unfortunately, when the seed paste is left

for a day or two, it ferments into a deadly pulp
which has killed many people.

6

The fleshy red part of **rhubarb** makes a tasty ingredient
for a pie, but the leaves are very poisonous and must
never be eaten. The leaves of potato and tomato plants
are also both harmful.

7

As part of the defence against the rigours of the Arctic
lifestyle, the polar bear stores large amounts of vitamin A
in its **liver** – so much, in fact, that eating the liver is
dangerously toxic to humans and other animals.

8

The fugu, a Pacific **blowfish**, is responsible for around
50 diner deaths each year in the Far East. It contains a
toxin, a drop of which can be lethal when it meets the
nervous system. Chefs must be licensed to laboriously
prepare and cook the fish, which is predictably
expensive.

9

Learning to tell edible fungi from their poisonous and
emetic cousins can be difficult, but there are often clues
in the names – death cap, death angel, panther cap,
destroying angel. And the **sickener** mushroom will, as
you might imagine, make you vomit.

10

Some poisonous plant names also contain clues –
deadly nightshade, bleeding heart, dogbane,
devil's trumpet. Since the mountain laurel shrub
is also known as **lambkill**, calfkill and
sheepkill, you might want to keep your farm
animals away from it.

CIN CITY

Twenty US cities which have given their names to movies

1. *New York* (1927)
2. *San Francisco* (1936)
3. *Honolulu* (1939)
4. *Reno* (1939)
5. *Pittsburgh* (1942)
6. *San Antonio* (1945)
7. *New Orleans* (1947)
8. *Albuquerque* (1947)
9. *El Paso* (1949)
10. *Tucson* (1949)
11. *Tulsa* (1949)
12. *Dallas* (1950)
13. *Fort Worth* (1951)
14. *Topeka* (1953)
15. *Nashville* (1975)
16. *Memphis* (1992)
17. *Philadelphia* (1993)
18. *Kansas City* (1996)
19. *Fargo* (1996)
20. *Chicago* (2002)

Traditional British sweets which *used to be sold in jars*

1 **bonbons** round lumps of sweet toffee in strawberry, lemon and caramel flavours, dusted with coloured icing sugar

2 **hoarhounds** dark, orangey-brown, tangy boiled sweets made from a medicinal plant and used as cough sweets

3 **barley sugar** clear, rich orange sticks, twists or lumps of boiled sugar, formerly containing an extract of barley

4 **bull's eyes** despite the name, these are black-and-white striped twisted lumps of hard, minty candy

5 **soor plooms** a Scottish favourite: sticky green balls with a tart plum flavour

6 **sports mixture** small fruit gums in the shapes of cricket bats, footballs and so on

7 **chocolate limes** luminous green boiled casings, each enclosing a lump of sticky chocolate

8 **ginger creams** crunchy, beige lumps with a strong-tasting ginger fondant centre

9 **pan drops** another Scottish sweet: large, flat and rounded peppermints with a shiny shell, forever to be found in the bottom of granny's handbag

10 **strawberry sherbets** red, rounded lozenges of berry-flavour boiled sweet with a sharp sherbet centre

11 **fairy drops** buttons of white chocolate covered in multicoloured sugar strands, aka 'hundreds and thousands'

12	**kola cubes**	delicious dark-red cola-flavour cubes with a sugar frosting
13	**Berwick cockles**	minty pillow-shaped hard boiled sweets, white-striped with red, originally made in the border town of Berwick
14	**coulter's candy**	irregular lumps of dark, hard toffee with a slightly burnt taste
15	**Everton mints**	old-fashioned striped mints with a chewy mint toffee centre
16	**sherbet lemons**	lemon-shaped boiled sweets laced with a dose of sherbet powder
17	**pomfret cakes**	coin-shaped pieces of liquorice from the Yorkshire town of Pontefract
18	**kopp kopps**	small, hard, black sweets with a sugar frosting which gave way to a pungent, medicinal flavouring
19	**midget gems**	tiny, cylindrical fruit-flavoured gum sweets
20	**pear drops**	pear-shaped boiled sweets with a tangy flavour similar to ethanol ester
21	**rhubarb rock**	sliced lumps of rock with a sharp red coating and a sweeter yellow centre
22	**teacakes**	small and flattened lumps of coconut and marzipan with a sugar frosting
23	**comfits**	capsule-shaped sweets with coloured sugar cases and liquorice inside
24	**brandy drops**	large red-brown boiled sweets with a rich winey taste
25	**satins**	multi-coloured pillow shapes of boiled candy, with various fruity flavours
26	**butternuts**	bright orange sucking sweets with a buttery taste, like miniature gobstoppers
27	**raspberry ruffles**	mixed coconut and raspberry fondant inside a shell of quite dark chocolate

28	**oddfellows**	large, spiced lozenges in pastel colours, slightly aromatic-tasting and crunchy
29	**rosebuds**	tiny pink and yellow fruit-flavoured boiled sweets
30	**sherbet pips**	very small and round sherbet sucking sweets in sharp citrus flavours
31	**poor bens**	small ribbed black pastilles with a liquorice and aniseed flavour
32	**chewing nuts**	chocolate nut-sized lumps with hard stickjaw toffee inside
33	**Army and Navy**	liquorice lozenges used for soothing a sore throat
34	**pineapple chunks**	similar to kola cubes, but with a pineapple flavour
35	**sweet peanuts**	buttery, nut-flavoured boiled sweets shaped like a peanut shell, with a soft, crunchy centre
36	**floral gums**	midget gem-style gums flavoured with rose and other floral and aromatic scents
37	**iced caramels**	soft toffees inside an iced shell in pastel colours
38	**sugared almonds**	consisting of a nut inside a brittle, coloured candy coating
39	**granny sookers**	triangular boiled apple-flavour sweets, supposedly beloved of older women
40	**wine gums**	fruit-flavoured chewy gums, originally shaped like wine bottles, glasses, etc

BEAST BEHAVIOUR

Some former folk beliefs about animals

1   It was once believed that snake bites and insect stings could be treated by climbing onto a donkey's back the wrong way round. **Dead donkeys** were leaped over for luck: they were considered extremely rare, since the common belief was that a donkey at death's door would sneak off and conceal itself.

2   People used to believe that the opossum had the following, most unusual, method of **reproduction**: the male would copulate with the female's snout, then blow in her mouth and nose, thus sending the sperm down into her pouch.

3   A **billy goat** used to be kept with horses since the company, and especially the smell, was thought to keep horses calm and disease-free (whereby, it has been suggested, may come the phrase 'to get someone's goat', since stealing a racehorse's companion was said to put it off its race.)

4   Bats' hearts and badgers' teeth were both considered lucky **charms** by gamblers.

5   The ancient Egyptians revered cats so much that they shaved their **eyebrows** off when a pet died, hoping this would help speed the puss to the feline afterlife.

6   Inhaling **cows' breath** was commonly thought to be good for us; it was claimed that dairy farmers never suffered from lung diseases.

7 Whereas nowadays a banknote stuffed into the waistband of hot pants will cause certain women to gyrate and undress, in the 14th century the preferred method was to write your name on parchment in owl's blood and **mole's sperm** and shove it under a woman's door. This would soon entrance her into dancing naked.

8 A medieval substitute for an alarm clock was to eat **hare's brain** stewed in wine. This was thought to prevent you from sleeping in the next day. Others were convinced that eating hare would make you melancholic.

9 The origin of the phrase '**hair of the dog** that bit you' is quite literal: people felt that a dog bite would heal more quickly if dressed with some fur from the offending cur.

10 People used to test their luck by throwing a **pig's nose** over their house with their backs to the door. Failure to clear the roof was a bad omen. Meanwhile, a wild pig's tusks were said to light up and glow demonically red during a hunt.

11 It used to be thought that eating weasel meat would be an antidote to snake poison. However, consuming **venison** could cause such poisoning, since it was believed that snakes were a major part of a deer's diet.

12 Even today in some places, fried fieldmouse is thought to be a fast and effective cure for whooping cough. Various illnesses were 'cured' by tying sheep's lungs or **spleens** to the feet.

13 **Bears** were formerly thought to mate just once every seven years but make so much noise doing so that farm animals would miscarry in fear.

LONG LIVE THE KING!

People and things which have been acclaimed as kings*

Kings of food and drink

1	King of Beers	Budweiser®
2	King of Rice	basmati or carnaroli
3	King of Nuts	almond
4	King of Stout	Guinness®
5	King of Puddings	4 eggs, 1pt milk, 8oz sugar, 4oz breadcrumbs, 4tbsp jam, 1tsp vanilla essence
6	King of Wines	Tokay or champagne
7	King of Fruits	mango or durian
8	King of Spices	pepper
9	King of Cheese	parmigiano reggiano
10	King of Red Wine	Cabernet Sauvignon
11	King of English Cheeses	stilton
12	King of Mushrooms	shiitake or maitake
13	King of White Wine	Chardonnay
14	King of 'Winter Taste'	echizen crab (Japanese delicacy)
15	King of Italian Wines	Barolo

Kings of the natural world

1	King of Beasts or the Jungle	lion
2	King of the Sea	herring
3	King of Woods	teak
4	King of Terriers	Airedale
5	King of Birds	wren or eagle
6	King of Trees	oak

7	King of Hair	bhringaraj ('hair-restoring' herb)
8	King of Hunting Dogs	Weimaraner
9	King of the Mountain	tiger
10	King of Herbs	ginseng
11	King of the Garden	rhododendrons
12	King of Fish	salmon or sturgeon
13	King of Flowers	peony
14	King of Dyes	indigo
15	King of the Forest	oak or Scots pine
16	King of Waters	River Amazon

Some fictitious monarchs

1	King of New York	gangster. Frank White (as played by Christopher Walken)
2	King of the Jungle	Tarzan (one of the monkeyman's monickers)
3	King of the Hill	Hank Hill (animated redneck with a conscience)
4	King of Comedy	Rupert Pupkin (wannnabe in the movie of the same name)
5	King of the Fairies	Oberon (Shakespeare's fairy king)
6	King of Terror	? (Nostradamus's unidentified apocalyptic leader)
7	King of the Trows	Broonie (troll leader in Scottish folklore)

Some things which are kings of their domains

1	King of Gems	ruby
2	King of Trails	Highway 75 from Winnipeg to Galveston
3	King of Craftsmen	blacksmith

4	King of Instruments	trombone or pipe organ
5	King of Crystals	diamond
6	King of Trains	the Orient Express
7	King of Scents	amber resin
8	King of Metals	gold

Some other people nicknamed or self-styled as kings

1	King of Steel	Andrew Carnegie (magnate from Fife)
2	King of One-Liners	Henry Youngman (US comic)
3	King of the Pulps	Max Brand (writer of westerns)
4	King of the Witches	Alex Sanders (British mystic)
5	King of the Mini-Series	Richard Chamberlain
6	King of Clout	Babe Ruth (baseball basher)
7	King of Off Broadway	Edward Albee (US playwright)
8	King of the Wild Frontier	Davy Crockett (pioneer and folk hero)
9	King of Beige	Giorgio Armani (fancy togmaker)
10	King of Hops	Michael Jackson (beer expert, a pun on his namesake)
11	King of Hollywood	Clark Gable
12	King of Welsh Rugby	Barry John
13	King of Showmen	Pat Collins (fairground legend)
14	King of the Ice	Elvis Stojko (skater)
15	King of Paparazzi	Rino Barillari
16	King of Hay-on-Wye	Richard Booth (self-styled king of town on English–Welsh border famous for its many bookshops)
17	King of Clowns	Felix Adler

18	King of Blood	Edwin Cohn (biologist)
19	King of Stonehenge	the Amesbury Archer (ancient skeleton)
20	King of Mystery	John Dickson Carr (crime writer)
21	King of the Ferret Leggers	Reg Mellor (top man of arcane and painful sport)
22	King of X	John Holmes (well-endowed tragic star of naughty films)
23	King of Horror	Stephen King
24	King of the Gypsies	Bampfylde Moore Carew (English vagabond)
25	King of the Cowboys	Roy Rogers
26	King of Kings	Jesus Christ
27	King of Chefs ·	Auguste Escoffier
28	King of Cocktails	Dale DeGroff (mover and shaker)
29	King of Handcuffs	Harry Houdini
30	King of Pirates	Edward Teach (aka Blackbeard)
31	King of Spam	Alan Ralsky (bulk emailer)
32	King of the Wildcatters	Hugh Roy Cullen (oil prospector)
33	King of the Stretford End	Denis Law (60s and 70s Scottish soccer star for Manchester United)
34	King of Bark	Christopher III of Scandinavia (added tree bark to his subjects' food during a famine)
35	King of Runners	Paavo Nurmi (aka the Flying Finn)
36	King of painters	Parrhasius (ancient Greek dauber)

*Many of these titles are hotly contested.

DEATH DISCO

Twenty curiously-titled death metal and grindcore songs

'Thorns of Crimson Death' (by Dissection)

'Hammer Smashed Face' (by Cannibal Corpse)

'Slowly We Rot' (by Obituary)

'Lustmord and Wargasm (The Lick of Carnivorous Winds)' (by Cradle of Filth)

'Purulent Bowel Erosion' (by Fleshcrawl)

'Ants (Nemesis Ride)' (by Cancer)

'Swarming Vulgar Mass of Infected Virulency' (by Carcass)

'Dawn of Perishness' (by Therion)

'A Succubus in Rapture' (by Dimmu Borgir)

'Impulsive Necroplasma' (by Edge of Sanity)

'Remnants of Withered Decay' (by Malevolent Creation)

'Future Breed Machine' (by Meshuggah)

'Liege of Inveracity' (by Suffocation)

'Of Blindness and Subsequent Seers' (by Emperor)

'Black Stone Wielder' (by Candlemass)

'Voice of a Tortured Skull' (by Mayhem)

'Disconnected Magnetic Corridors' (by Hypocrisy)

'Rivalry of Phantoms' (by Borknagar)

'Transmigration Macabre' (by Arch Enemy)

'Goliaths Disarm Their Davids' (by In Flames)

ROLL UP!

The text on a nearby 'milestone' explaining the Electric Brae experience

'The Electric Brae', known locally as Croy Brae. This runs the quarter mile from the bend overlooking Croy railway viaduct in the west (286 feet Above Ordnance Datum) to the wooded Craigencroy Glen (303 feet A.O.D.) to the east. Whilst there is this slope of 1 in 86 upwards from the bend to the Glen, the configuration of the land on either side of the road provides an optical illusion making it look as if the slope is going the other way. Therefore, a stationary car on the road with the brakes off will appear to move slowly uphill. The term 'Electric' dates from a time when it was incorrectly thought to be a phenomenon caused by electric or magnetic attraction within the Brae.

The Electric Brae is on the A719 in Ayrshire, Scotland. I recall experiencing the strange sensation as a child during a family holiday.

A WOMAN'S WORK

Eleven tips for male supervisors on 'getting more efficiency out of women employees', from the July 1943 issue of *Mass Transportation* magazine

1 If you can get them, pick young married women. They have these advantages, according to the reports of western companies: they usually have more of a sense of responsibility than do their unmarried sisters; they're less likely to be flirtatious; as a rule, they need the work or they wouldn't be doing it – maybe a sick husband or one who's in the army; they still have the pep and interest to work hard and to deal with the public efficiently.

2 When you have to use older women, try to get ones who have worked outside the home at some time in their lives. Most transportation companies have found that older women who have never contacted the public, have a hard time adapting themselves, are inclined to be cantankerous and fussy. It's always well to impress on the older woman the importance of friendliness and courtesy.

3 While there are exceptions, of course, to this rule, general experience indicates that 'husky' girls – those who are just a little on the heavy side – are likely to be more even-tempered and efficient than their underweight sisters.

4 Retain a physician to give each woman you hire a special physical examination – one covering female conditions. This step not only protects the property against the possibility of lawsuits but also reveals whether the employee-to-be has any female weaknesses which would make her mentally or physically unfit for the job. Transit companies that follow this practice report a surprising number of women turned down for nervous disorders.

5 In breaking in women who haven't previously done outside work, stress at the outset the importance of time – the fact that a minute or two lost here and there makes serious inroads on schedules. Until this point is gotten across, service is likely to be slowed up.

6 Give the female employee in garage or office a definite day-long schedule of duties so that she'll keep busy without bothering the management for instructions every few minutes. Numerous properties say that women make excellent workers when they have their jobs cut out for them but that they lack initiative in finding work for themselves.

7 Whenever possible, let the inside employee change from one job to another at some time during the day. Women are inclined to be nervous and they're happier with change.

8 Give every girl an adequate number of rest periods during the day. Companies that are already using large numbers of women stress the fact that you have to make some allowance for feminine psychology. A girl has more confidence and consequently is more efficient if she can keep her hair tidied, apply fresh lipstick and wash her hands several times a day.

9 Be tactful in issuing instructions or in making criticisms. Women are often sensitive; they can't shrug off harsh words in the way that men do. Never ridicule a woman – it breaks her spirit and cuts her efficiency.

10 Be reasonably considerate about using strong language around women. Even though a girl's husband or father may swear vociferously, she'll grow to dislike a place of business where she hears too much of this.

11 Get enough size variety in operator uniforms that each girl can have a proper fit. This point can't be stressed too strongly as a means of keeping women happy, according to western properties.

PEEL ME

The Greatest Hits — if the Velvet Underground had been Scottish

1 'I'm Wee Free'
2 'Sweet Ginger'
3 'White Land/White Hill'
4 'Run, Run, Runrig'
5 'Foggy Nation'
6 'I'll Be Your Record'
7 'Sandy Says'
8 'Pale Red Hair'
9 'Whit Gangs Oan'
10 'Caledonian Son to Hugh MacDiarmid'
11 'Sister Rhona'
12 'Lady Macbeth's Operation'
13 'All Tomorrow's Ceilidhs'
14 'Venus in Largs'

CRUSHED TO DEATH

The ten degrees of intensity of passion for another man's wife according to the *Kama Sutra*

1 love of the eye
2 attachment of the mind
3 constant reflection
4 destruction of sleep
5 emaciation of the body
6 turning away from objects of enjoyment
7 removal of shame
8 madness
9 fainting
10 death

Roddy's tip — avoid the inevitability of number ten by skipping number five! It works for me!

The 36 most Dickensian Dickensian characters

MUTUAL FRIENDS

1 Nicodemus Dumps
2 Augustus Moddle
3 Wackford Squeers
4 Hannibal Chollop
5 Fanny Cleaver
6 Alderman Cute
7 Phil Squod
8 Sampson Brass
9 Nathaniel Pipkin
10 Montague Tigg
11 Affery Flintwinch
12 Conkey Chickweed
13 Jarvis Lorry
14 Caddy Jellyby
15 Canon Septimus Crisparkle
16 Anastasia Veneering
17 Toby Crackit
18 Dot Peerybingle
19 Simon Tappertit
20 Volumnia Dedlock
21 Sir Barnet Skettles
22 Noah Claypole
23 Zephaniah Scadder
24 Abel Magwitch
25 Ned Cheeryble
26 Mercy Pecksniff
27 Diggory Chuzzlewit
28 Newman Noggs
29 Pleasant Riderhood
30 Cecilia Bobster
31 Henerietty Boffin
32 Quebec Bagnet
33 Lord Decimus Tite Barnacle
34 Hiram Grewgious
35 Luke Honeythunder
36 Prince Turveydrop

QUOTIDIAN CACOPHONY

One hundred and one people's most hated words

bamboozle	brouhaha
whore	incent
soulmate	bitch
apoplexy	progressive
blurt	pimp
kidnap	sofa
obfuscate	slather
tracheotomy	usability
haggis	taboo
ointment	rectum
flaccid	gauche
pelmet	haemorrhage
heuristic	proactive
puppies	piss
barf	classical
chipotle	sucks
hyperbole	timeous
regimentation	musings
moustache	moist
phlegmy	flesh
memo	fidget
pagination	blagging
sewage	couscous
retiree	schmuck
webmaster	chestnut

suckle
deplane
cute
pamphlet
carbuncle
abortion
genre
landlord
shall
exchequer
filthy
knickers
clique
stylish
nostrils
inchoate
barbarous
ordure
gunman
sup
ambient
cathartic
pus
journalling
nausea
showcase

poodle
bald
scrotum
nougat
chore
panties
juggler
stinky
cummerbund
gimmick
downsizing
period
commentator
blockade
cretin
lush
flapjack
maestro
squelch
retired
fannypack
anorak
ladies
soundscape
stumer

**My own would have to include gobsmacked,
cloaca, hubby and spirituality.**

KIDS IN AMERICA

The basic ingredients of American 'coming of age' films

- A voiceover by the main character at the start of the film ('That was the summer I was 14 years old …') as the camera follows them cycling along a street, standing up on the pedals.

- Perfect summer weather, bar one terrible storm.

- A massive unrequited crush on someone way, way out of the main character's league, who will look at them with renewed interest ten minutes before the end of the film.

- Two cars full of teenagers pulling up alongside each other at some red lights, and a whole lot of threatening eye contact.

- A dog that is never on a lead, knows loads of tricks and can put its head on one side.

- A bitchy girl who is haughtily beautiful, with a coterie of henchwomen, each uglier than the next, who will at some point all be soaked in some kind of liquid.

- A mom who only ever comes in with groceries and or goes out to dinner, conveniently leaving the house empty for teenage mayhem. Sometimes she will put on make-up, although she is already wearing lots.

- An emotionally absent father, prone to making stilted conversation and taking off his glasses to polish them.

- A crucial sports fixture. One point needed in the final minute. An unlikely hero hoisted on the shoulders of his teammates.

- A geeky girl who is actually flawless, but has braces like oil rigs on her teeth and large bunches.

- A geeky boy in glasses who walks leaning forwards from the waist and regularly falls over.

- Small stones thrown at a window which is soon escaped from via the branches of a tall tree.

- An improbable gadget wired up by the geeks to soak, trip or strip clothes from the bully gang.

- Parents looking with concern at a door slamming behind their teenage offspring and then at each other in silence. They will be holding cutlery above an uneaten meal. They just don't understand.

- Social humiliation – like tissue paper falling out of a bra – followed by a sprint down a locker-lined corridor and a shot over the walls of a toilet cubicle down onto sobbing girl.

- Fluffy jumpers, usually accessorized with a pile of books clasped close to budding teenage breasts.

- A dead body. And nobody must know.

- An older tearaway character with a flash motor, James Dean hair, a leather jacket and a hidden heart of gold.

- A test of friendship, like a bitter row where one of the friends storms off, usually into a dangerous situation like driving towards a canyon with a missing bridge.

- The local cop with mirror shades and thick tash who glowers from beneath his peaked cop cap. Will later drive into fire hydrant causing it to gush.

- A nasty sibling who is really mean but manages not to get into trouble. Usually seen menacingly thumping a baseball mitt if male, or going out to the prom with a smug expression if female.

155

- A wise character with an old spirit, even if not actually old, often a worn-down waitress or janitor, who watches proceedings and occasionally comments sagely on them while shaking head.

- A soundtrack involving soul staples.

- Cheerleaders and all the complex social hierarchy they imply.

- An embittered sports coach eventually revealed to be a bullying fraud, resulting in school sports star being emotionally crushed by loss of father figure.

- A yearning shot of a smiling girl walking in slo-mo from left to right, her ponytail bobbing in the sunshine, in the company of Butch/Brad/Brawn/Brick, the spunk on the high-school football team. She will glance over her shoulder at the star-struck central character.

- A bicycle chase.

- Hilarious dining room incident involving the central character, a sporty jock (if main character is male) or head cheerleader (if main character is female) and a milk carton, swiftly followed by extreme physical pain and/or severe humiliation.

- Milk carton incident duly noted by good-natured and rather shy girl/boy who feels sorry for our hero/heroine.

- Shy person and main character collide coming round a corner, scattering their school books all over the floor; much bending down, apologizing and awkward silences ensue, but love is in their eyes.

- A voiceover by the main character at the end of the film as the camera pans up and away from the street where it all began.

BERRY BERRY FEVER

Twenty-one strawberry-flavoured infowisps from the world of arts and entertainment

1   *I My Me! Strawberry Eggs* is a curiously-titled Japanese animation series in which the hero poses as a woman in order to secure a job at a school which employs only female teachers.

2   In **Othello**, the notorious handkerchief which leads to Othello's downfall is 'spotted with strawberries', a pattern which symbolizes fidelity and virginal blood.

3   In the book and film **The Caine Mutiny**, Queeg's madness is exacerbated by the theft of a quart of frozen strawberries by someone else on the ship.

4   The 1982 LP **Strawberries**, by pop punks **the Damned**, came with a scratch and sniff lyric insert which smelled of the eponymous fruit.

5   Over 20 films have name-checked the red berry, including *Strawberries and Wine*, *Strawberry Flavour*, *Strawberry Spring* and *The Strawberry Blonde*, starring James Cagney, Olivia de Havilland and **Rita Hayworth**.

6   '**Strawberries**' and other favourite love poems by Edwin Morgan were somewhat reassessed when Morgan 'came out' rather late in life. 'Let the storm wash the plates.'

7 In the Bergman film **The Seventh Seal**, the characters Block and Jof discuss the plague and eat a bowl of fresh strawberries – heavily symbolic, no doubt.

8 Sitcom characters **Frasier** Crane and Private **Fraser** may both be berry men, the names perhaps being originally derived from a French surname meaning strawberry.

9 Strawberry Studio, in **Stockport**, was used to record many well-known LPs, including ones by **10cc**, **Ramones** and **Joy Division**.

10 Strawberries have appeared in the titles of both Harry **Secombe's** autobiography and a book about sex by Vanessa **Feltz**.

11 **Ruth Rendell** wrote *The Strawberry Tree* for television. It starred Eleanor Bron and Simon Ward.

12 Strawberries have cropped up (excuse the pun) in LP titles by Pat **Benatar**, Johnny **Cash** and Paul **Butterfield**.

13 Strawberries make regular appearances in children's literature. Favourites include the cutesy **Strawberry Shortcake** character, *Flicka, Ricka, Dicka and the Strawberries*, and **Strawberry Girl**, Lois **Lenski's** homely classic telling of the struggles of a Florida frontier family.

14 Jessica Stirling, leading author of romances such as *The Strawberry Season*, is actually an elderly Scotsman named **Hugh Rae**.

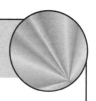

15 In *Henry V*, **Shakespeare** notes metaphorically that 'the strawberry grows underneath the nettle'.

16 *Wild Strawberries*, the Bergman film, is properly known as *Smultronstället*.

17 The folk song 'Strawberry Fair' evolved into the song '**Scarborough Fair**'. Both are derived from the old ballad 'The Elfin Knight'.

18 The Fragaria fruit has found its way into many band names, including the **Strawbs**, Strawberry Alarm Clock, Wild Strawberries, Strawberry Minds, Strawberry **Switchblade** and Strawberry Slaughterhouse.

19 In the Peter Weir film *Fearless*, Jeff Bridges's character believes he is invincible after surviving a plane crash. To prove it, he eats strawberries, to which he previously had a chronic allergic reaction.

20 Part of New York City's **Central Park** was renamed Strawberry Fields after the shooting, outside the nearby Dakota Building, of John Lennon.

21 In the movie industry, the term **strawberry filter** supposedly refers to a situation when a director needs to pretend to film someone, for example when a star demands to reshoot a scene against the director's wishes. They call for a strawberry filter, and the cameraman knows they should empty the camera of film.

NO BUSINESS

Fifty showbiz nicknames

1   The Divine Miss M (Bette Midler)

2   The Master of Suspense (Sir Alfred Hitchcock)

3   The Duke (John Wayne)

4   Mr Saturday Night (Jackie Gleason)

5   Satchmo (Louis Armstrong)

6   The Muscles from Brussels (Jean-Claude van Damme)

7   The Peter Pan of Pop (Sir Cliff Richard)

8   Mozzer (Morrissey)

9   The Velvet Fog (Mel Tormé)

10 The Purple One (Prince)

11 Our Gracie (Dame Gracie Fields)

12 Mr Toothpaste (Pat Boone)

13 Bird (Charlie Parker)

14 The Old Groaner (Bing Crosby)

15 The Hockey Stick (Dame Julie Andrews)

16 The Pelvis (Elvis Presley)

17 Posh (Victoria Beckham)

18 The King of Cool (Steve McQueen)

19 Saint Bob (Bob Geldof)

20 The Kid (Warren Beatty)

21 The Big Yin (Billy Connolly)

22 Bud (Marlon Brando)

Q HE?

A list of noted people
with the Q factor

1	François Quesnay – French economist
2	Randy Quaid – US actor and comic
3	Willard Quine – US philosopher
4	Edgar Quinet – French writer and statesman
5	Niall Quinn – Irish footballer
6	Aileen Quinn – US child actor who played 'Annie'
7	Mary Quant – English fashion designer
8	Raymond Queneau – French novelist
9	Robin Quivers – US radio presenter
10	Dennis Quaid – US actor
11	Anthony Quinn – US actor
12	Gene Quill – US saxophonist
13	Dan Quayle – US politician
14	Joanna Quinn – English animator
15	Sir Peter Quennell – English biographer and historian
16	Salvatore Quasimodo – Italian Nobel prize-winning poet
17	Denis Quilley – English actor
18	Manuel Quintana – Spanish classical poet
19	Serafin Quintero – Spanish playwright
20	Aidan Quinn – US actor
21	Marcus Quintilianus – Roman thinker
22	Kathleen Quinlan – US actor

23	Dan Quisenberry – US baseball star
24	Vidkun Quisling – Norwegian politician
25	Francisco Quevedo y Villegas – Spanish satirist
26	Tommy Quickly – English singer
27	William Quantrill – US soldier
28	Johann Joachim Quantz – musician and composer
29	Roger Quilter – English composer
30	James Quin – early English theatre actor
31	Franck Queudrue – French footballer
32	Finlay Quaye – Scottish pop singer
33	Manuel Quezon – first Philippine president
34	Suzi Quatro – actor and pop singer
35	Josiah Quincy – US anti-slavery congressman
36	Anthony Quinn – US actor
37	Sir Arthur Quiller-Couch – English writer and academic
38	Ed 'Snoozer' Quinn – US guitarist for Bix, Bing etc
39/40	Stephen and Timothy Quay – US animators
41	Ivy Queen – US rapper
42/43	Artus and Arnold Quellin – Belgian sculptors
44	Eimear Quinn – Irish singer
45	Diana Quick – English actor
46	Alvin Queen – US jazz drummer
47	Francis Quarles – English 17th-century poet
48	Harriet Quimby – US aviator and journalist
49	Fernand Quinet – Belgian composer
50	Caroline Quentin – English actor and comedian

FIFTY FIFTY

US state nicknames

Alabama	The Yellowhammer State • The Camellia State • The Heart of Dixie
Alaska	The Last Frontier • The Mainland State
Arizona	The Grand Canyon State • The Apache State
Arkansas	The Natural State • The Bear State • The Land of Opportunity
California	The Golden State
Colorado	The Centennial State
Connecticut	The Constitution State • The Nutmeg State
Delaware	The First State • The Diamond State
Florida	The Sunshine State • The Everglade State
Georgia	The Peach State • The Empire State of the South
Hawaii	The Aloha State
Idaho	The Gem State
Illinois	The Prairie State • The Land of Lincoln
Indiana	The Hoosier State
Iowa	The Hawkeye State • The Corn State
Kansas	The Sunflower State • The Jayhawker State
Kentucky	The Bluegrass State
Louisiana	The Pelican State • The Creole State • The Sugar State
Maine	The Pine Tree State
Maryland	The Old Line State • The Free State
Massachusetts	The Bay State • The Old Colony
Michigan	The Great Lakes State • The Wolverine State
Minnesota	The North Star State • The Gopher State

Mississippi	The Magnolia State • Big Sky Country
Missouri	The Show Me State • The Bullion State
Montana	The Treasure State
Nebraska	The Cornhusker State • The Beef State
Nevada	The Silver State • The Sagebrush State
New Hampshire	The Granite State
New Jersey	The Garden State
New Mexico	The Land of Enchantment • The Sunshine State
New York	The Empire State
North Carolina	The Tar Heel State • The Old North State
North Dakota	The Peace Garden State • The Flickertail State • The Sioux State • The Roughrider State
Ohio	The Buckeye State
Oklahoma	The Sooner State
Oregon	The Beaver State • The Sunset State
Pennsylvania	The Keystone State
Rhode Island	The Ocean State • The Plantation State • Little Rhody
South Carolina	The Palmetto State
South Dakota	The Mount Rushmore State • The Coyote State • The Sunshine State
Tennessee	The Volunteer State
Texas	The Lone Star State
Utah	The Beehive State • The Mormon State
Vermont	The Green Mountain State
Virginia	The Old Dominion State • The Mother of Presidents
Washington	The Evergreen State • The Chinook State
West Virginia	The Mountain State • The Panhandle State
Wisconsin	The Badger State • America's Dairyland
Wyoming	The Equality State • The Cowboy State

VILLAGE PEOPLE

Some fictional UK or Irish villages from literature, films, radio and television

1. Tannochbrae (TV's *Dr Finlay's Casebook*)
2. Highbury (*Emma*)
3. Manteg (Caradoc Evans' *My People* stories)
4. Glendarroch (soap *Take the High Road*)
5. Ballykissangel (light drama series)
6. Ulverton (Adam Thorpe's novel)
7. Walmington-on-Sea (*Dad's Army*)
8. King's Oak (soap *Crossroads*)
9. Darrowby (*All Creatures Great and Small* books and TV series)
10. Ballybeg (plays of Brian Friel)
11. Royston Vasey (TV comedy *The League of Gentlemen*)
12. Tickle on the Tum (toddlers' TV series)
13. Dibley (sitcom *The Vicar of Dibley*)
14. Llareggub (Dylan Thomas's *Under Milk Wood*)
15. Grimpen (*The Hound of the Baskervilles*)
16. Ambridge (radio soap *The Archers*)
17. Greendale (home of *Postman Pat*)
18. Midsomer Worthy, Midsomer Norton, Midsomer Parva (TV's *Midsomer Murders*)
19. Some Tame Gazelle (oddly-named village in a Barbara Pym saga)
20. Furness (film *Local Hero*)
21. St Mary Mead (Miss Marple mysteries)
22. Puckoon (Spike Milligan's comic novel)
23. Cardale (TV doctors show *Peak Practice*)

24 Lochdubh (TV series *Hamish Macbeth*)

25 East Proctor (*An American Werewolf in London*)

26 Pontypandy (*Fireman Sam*)

27 Beckindale (soap *Emmerdale*)

28 Kirrary (*Ryan's Daughter*)

29 Barbie (*The House with the Green Shutters*)

30 Raveloe (*Silas Marner*)

31 Lambton (*Pride and Prejudice*)

32 Chigley/Trumpton/Camberwick Green (related kids' TV shows)

33 Sweet Auburn (Goldsmith's *The Haunted Village*)

34 Abbot's-Cernel (*Tess of the D'Urbervilles*)

35 Styles St Mary (*The Mysterious Affair at Styles*)

36 Kinraddie (Lewis Grassic Gibbon's *Sunset Song*)

37 Cwmderi (Welsh soap *Pobol y Cwm*)

38 Aidensfield (TV's *Heartbeat*)

39 Ottery St Catchpole/Little Whinging/Hogsmeade (Harry Potter books)

And a few from overseas ...

1 Avonlea (*Anne of Green Gables*)

2 Amity (*Jaws*)

3 Lansquenet (*Chocolat*)

4 Schabbach (*Heimat*)

5 Macondo (*100 Years of Solitude*)

6 Whoville (Dr Seuss)

7 Cicely (*Northern Exposure*)

8 Anatevka (*Fiddler on the Roof*)

9 Cabot Cove (*Murder She Wrote*)

10 Ramelle (*Saving Private Ryan*)

11 Lake Wobegon (tales by Garrison Keillor)

12 Dorfli (*Heidi*)

13 Spoon River (E L Masters's pithy poems)

BLADES OF THE DALES

Some beautifully-named European wild flowers

meadow clary
agrimony
spiked rampion
thrift
wood avens
selfheal
clustered bellflower
forking larkspur
early goldenrod
livelong saxifrage
black medick
enchanter's nightshade
comfrey
mouse-ear hawkweed
touch-me-not balsam
Venus's looking-glass
purging flax
sanicle
dog's mercury
lady's slipper
oxeye
bittersweet
red helleborine
sainfoin
kidney vetch
cypress spurge
spring snowflake
lords and ladies
wood forget-me-not
frogbit
meadow cranesbill
creeping cinquefoil

ragged robin
eyebright
hop trefoil
dark mullein
feverfew
trumpet gentian
burning bush
summer pheasant's-eye
sundew
biting stonecrop
shepherd's-purse
tufted-loosestrife
ribbed melilot
corn spurrey
tormentil
columbine
tansy
slender speedwell
twayblade
wintergreen
moor-king
Solomon's seal
sun spurge
Scottish asphodel
lady's mantle
nodding bur-marigold
mignonette
mare's tail
annual knawel
water-soldier
sticky catchfly
sheep's sorrel
hoary cress
cow parsley
yarrow
hairy violet
betony

OLD MASTERS

Fourteen dogs belonging to famous writers of yesteryear

1	Alexander Pope	Bounce
2	Elizabeth Barrett Browning	Flush
3	Charles Lamb	Dash
4	Sir Walter Scott	Maida
5	Lord Byron	Boatswain
6	Charles Dickens	Turk
7	Thomas Hardy	Wessex
8	Emily Brontë	Keeper
9	Eugene O'Neill	Blemie
10	Matthew Arnold	Geist
11	Walter Savage Landor	Giallo
12	Anne Brontë	Flossy
13	Robert Burns	Luath
14	John Steinbeck	Charley

The ten most popular pet names for cars in the UK

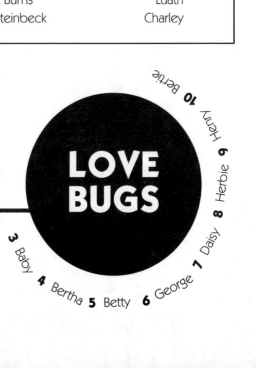

LOVE BUGS

1 Betsy/Bessie **2** Fred **3** Baby **4** Bertha **5** Betty **6** George **7** Daisy **8** Herbie **9** Henry **10** Bertie

SORE THUMBS

A list of unlikely words which have turned up in the lyrics of UK Number One hit songs

enchilada ('Mambo Italiano' by Rosemary Clooney)

fuzzy ('All Shook Up' by Elvis Presley)

plumb ('Claudette' by the Everley Brothers)

cement ('Mack the Knife' by Bobby Darin)

lulu ('Rock-a-Hula Baby' by Elvis Presley)

snitch ('Little Children' by Billy J Kramer and the Dakotas)

farmyard ('Little Red Rooster' by the Rolling Stones)

socks ('Eleanor Rigby' by the Beatles)

merry-go-round ('Puppet on a String' by Sandie Shaw)

seasick ('Whiter Shade of Pale' by Procol Harum)

eskimo ('The Mighty Quinn' by Manfred Mann/'Hit Me With Your Rhythm Stick' by Ian Dury and the Blockheads/'The Chicken Song' by Spitting Image)

tavern ('Those Were the Days' by Mary Hopkin)

paraffin ('Lily the Pink' by the Scaffold)

embassy ('Where Do You Go To, My Lovely?' by Peter Sarstedt)

Clyde ('Israelites' by Desmond Dekker)

acorns ('The Ballad of John and Yoko' by the Beatles)

playmate ('Two Little Boys' by Rolf Harris)

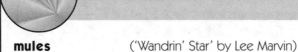

mules	('Wandrin' Star' by Lee Marvin)
Pagliacci	('Tears of a Clown' by Smokey Robinson and the Miracles)
smog	('Woodstock' by Matthews' Southern Comfort)
Chaplin	('Grandad' by Clive Dunn)
yoghurt	('Ernie (The Fastest Milkman in the West)' by Benny Hill)
corkscrew	('Telegram Sam' by T Rex)
linen	('Vincent' by Don McLean/'Bring Your Daughter to the Slaughter' by Iron Maiden)
bugle	('Fernando' by Abba)
apron	('No Charge' by J J Barrie)
khaki	('Up Town Top Ranking' by Althia & Donna)
Ancoats	('Matchstalk Men and Matchstalk Cats and Dogs' by Brian & Michael)
Arapaho	('Hit Me With Your Rhythm Stick' by Ian Dury and the Blockheads/'The Chicken Song' by Spitting Image)
bullhorn	('I Don't Like Mondays' by the Boomtown Rats/'Rubber Bullets' by 10cc)
manure	('Too Much Too Young' by the Specials)
textbooks	('Going Underground' by the Jam)
towel	('Geno' by Dexy's Midnight Runners)
Glasgow	('Super Trouper' by Abba)
Gorgon	('House of Fun' by Madness)
combie	('Down Under' by Men At Work)

Renoir	('The Reflex' by Duran Duran)
Doris	('Wake Me Up Before You Go-Go' by Wham!)
biscuits	('Two Tribes' by Frankie Goes To Hollywood)
starboard	('Star Trekkin'' by the Firm)
capitan	('La Bamba' by Los Lobos)
Cebu	('Orinoco Flow' by Enya)
gallow	('Belfast Child' by Simple Minds)
copywritten*	('The Power' by Snap)
pompatus**	('The Joker' by Steve Miller Band)
mothballs	('Do The Bartman' by the Simpsons)
Sierra	('Deeply Dippy' by Right Said Fred)
squirrel	('Oh Carolina' by Shaggy)
fireplace	('Don't Look Back in Anger' by Oasis)
psychosomatic	('Breathe' by the Prodigy)
sangria	('Perfect Day' by Various Artists)
bosom	('Brimful of Asha' by Cornershop)
huff	('C'est La Vie' by B*Witched)
Christianity	('Survivor' by Destiny's Child)
chinchilla	('Crazy In Love' by Beyoncé)

* A word which does not really exist.

** The story behind this odd word is complex but, in a nutshell, Miller misheard and borrowed the word from an old song by a band named the Medallions. The actual word sung was 'puppetutes', a word coined by the song's writer and meaning 'good-looking girls'.

JOIN THE CREW

The 'canting crew' was the name given to those types of people who lived in the rougher parts of old London and who commonly used low and criminal slang (sometimes called 'pedlar's French'). These divisions were first set out in the mid-1500s by one Thomas Harman (in a tract called *A Caveat Or Warning For Common Cursetors Vulgarly Called Vagabond*). Some of the categories are now somewhat obscure but, in many respects, not much has changed ...

Men

1   **Rufflers** (the criminal elite; sometimes, those who gained money by pretending to be injured soldiers)

2   **Upright Men** (tough gang leaders whose privilege was to deflower young prostitutes)

3   **Hookers** or **Anglers** (petty thieves who used a stick and hook to steal goods through windows)

4   **Rogues** (common criminals)

5   **Wild Rogues** (those who have been criminal since early childhood)

6   **Priggers of Prancers** (horse thieves; those who stole hens were 'priggers of cacklers')

7   **Palliardes** (ragged beggars from a begging dynasty, especially those who employed false sores and injuries)

8   **Fraters** (those who used false papers and patents in their begging)

9   **Jarkmen** (those who manufactured false documents for use in begging)

10 **Fresh Water Mariners** or **Whip Jack(et)s** (those who begged by pretending to be shipwrecked sailors trying to get back to port or home)

11 **Dummerers** or **Drummers** (those who feigned dumbness; those who travelled selling cheap or stolen goods)

12 **Drunken Tinkers** (itinerants who sold small goods for beer money)

13 **Swaddlers** (violent muggers)

14 **Abrams** (those who begged by pretending to be mad or disturbed)

15 **Patricoes** (low or unprincipled priests who conducted marriages for the poor; these ceremonies often took place with the couple either side of a dead animal, to symbolize 'till death do us part')

Women and Children

1 **Demanders for Glimmer** or **Fire** (women who begged for charity claiming to have been the victims of fire)

2 **Bawdy Baskets** (thieves who also sold small goods and obscene books)

3 **Morts** (molls; unmarried women of generally low morals)

4 **Autem Morts** (married beggars using borrowed children to gain sympathy)

5 **Walking Morts** (those who sold cheap or stolen goods in the street or door to door)

6 **Doxies** (older prostitutes who also begged)

7 **Delles** (prostitutes, especially young attractive ones)

8 **Kinching Morts** (girls trained in pickpocketing, etc)

9 **Kinching Coes** (orphans or beggars' children trained in various criminal acts)

There are around 5,000 islands and islets which make up the British Isles, though only a few per cent of these are inhabited and many are not even named. Here are some of the more interesting island names from around the British and Irish coasts

Valentia	Staffin Island
Green Scar	Fidra
Wiay	Herm
Mousa	Middle Mouse
Samphrey	Swona
Mutton Island	Piel Island
Texa	Eorsa
Haaf Gruney	Samson
Guillamon	Cava
Isle Ristol	Rat Island
Eilean Flodigarry	Tory Island
Dursey	Osea Island
Muckle Flugga	Gola
Huskeiran	Yell
Calf of Man	Little Shillay
Floddaybeg	Eilean a' Bhreitheimh
Gorumna	Soa
Gigalum	Vementry
Wart Holm	Inishbofin
Inchmickery	Inishark
Rumble	Carna
Coomb	Hildasay
Gugh	Campay
Quinish	Isle of Ewe
Lunga	Oldany Island
Kishorn	Papa Little
Pladda	

SCEPTRED ISLES

THE NEW ROCK AND ROLL

In the early 90s, the broadcaster Janet Street-Porter described comedy as 'the new rock and roll', thereby ushering in a popular buzz phrase of the decade. Since then, it appears to have been applied to gardening more than anything else, but here is a selection of other things which have been tarred with the epithet the New Rock and Roll

greyhound racing • brown • mathematics • weblogging cookery • art • bingo • being a father • chess • coffee film-making • football • public speaking • poetry • fishing comics • medicine • gaming • DIY • living space design entrepreneurs • languages • hypnosis • retro • debt restructuring • outsiders • sexual fetishism • coughing sci-fi • ballet • e-business • Cardiff • toilet humour cabaret • Java® • preaching • gas contracts • modelling image • English porn • cushions • farming • education lawnmower racing • niche marketing • animation • dying food • soaps • custard pie fighting • enterprise portals life after death • housewares • the Net • philosophy hard-boiled fiction • genomics • fashion • flamenco nautical facial hair • anti-globalization • Pokémon newspaper columns • porridge • theatre • technology geology • jellied eels • birth control • care of the elderly online radio • banjos • day trading • graphics cards self storage • climbing • tropical fish • rock and roll

The unusual phrase 'twenty

TWENTY THREE SKIDOO

three skidoo' (meaning, broadly, no chance, get lost or sometimes 'let's go') became 'perhaps the first truly national fad expression' in the USA at the beginning of the 1900s, and remained popular for a decade or two. Its origin (as with that of 'OK') has been much discussed by word enthusiasts. The 'skidoo' part seems to be related to the word skedaddle (probably a 19th-century variant on 'skid' and 'scuttle'), meaning to run off. Here are some possibilities for the phrase's derivation

1 It comes from *A Tale of Two Cities*, in which a female character counts the many prisoners heading for the **guillotine**. The hero Carton was number 23, and when the novel was turned into a play, the weepy cry of this number became a Broadway catchphrase and came to mean 'let's get out of here while we can.'

2 The phrase may have been coined and popularized by Thomas Aloysius Dorgan (TAD), a popular **cartoonist**, around 1900. But it is also claimed that he never made use of the phrase.

3 The word and the number were both displayed on pennants, armbands and memorabilia at seashore **resorts** (for unremembered reasons) around 1900 and the two got added together to form the nonsense phrase.

4 'Twenty three' as a euphemism for 'get lost' originates in a play called ***Little Johnny Jones*** by George M Cohan, where the phrase is used as a catchphrase by one character.

5 It is a version of SKYDDU, a mysterious word painted on walls as a **rain charm** or omen (a pun on 'sky dew').

6 The phrase arose in the **borax** mining industry in California's Death Valley. Skidoo was the name of the place where the mineral was loaded onto trains and it supposedly took 23 mules to haul the carts there. Another possibility is that it was a miner's drinking cry, used when they intended to visit each of the 23 canvas taverns in the town.

7 Another suggestion has to do with the **Flatiron** building in NYC, a wedge-shaped block which stands on the corner of Broadway and 23rd Street. It is said that strange wind currents roused by the building's shape would cause ladies' skirts to be blown up. Hence policemen would shoo voyeurs with '23 skidoo!' Sometimes the phrase meant the skirt-blowing phenomenon itself.

8 It was once part of a telegraphic **code** where numbers stood for common phrases; 23 was the code for 'away with you!', or perhaps may have referred to an extremely urgent message.

KHALSA BUSINESS

The five symbols of the khalsa or Sikh brotherhood

1 kirpan (a dagger)
2 kara (an iron wristband)
3 kesh (uncut hair)
4 kacha (short trousers)
5 kanga (a comb worn in the hair)

These symbols, the 'five Ks', have been restyled by the London-based poet Daljit Nagra as the 'five Bs': 'blade, bangle, barnet, boxers and brush'.

SHE SELLS ...

Sixty-seven exceptional seashells

warty egg cowry
glory-of-the-sea
superb gazza
lovely slit
horny cyclas
strawberry goblet
swollen pheasant
wobbly keyhole
bursa frog
beaded sundial
orange-mouth olive
few-wrinkled bonnet
lima file
thick-lipped drill
babylon turris
grimy volute
frilled dog winkle
drab horse conch
pinpatch
rhinoceros vase
bullmouth helmet
sunburst carrier
tapestry turban
fearful nutmeg
bear paw
exquisite harp
funereal whelk
glistening Margarite
bubble turnip
spiny cup-and-saucer
partridge tun
near colus

ass's ear abalone
wedding cake venus
old maid
fat neptune
flamingo tongue cyphoma
bleeding tooth
giant knobbed cerith
coat-of-mail
precious wentletrap
Evelyn's auger
commercial top
turkey wing ark
gloomy thorn drupe
Western noddiwink
sunrise tellin
fragile geography cone
wrinkled slipper
Jacqueline bolma
Adam's baby bubble
Beau's phos
papery rapa
double-snouted volva
spiny vase
lumpy morum
Panama swamp cassidula
hailstorm prickly winkle
lisping caurica
remarkable ostrich foot
Tankerville's ancilla
McGinty's distorsio
roostertail
colourful Atlantic moon
walkway babylon
miraculous Thatcheria
bloody trivia

SHORT CUTS

Thirty-seven bands which shortened their names

1	Santana Blues Band → Santana
2	Arabacus Pulp → Pulp
3	Balaam and the Angel → Balaam
4	Chicago Transit Authority → Chicago
5	The Silver Beatles → The Beatles
6	Tripsichord Music Box → Tripsichord
7	Wah! Heat → Wah!
8	Ambrose Slade → Slade
9	X Mal Deutschland → X Mal
10	Generation X → Gen X
11	The Fatback Band → Fatback
12	The Easy Cure → The Cure
13	Hawkwind Zoo → Hawkwind
14	Southern Death Cult → The Cult*
15	Tyrannosaurus Rex → T Rex
16	The Leyton Buzzards → The Buzzards
17	The Nipple Erectors → The Nips**
18	The Moody Blues Five → The Moody Blues
19	The Guildford Stranglers → The Stranglers
20	Silmarillion → Marillion
21	Pogue Mahone → The Pogues**
22	Clan of Xymox → Xymox
23	Kajagoogoo → Kaja
24	Spirits Rebellious → Spirit
25	The Count Bishops → The Bishops
26	The Cranberry Saw Us → The Cranberries

27	The Glitter Band → The G Band
28	Nitty Gritty Dirt Band → The Dirt Band
29	J Geils Band → Geils
30	The Heavy Metal Kids → The Kids
31	Mott the Hoople → Mott
32	The Special AKA → The Specials
33	The Jazz Crusaders → The Crusaders
34	Dalek I Love You → Dalek I
35	The Bonzo Dog Doo-Dah Band → The Bonzo Dog Band
36	The Sweetshop → Sweet
37	The Troglodytes → The Troggs

There are many reasons to change a name – often the original was too long or silly or pretentious (note the large number of glam and goth bands on the list.) Some bands changed due to the too-rude-for-radio factor of the original name (**mostly bands featuring Shane McGowan). Some even changed twice (*Southern Death Cult becoming Death Cult becoming the Cult). Other name changes (see Kaja, Mott) seem to be due to a last gasp attempt at staying on the pop map, or perhaps a legally caused adaptation of a debated name. Here are six further types of name shortening which I ignored when making the list:

1	Name changes where the band essentially, aesthetically, became a new band, eg the Small Faces to the Faces.
2	Changes due, perhaps, to extensive line-up changes, eg the Rollers, the Tops, later versions of the Bay City Rollers/ the Four Tops.
3	Official adoption of comon abbreviations, eg OMD, NKOTB.
4	Shortenings used for legal reasons (eg conflict with brand names, existing groups with similar names) in other countries, eg Yazoo, Comsat Angels (Yaz, CSAs in the USA).
5	'XY and the Zs' becoming just 'The Zs' or, say, Patti LaBelle and the BlueBelles changing to LaBelle.
6	Shortenings caused by personnel changes, eg S Club (S Club 7).

THREE LEGS GOOD
MANX FOR BEGINNERS LESSON 19

Here are the vocabulary words to learn from this week's story

aachummey stronney	rhinoplasty
jyst soo	jam dish
possan lhiggee	firing squad
aane voiddee	cod liver
faagail gyn vree	to stultify
fadeyrag padjerey	praying mantis
radlin	balustrade
wagaantagh keiy	wharf rat
quallian	puppy
sooslagh feeackle	toothpaste
keanagh	cotton
smooidraght	drizzle
putage ghoo	black pudding
mee-chummit	deformed
flibbag	earlobe
quing-raa	zeugma
daa-cheintssaght	bisexuality
aggle straiddey	agoraphobia
casag ghlare-eddin	kiss-curl
yn chiass	gonorrhoea
shenn-chaillagh	harridan
smarree	greasy
kiark cholgagh	shuttlecock
smittag	a smooch
maghouin marrey	polar bear
Immee gys Niurin!	go to Hell!

YOUR TIME IS NOW

Thirteen variations on *carpe diem*

* Ndebele version.
** Popularized by T S Eliot in 'The Love Song of J Alfred Prufrock'.

THE DROWNERS
Some nasty water spirits from British folklore

Rawhead or **Bloody Bones**
A boggart or water goblin who lurks in water, waiting to pull in passing strangers.

Jenny Greenteeth
Northern English water witch who can be detected by green scum or weed on the top of deep water. Those, particularly children, getting too close will be yanked in and held under until they drown.

Nelly Long-arms
Similar to the above, but with the emphasis on long rubbery arms which will envelop any over-curious child or traveller.

Peg-a-lantern
A bog sprite who uses a light to waylay night travellers, who are entranced into following the light until swallowed by the swamp.

The **Hedley Kow**
A Northumbrian imp, one of whose many deviant pleasures was tricking the unwary into drowning. A favourite ploy was to shape-shift into the form of two comely young women who would lure men to a wet, weedy grave. The **Sprite of Nikkesen's Pool** on the Isle of Man was a similar creature who would impersonate a handsome young man in order to drown passing maidens.

The **Water Cow**
A Scottish water spirit which lowed like a cow and could change shape in order to lure the doomed into lochs.

Peg Powler
A nixie, or bad water nymph who delighted in snatching and drowning anyone who got too close to deep water or fast rivers, especially children of course.

The **cabbyl ushtey**
A Manx water horse with back to front hooves which would carry anyone who mounted it deep into a nearby river. The **tarroo ushtey** was a similar bovine creature.

The **Doolie**
This Scottish spirit, perhaps a relative of the kelpie, or ghostly water horse, tended to wait by fords, trying to entice those crossing to take the most treacherous path across the river.

The **fuath**
A sort of northern Scottish equivalent of Greenteeth, with green clothes, webbed feet and bright yellow hair. But the intention was the same. Drown and drown and drown.

DANCING AROUND THE WORLD

An international alphabet of dances

Abuang (Indonesia)
Bergomask (Italy)
Calinda (Congo)
Debka (Israel)
Ezcudantza (Basque region)
Fackeltanz (Austria)
Gunnesbopolka (Sweden)
Hanacca (Moravia)
Ijswals (The Netherlands)
Jabadao (Brittany)
Kolomyjka (Ukraine)
Lezginka (Iran)
Maxixe (Brazil)
Numba (Kenya)
Okina (Japan)
Planxty (Ireland)
Quadrille (France)
Redowa (Bohemia)
Springer (Norway)
Tango (Argentina)
Urva Franka (Macedonia)
Verbunkos (Hungary)
Wireng (Java)
Xacaras (Portugal)
Yumari (Mexico)
Zapateado (Spain)

187

PURE DEAD BRILLIANT

Eleven examples of Glaswegian slang

1 mollicate

In Glasgow, this means to defeat, to batter or tear to pieces, as in 'ony mair o' yer lip, Carole Ann, ye wee scunner, an' ahm comin through tae mollicate ye' or 'Ahm no goan back tae see Thistle, they aye get mollicatit.'

2 no danger!

Easy, no problems, no worries, it's apples, don't fret, everythin's gonna be all right baby! As in, 'ah cud len ye a fiver no danger, big man.'

3 varicose veins

Children. This is Glaswegian rhyming slang: veins = weans = children.

4 big man

Take a few centuries, add Italians and the Irish to an already short Scots stock and you have an average male adult height of 5ft 5in. Hence, anyone (or family pet or inanimate object) over this height is referred to as 'big man'. As in, 'Yawrigh, big man? Seez wan ae yer oven chips.'

5 the wee Malkie

A bogeyman, or anything nasty or sinister. Why a small person called Malcolm should be Glasgow's bogeyman is a mystery. The term 'malkie' is also used for that most Glaswegian of pleasantries, the headbutt or 'Glasgow kiss'.

6 this is me since yesterday!

Meaning I'm exhausted and I've been non-stop busy for the whole day. Said exclusively by elderly women on public transport. It might make a good replacement for Glasgow's former slogan 'Glasgow's Miles Better', which has been cynically reinterpreted elsewhere as 'Glasgow's Smile's Bitter' and 'Glasgow's Males Batter'.

7 ya dancer!

A cry of triumph. Apparently short for dancing bear. What dancing bears have to do with it, I do not know. See also 'ya beauty!' which is not strictly Glaswegian.

8 ginger

The term for any fizzy drink, no matter the colour or flavour, but particularly Barr's Irn Bru®, the ginger-coloured soda with the hard-to-describe taste which is rife in Glasgow (one of the few world cities where cola is not the bestselling soft drink). As in 'Haw Shug, goan get's a bottly ginger, by the way.'

9 ahwsl'ah!

A slurred shortening of 'I was like that', accompanied by the suitable facial expression (triumph, disgust, yawn), used when recounting a piquant adventure from recent history, eg 'he goes to me aye, that Gucci suit is hauf price and ahwsl'ah' (grins ear to ear).

10 see you!

An angry or mock-angry accusation or way of getting someone's attention: 'See you, Davie, yer a toerag an' a patter merchant an' ah mean it!'

11 defiNATEly!

A word implying emphasis, still widely used despite the fact that 12% of Glaswegians now know the word 'definitely' is not spelt with an 'a'.

INITIALS BB

Twenty-eight 'BB' types and stereotypes

1 **bovver boy**
a thuggish young male, especially wearing skinhead fashion including bovver boots (UK, early 70s).

2 **brown breader**
someone given over, superficially at least, to 'healthy eating'. By extension, any hippie or liberal.

3 **beach bum**
someone who lives the surfing or sand hobo lifestyle.

4 **Busby babe**
one of the Manchester United soccer team of the late 50s, managed by Matt Busby, many of whom were killed in an air crash in West Germany.

5 **brain box**
a nickname for a child of high intelligence.

6 **big brother**
an imposing and sinister head of state or any organization; from Orwell's *Nineteen Eighty-Four*.

7 **Baron Bung**
an old expression for the host of a drinking party.

8 **bunny boiler**
a woman who becomes obsessive and behaves irrationally or violently during a relationship, especially an adulterous one; from the sleazy thriller *Fatal Attraction*.

9 **bathing belle** a contestant in a seaside beauty competition, particularly circa the 30s.

10 **bridled bear** a young nobleman who was chaperoned by a tutor.

11 **buttered bun** a sexual partner who has recently had intercourse with someone else.

12 **blonde bombshell** a glamorous blonde-haired woman, especially a model or movie star of yesteryear; now used mostly ironically for any gender.

13 **Bungalow Bill** a man who has 'little up top'.

14 **barrow boy** one who sells goods, especially fruit and veg, from a stall in a market; any loud, loquacious or uncouth man.

15 **Bible basher** a fundamentalist or evangelical Christian, especially one who is over-enthused with biblical moralizing.

16 **backroom boy** a scientist, theorist or technician who makes things happen 'backstage' or away from the politicians or generals.

17 **boot black** one who shines shoes for a living.

18 **blue bottle** an old name for a beadle or a police constable.

19 **back bencher** a member of the British parliament who does not hold office.

20 bachelor boy a young unmarried man; by extension, one who is such by reasons of homosexuality.

21 Blair babe one of the many female MPs brought into UK government by Tony Blair's late 90s New Labour.

22 brown bagger one who brings their own booze, or carries it out of the shop in a brown bag; one who drinks alcohol in public from a brown bag due to bylaws.

23 bawdy bard a penner of erotic verse or comic smut.

24 Billy Bunter any greedy person, foodwise; from a British schoolboy character of that name.

25 Billy boy an Irish or Scots Protestant, from their historical support for King William (Billy); a football supporter of Protestant teams such as Glasgow Rangers.

26 blue bonnet an old name for any Scotsman, from a regiment which wore them.

27 ball breaker a slang name for a tough, manipulative or man-hating woman.

28 baby boomer one who was born in the post-war baby boom; broadly, those who were young in the 60s and early 70s.

The equator crosses the land mass of ten major countries

Ecuador

Colombia

Brazil

Gabon

Republic of the Congo

Democratic Republic of the Congo

Uganda

Kenya

Somalia

Indonesia

MIDDLE EARTH

START THE DAY

Three idiomatic breakfasts

A **Whore's Breakfast**
two coffees and four cigarettes

A **Dingo's Breakfast**
a piss and a sniff around

A **Mexican Breakfast**
a cigarette and a glass of water

An old BBC record, *Silly Songs of the 20s and 30s*, **offers an insight into the wacky humour of that era. Here are twelve things which people apparently found hilarious between the wars**

SILLY SEASONS

1 Flatulence

Eek! Sadly, anything to do with roughage, rumbling or raspberries was top-notch humour material in the age of the flapper. Witness the fruit-obsessed song (later revived by Spike Milligan) about the village 'pétomane', who made a musical performance of his flatulence:

> *Though it isn't very pretty, you've got to admit it's cute,*
> *So all together, let it go* [sundry kazoo noises], *eat more fruit!*

'Le Pétomane' was a French music-hall entertainer, famous for his capacity for breaking wind. His unusual act topped the bill at the Moulin Rouge, but then he opened his own theatre in 1895. Three years later he sued the Moulin Rouge for presenting a female 'Pétomane', but before the case came to court she was exposed as a fraud, having concealed various whistles and bellows in her skirts. Pétomane retired from the stage in 1914 when the outbreak of World War I made his speciality act of mock artillery barrages seem inappropriate.

2 Ethnic Sorts

Chinamen, Arabs, 'cannibal' natives – yee ha! But funniest of all back then was the humble Eskimo, subject of many a ribald song and poem. How about 'I Scream, You Scream, We All Scream for Ice Cream' (I can just see Lionel Blair having a dicky ticker moment on *Give Us a Clue* trying to do that as a charade), which explains:

> *When he says come on let's go, though it's 45 below,*
> *Listen what those Eskimos all holler:*
> [all together!] *I scream you scream, we all scream for ice cream, ra! ra! ra!*

3 Funny Voices

Men with tight-trousered falsettos, little big-band sidekicks specially kept for their ability to dip to a rasping duck-honk; anything juddering, lisping, stammering, camp, Italiano or cod-horror – they lapped it up. I blame the Marx Brothers. For everything.

4 Wigan

We all need a joke town to namecheck, but why Wigan, all but as reviled now as back in them days?

> *Oh you live up in Wigan?*
> *Well, don't blame that on me …*

… claims a copper in the deliberately irritating ditty 'Shut the Door, They're Coming Through the Window'. Wigan pier, Wigan kebabs, Wigan as the epicentre of 'circus skills' dancing. Ooh, stop it or I'll send you up to Auntie Edith in Wigan! She'll sort you.

5 Prunes

Oh, what better than a fruit (hurrah!) that has bowel (twice hurrah!) connotations? And it's wrinkly! And it has a silly name that sounds mildly rude! Join me now as I croon:

> *No matter how young a prune may be,*
> *It's always full of wrinkles.*
> *We may get them on our face,*
> *Prunes get 'em every place!*

Prunes have been butt of the joke and on the menu of connotations for many a century. In the Elizabethan era, they symbolized the wrinkling of the skin of those who soaked in the bath houses, which were often fronts for prostitution. In fact, bottles of prunes were used in the windows of brothels to let passing customers know what sort of business lay within.

6 A Glimpse of Stocking

Nowadays, young college babes aiming to shock bother metal detectors with multi-piercings, wear thongs (is there anything less erotic than the thong?) just below their shoulder blades and feed us with blogs about their love lives, but back in the 20s, a fad appeared which shocked and awed America – the sock! Yes, rad college girls would roll their stockings down to look like male socks, hence giving American males the first ever sight of the lightly-downed female patella, hence the song 'Roll 'Em, Girls':

Roll 'em down and show your pretty knees.
Even grouchy traffic cops get jolly,
When they see you step on to a trolley!

7 Belly Dancing

It's got sex, it's got ethnicity, it's got timpani – it's a roll-over scream! Princeton gals may have offered a downy knee, but cor, those middle Eastern ones, they had their tummy buttons out and about and everything! Here's what 'Egyptian Ella' was capable of when she shook her breadbasket at the locals:

Every sheikh in the audience
Jumps up and offers her love intense [in tents?]
Oh how they love Egyptian Ella!

8 Foreign Climes

Ah, Timbuktu, so much to answer for! Sir Noël Coward knew that he had a sure-fire hit if he namechecked a bucketload of far-flung locations, a spattering of gurning natives and Johnny Englishman offering his rosy stiff upper lip to the dazzling sun:

In Bangkok, at twelve o'clock
They foam at the mouth and run
But mad dogs and Englishmen
Stay out in the midday sun!

The Eskimo, not eligible for this song on a technical point, had to make do with a comeback in the puerile but jaunty rival travelogue 'When it's Night-time in Italy, it's Wednesday Over Here'.

9 Naturists

Always a fair and square figure of fun, long before the fad for 'nudist films', there were songs such as 'Nellie the Nudist Queen' which pitches bawdy puns seldom found outside of the George Formby songbook. Naughty naked Nell manages to escape the attentions of some auditors – how? Well:

When she showed her assets,
Boy, her assets were immense!

10 Yodelling

Somewhere on this earth, there are isolated pockets where yodelling is taken seriously. But 'The Yodelling Chinaman' has it all – silly voices, ethnicity, and, boom boom, trump card, it has yodelling! The song begins:

In the café the other day, down in Chinatown
There I sat in a Chinese hat with black men, yellow and
brown.
Plinky Plinky Poo said, 'Quietness please'
Pakee Pakee Poo will sing …

and soon we are treated to a fine exhibition of high-pitched comedy yodelling, never since equalled. Mildly offensive it may be, but few will fail to grin a little.

11 Homosexuality

Still all very codified, back then, but few were in doubt of the real subject matter behind 'Let's All be Fairies', in which a singer as camp as a red squirrel tells of two 'great big burly boxers' who decide to throw the fight because they secretly want to be fairies (*'Don't be afraid if I shove you, you can't imagine how I laaaave you'*):

We'll go wimsy wamsy, on tiptoe, we'll say dash dash!
Let's all be fairies – tinkle tinkle, crash crash crash!

12 Prostitution

Nudge nudge, wink wink. Rewriting myths and fairy tales from a feminist perspective, eh? Long before the masses of contemporary female writers found their subject, it was being done by jazz big bands. Witness, this tale of Red Riding Hood empowering herself:

How could Little Red Riding Hood have been so very
good
And still keep the wolf from the door?
Why was she dressed up in bright flaming red
    Unless she expected to knock someone dead?

PSEUDONYMS CORNER

Eleven groups of people who generally don't use their real names

1 Magicians

Though some prestidigitators have ever felt it beneath them, most still agree that a good and silly stage name looks tidy on a poster, for example Mephisto, the Great Cardini or the Mighty Kazimir.

2 People in chatrooms

As long as you understand that dookiedawg21 did not receive that soubriquet from his parents, and that deedee is actually a hanky-happy, spotty adolescent called Josh, then all's fair.

3 Rappers

Since many rappers were saddled with questionable names like Tracy, Marshall and Duwayne, it's understandable that when toting their phat wares, they prefer to be, say, Da Professah, Foxee-D or Badd Dogg.

4 Gossip columnists

Especially of the political sort, they need to protect their sources and their delicate nosebones, and to avoid legal fees, so they become Peterborough, Monteith or Smallweed.

5 Brazilian footballers

Since the Portuguese language encourages speakers (in much the way the German language loves compound nouns like Selbstbedienungslebensmittelgeschäft) to build their names until they are something like Arnoldo di Salvo Famagusta di Argumento, and since room on shirtbacks is limited, Brazilian kickers tend to stick to being Ernesto, Zico and Vamosinho.

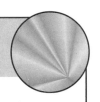

6 Performance poets

These are often magnetically drawn to performance names which tag their style – see Mr Social Control, Skorpio the Nemesis, Salena Saliva.

7 Romantic novelists

It is the unbreakable law that they should have wistful or fluffy names such as Candida Somerset, Cressida Woodruffe or Maureen O'Malley, a law punishable by three years in the febrile grip of a buckle-swinging cad, even for those – the majority of them – who are actually elderly men.

8 Crossword setters

The reason for setter names is lost in the mist, but may be to do with tax, or the fact that many early setters were clergymen, who felt such fripperies as puzzles needed to be kept a secret. A setter should aim for a plucky and important sounding name such as Ximenes or Ganymede or a short one like Pod.

9 Clowns

The ringmaster screams, let's hear it for Trevor Jenkins and Phil Smith everybody! No, doesn't ring quite right (excuse the pun). And so clowns are Cocky, Magnifico or, more often than not, Joey.

10 Racing tipsters

For obvious reasons, ie the no-win problem of your house being staked out either by sore bookies or skint punters carrying baseball bats, tipsters tend to use names such as Nap, Racecard or Bert.

11 Spies and terrorists

For reasons even more obvious! Good spy names might be Clarion, Goshawk or Five-One-Zero. Good terrorist names are Brendan 'the Babyeater' Flanagan and Pepe the Hyena.

FLOAT ON

The word 'floater' is a surprisingly versatile one; here are 36 meanings it can have

1 a late night takeaway delicacy from South Australia – a meat pie and ketchup served in pea soup

2 a type of candle

3 a serve in volleyball

4 a person who is unsure who to vote for in an election

5 a general term for those who boat or canoe on rivers

6 a type of glider

7 an order to leave a place

8 a song by Bob Dylan (from *Love and Theft*)

9 a person who drifts between casual jobs

10 a person who does skilled temporary work, ie a locum

11 a type of golf ball

12 a slang name for the drug Quaalude®

13 a complex component of a racing car

14 a blunder or cock-up

15 a type of dumpling

16 a member of the Floaters, famous for their big hit 'Float On'

17 something nasty which won't flush away

18 a dark speck that appears before one's eyes

19 an old word for 'penis' from the 1800s

20 a slang term for a carcase at sea or on a river

21 a term in investment, erm, something to do with a short-term rate

22 a person employed in espionage, but only on an occasional basis

23 a coin that doesn't spin in an Antipodean 'heads or tails' game

24 a type of all-weather coat

25 a specific move in surfing

26 a homosexual prostitute

27 an aerator for keeping fish bait alive

28 an infuriating text frame which moves as you do on an internet page

29 a book or magazine that is surreptitiously passed between prisoners

30 a device used in stretching a canvas/picture framing

31 a buoyancy aid to help meditation or wading

32 a form of insurance policy for moveable property

33 a sort of large North American mussel

34 a fried scone from New Zealand which supposedly floats in the cooking oil

35 a crumb in a bottled drink

36 a short, high shot in golf or basketball

LIFF REVISITED
PART TWO

Some more new words in the style of *The Meaning of Liff*

MALCOLM'S POINT (*n, math*) this mathematical theorem describes the relationship between the space given to an ingredient on packaging and the actual amount in the food within, eg the delicious picture of chunks of gammon and the large word HAM on a 'Cheese and Ham Slice', and the tiny words 'ham (4%)' on the ingredients list

MAMBLE (*n*) an awkward dance, often wrongly called salsa, which is performed by a herd of women with cloughs (qv) at arts centre evening classes

MENABILLY (*n, rare*) a short-lived musical genre (c.1973–4), a cross between rockabilly and Welsh male voice choir singing, the best remembered example being 'Valley Cat' by the Teds of Tredegar

MIDDLEZOY (*n, dial*) a Yorkshire term for a middle child, one who can lay no claim to the winsome terms 'our eldest' and 'the babby of t' family'

MOFFAT (*n*) an understandable error, such as mixing up Cole Porter and Irving Berlin during a game of Trivial Pursuit®

MOSTYN (*n*) an annoying boy in glasses who remembers you

NYBSTER (*n*) a small, flat ethnic hat often found atop a clough (qv)

PLAXTOL (*adj, vb*) jaunty; to jauntily drum along with music (derived from the technical percussion term for the clappy bit in the *Friends* theme tune)

PLUMSTEAD (*n*) the sort of middle-aged man who shows himself a fool by declaring that he 'doesn't suffer fools gladly'

QUILQUOX (*vb, rare*) to attempt to calculate the likely percentage of people alive who have impersonated a chicken

RAGNALL (*n*) the one tattered magazine used as bait by a bogus *Big Issue* seller

SKIPWITH (*n*) a recent form of frothy repetitive jazz music invented solely for use in the dull bits of DIY and antiques programmes

SLAD (*vb*) to be wilfully obese

SNAVE (*vb*) to hit 'Send & Receive' again, convinced that you are far too popular and important not to have any email

STANBOROUGH (*n*) a particularly hard game of Freecell

STARBOTTON (*n*) a meteorite which almost certainly won't hit and destroy the Earth in a few decades' time, but which is a good excuse for filling a space in a newspaper

TATTERSET (*n*) a display of merchandise (eg sweatshirt, key rings, own brand condiments) on sale in a trendy bar, which no one wants

TAUCHERS (*n pl*) the two stinkers in an otherwise good book of short stories

TREEN (*vb*) to find yourself legitimately but uncomfortably in a hotel above your station

TRETHARGY (*n*) the process whereby a fizzy drink goes into your mouth and straight back out of your nose

TRISLAIG (*n*) the trinity of wide-brimmed hat, salt-and-pepper beard and checked cream shirt worn at jazz gigs and weekend parties by newly-retired, middle-class men

TULLOES (*n*) the quivering in the jaw of someone who has been listening to a chatsworth (qv) for more than an hour

TURVEY (*n*) the artistic hobby of a non-artistic person

UNDERHOULL (*vb, rare*) to cook too little rice or pasta

WARMWELL (*n*) the particular contentment felt by two local historians who meet and fall in love

WENDLING (*n*) the uneasy electrical sensation felt in the index finger when having to use an old-fashioned phone with a dial

WIGTOFT (*n*) the correct name for the terrifying teenage hairstyle nicknamed the 'Hoxton fin'

WIRRAL (*n*) the near invisible cut end on a roll of tape

YARLET (*n*) a young woman who dances near a swimming pool in a rap video

CINEMAPERISCOPE

Thirty-four films about or set on submarines

1 *Men Without Women* (1930)
2 *Men Like These* (1931; aka *Trapped in a Submarine*)
3 *Morgenrot* (1933)
4 *Hell Below* (1933)
5 *Submarine D-1* (1937)
6 *49th Parallel* (1941)
7 *Submarine Raider* (1942)
8 *Crash Dive* (1943)
9 *We Dive At Dawn* (1943)
10 *Destination Tokyo* (1943)
11 *Les Maudits* (1947)
12 *Morning Departure* (1950)
13 *The Flying Missile* (1950)
14 *Operation Pacific* (1951)
15 *Submarine Command* (1952)
16 *Torpedo Alley* (1953)
17 *20,000 Leagues Under the Sea* (1954)
18 *The Enemy Below* (1957)
19 *Hellcats of the Navy* (1957)
20 *Run Silent, Run Deep* (1958)
21 *Torpedo Run* (1958)
22 *On the Beach* (1959)
23 *Operation Petticoat* (1959)
24 *Up Periscope* (1959)
25 *The Bedford Incident* (1965)
26 *Assault on a Queen* (1966)
27 *The Russians Are Coming! The Russians Are Coming!* (1966)
28 *Ice Station Zebra* (1968)
29 *Gray Lady Down* (1978)
30 *Das Boot* (1981)
31 *The Hunt for Red October* (1990)
32 *Crimson Tide* (1995)
33 *Down Periscope* (1996)
34 *U-571* (2000)

NORTHERN ENDURANCE

Some of the events and contests of the World Eskimo—Indian Olympics, which is held annually in Fairbanks, Alaska

One-Hand Reach
A game of balance and strength, where a person face down, balanced on one arm, must reach up to a target and return to the original position without collapsing.

Alaskan High Kick
In this game, contestants must spring from a balanced sitting position to kick a target up to two metres high and return to the ground with grace.

Indian Stick Pull
Two athletes compete to grab a greased baton from each other. The stick symbolizes a slippery fish.

Eskimo Stick Pull
Contestants sit with feet against each other's and their hands grasped around a stick. They then attempt to pull each other over.

Ear Pull
A painful test of stamina, this is a 'tug-of-war' between two people joined with string looped round their ears. Very rarely, players lose an ear.

Toe Kick
Players jump with feet kept together to kick over a stick which is moved further away until a winner emerges.

Kneel Jump
Contestants swing their arms to build up momentum for a jump from a kneeling position.

Greased Pole Walk
Competitors attempt to walk as far as possible on a slippery pole without falling.

Scissor Broad Jump
A distance event which mimics jumping from ice floe to ice floe.

Arm Pull
A test of strength where men with arms and legs locked attempt to pull each other over.

One Foot High Kick
Contestants must jump up and kick a suspended sealskin ball with one foot, then land on this same foot. There is also a **Two Foot High Kick** contest.

Ear Weight
Lead weights on a string (formerly flour sacks) have to be picked up using only the ear.

Blanket Toss (aka Nalakatuk)
A large circle made of animal skins is used by several people to toss the competitor several metres into the air. They are judged on balance and moves. It is thought that the practice may derive from a way of spotting game from a distance.

Drop the Bomb
This event involves three men carrying another, who has stiffened his limbs, by his hands and feet until he drops.

Four Man Carry
A distance event which mimics the carrying of a carcase after a hunt.

Knuckle Hop (aka Seal Hop)
A test of endurance to see how far contestants can travel by hopping with only their toes and knuckles allowed to touch the floor.

As well as these sports, there are also the following events:

The Race of the Torch
Seal Cutting Contest
White Man versus Native Woman Tug o' War
Muktuk Eating Contest*
Miss WEIO Pageant
Fish Cutting contest
Baby Contest (Indian and Eskimo)
Native Regalia Pageant
Sewing Contest
Dance Team

* Muktuk is whale skin and flesh, said to taste 'like fresh coconut'.

PLAYTIME

Some old Scots children's games (according to Alexander Warrack's *The Scots Dialect Dictionary* of 1911)

allicomgreenyie (girls' game of 'drop the handkerchief')
anthony-over (throwing balls over a house)
bars ('tag' game)
bellie-mantie (blindman's buff)
black-doggie ('drop the handkerchief'-style chasing game)
blanket (hide and seek game)
blind-bell (blindfold players try to catch a bell-carrier)
bogle-about-the-stacks (hide and seek played among haystacks)
bonnet-ba (played by boys with caps and a ball)
bulliheizilie (boys' wrestling game)
burley-whush (ball game)
buttony (players guess who has been given a button)
cat-beds (played with pieces of turf)
curcuddie (crouching and hopping)
dike-queen ('king-of-the-castle' game)
dilly-castle (standing on sandcastles until washed away)
dishaloof (hand covering game)
dumscum (like hopscotch)
foot an' a half (form of leapfrog)
funny (marbles game)
hap-the-beds (form of hopscotch)
henners (swinging game)
het beans and butter ('hunt the object' game)
hinkum-booby (singing game)
hornie (hand game)
horny-holes (batting game played with stick and sheep's horn)
huckie-buckie (sliding down a hill)
hunt-the-staigie (chasing game)

I dree, I dree, I dropped it (girls' singing game)
jinkie (chasing game)
keeky-bo (peekaboo)
kick-bonnety (game using a hat as a football)
kittlie-cowt ('hunt the object' game)
kypie (bat and ball game)
langie-spangie (marbles game)
line-him-out (boys take turns to beat each other with caps)
loup-the-bullocks (leapfrog)
moolie-pudding (boys' chasing game)
mump-the-cuddie (racing on haunches)
needle cases (singing game)
neivie-nick-nack (guessing game)
paipie (game using cherry stones)
pop-the-bunnet (game played with hat and pins)
rangiebus (cap-collecting game)
rin-'em-owre (chasing game)
robin-a-ree (game with a lighted stick)
row-chow-tobacco (a coiling line of boys)
sailor-lad (girls' dancing game)
salmon-fishers (singing game)
Scotch and English (rough team game)
sheep-race (rough boys' game)
spang-cockle (nut-flicking game)
spawnie (button-throwing game)
sunshines (singing game)
sweer-arse (one-to-one tug-of-war)
tappie-tousie (questioning game while holding
  another's hair)
tig-tow (chasing game)
titbo-tatbo (peekaboo)
troap (catching game)
tuilyie-wap (hand-grasping game)
widow (singing game)
Willy Wastell (rhyming game)
winnie (marbles game)

ALIAS

Presidential code names supposedly used by the US Secret Service

JFK	Lancer (Jackie was Lace)
LBJ	Volunteer (Lady Bird was Victoria)
Richard Nixon	Searchlight
Gerald Ford	Pass Key (Betty was Pinafore)
Jimmy Carter	Lock Master or Deacon (Rosalynn was Dancer)
Ronald Reagan	Rawhide (Nancy was Rainbow)
George Bush	Timberwolf (Barbara was Snowbank or Tranquility)
Bill Clinton	Eagle (Hillary was Evergreen and Chelsea was Energy)
George W Bush	Tumbler or Trailblazer

Other Secret Service code names have included ...

Queen Elizabeth II	Kittyhawk
Prince Charles	Unicorn or Daily
Frank Sinatra	Napoleon
Henry Kissinger	Woodcutter
Pope John Paul II	Halo

SKY HIGH

Reported accounts of the adventures of ten celebrated aviatresses

1 **Laetitia Sage** was an actress who became the first British woman to take to the air in the summer of 1785. The pioneer balloonist Vincent Lunardi had suffered some embarrassing failures and invited Mrs Sage to join him to generate some fresh publicity. The ascent was a great success, with the balloon travelling 30 miles from central London – nearly as far as Harrow. Lunardi had to first remove himself and a colleague to lighten the load but Laetitia (accompanied by the flight's sponsor) was soon waving and blowing kisses to the London crowds below. She later published an account of her experience.

2 **Lady Mary Heath** was at the heart of the trend for glamorous 20s aviatresses, which was taken up enthusiastically by the media of the day. She insisted on flying in furs and frills. When she flew solo to South Africa, her plane was painted to match her jewellery. On another long flight, the Air Ministry refused to escort her over the Mediterranean and she had to enlist the help of Mussolini. Although Irish by birth, she had once been part of the British Olympic athletics team.

3 It has been suggested that **Amy Johnson** may have first taken up flying lessons intending to commit suicide after an unhappy relationship. Instead, she found herself enthralled by flight. In 1930, she raised the money for an attempt at a solo flight to Australia. This was successful, but the subsequent publicity and another difficult relationship with a fellow celebrity pilot, buffeted her. During World War II, she was drowned after a plane she was transporting crashed into the Thames Estuary.

4 Bored with her job as a jobbing model and actress, **Sheila Scott** learned to

fly planes, winning the de Havilland Trophy only a few years after commencing her training. In the mid-60s, she made a solo round-the-world flight. In 1971, in a Piper Aztec, she became the first pilot to fly over the North Pole in a light aircraft (an American Arctic explorer, Louise A Boyd, had earlier flown over the Pole at the age of 68 in 1955). Scott wrote an autobiography *Barefoot in the Sky* about her air adventures. She died in the late 80s.

5   **Mrs Maurice Hewlett** (known as Hilda) was probably the first woman to fly solo and became the first licensed female pilot in 1911, teaching her son to fly soon after. She appears to have set the trend for unusual flying outfits and wore her hair unfashionably short. She went on to cofound an aircraft and engine company, Hewlett & Blondeau. She was something of an aesthete, having trained at art college and married a romantic novelist, and was also a pioneer of motoring with a taste for speed.

6   A restless and eccentric aristocrat, the **Duchess of Bedford** took up flying in her 60s, partly inspired by the way the shift in air pressure temporarily eased her deafness. She undertook several long-distance flights, often flying as low as possible to observe the landscape and nature of the foreign lands below. She died in an unexplained air accident in 1937.

7   **Amelia Earhart** was the first woman to fly the Atlantic (only as a passenger) in 1926. It was said that she was chosen partly due to a physical resemblance to Charles Lindbergh! She had been taught to fly by Neta Snook, one of the first woman air pioneers, and she later became the first President of the 'Ninety-Nines', an organization for women pilots. In 1932, she made the first successful solo transatlantic flight since Lindbergh's, landing in rural Ireland, sustained during the journey by a flask of soup and smelling salts. In 1935, she flew from Hawaii to California, but a round-the-world flight was her ambition and so she set off in her plane *Electra* in 1937. Despite a good start, the long-haul flight became draining and her plane was lost in the Pacific in July. There have been several conspiracy theories

about this most famous of woman fliers (that she was captured by the Japanese or went on to live happily on an island with a fisherman), but it seems likely that pilot error led to a crash into the sea or onto an atoll.

8   **Jean Batten** was a flier from New Zealand, known as 'Hine O Te Rangi' ('Daughter of the Skies') and the 'Garbo of the Air'. After two failed attempts (including a minor crash in India), in 1934 she managed to beat Johnson's record for flying to Australia from England by six days. Batten suffered from two common problems for fliers of the day. She was caught between the faddish glamour of being an aviatress and her feminism; she also suffered from the numbing loneliness of long-distance solo flying. Two years later she smashed the England–Australia record in both directions. Eye problems caused her to give up flying in the late 30s and she later lived a reclusive existence in Spain, dying from an infected dog bite in 1982.

9   **Pauline Gower** was the first English woman to receive a commercial pilot's licence in 1931. She sometimes flew with another aviatress, Dorothy Spicer, as copilot (as Anne Morrow Lindbergh had sometimes done with her famous husband.) During the war, she headed the women's division of the Air Transport Auxiliary (for whom Amy Johnson was serving when she was killed). Gower fought hard against the prejudices faced by women pilots during wartime and was proud of the safety record of her small band of pilots.

10   The original Miss Selfridge, **Violette de Sibour** was a daughter of Harry Gordon Selfridge, founder of the famous London department store which once sold small aircraft and gear for pioneer pilots. With her husband Jacques she undertook a 10,000 mile game hunting trip by air to India and the Far East. While most aviatresses preferred woollen balaclavas and leather suits, Violette never flew off on an adventure without a cache of gowns, lingerie and silk stockings. After one emergency landing in India, Violette was horrified to find locals making off with some of the choicest items from her clothing supplies.

DESTROY (YOUR IMAGE)

Ten not-very-punk moments for British punk heroes

1 Captain Sensible

1976 – mooning and mugging for the Damned

1982 – hits Number One with a novelty hit taken from the musical *South Pacific*

2 The Stranglers

1977 – sleazing and slapping anyone who wants some

2000 – upping the morale of the British troops during gigs in the Balkans

3 Howard Devoto

1976 – between boredom and breakdown with the Buzzcocks

early 90s – begins job as a photographic librarian

4 Paul Simenon

1977 – stripping and strutting behind Joe Strummer

2002 – exhibits his (rather good) landscape oil paintings in central London

5 Poly Styrene

1977 – pogoing and yelling with X-Ray Spex

early 80s – converts to Hare Krishna religion and later reportedly marries a priest

6 Elvis Costello

1977 – bristling and yodelling punk-power pop hits

1999 – sings a Charles Aznavour ballad for a slushy Hugh Grant movie

7 Feargal Sharkey

1978 – writhing and keening afront the Undertones

1998 – company managing director becomes a member of the Radio Authority panel

8 Richard Jobson

1978 – howling and high-kicking with the Skids

2002 – *The Guardian* film interviewer turns film director

9 John Lydon

1976 – gobbing and snarling for the Pistols

early 90s – is reported to be considering taking a degree in Marine Biology at a Californian university

10 Siouxsie Sioux

1978 – wailing and wiggling with the Banshees

1983 – releases pretty pop cover of a Beatles' number about a socialite

LUNCH LINES

A recent BBC survey on school dinners found that people in the UK had the worst memories about these ten foods

1
Tapioca

2
Cabbage

3
Overcooked vegetables

4
Lumpy mashed potato

5
Lumpy custard

6
Liver

7
Semolina

8
Gristly meat

9
Blancmange

10
Beetroot

Now, I do have some nasty memories about school dinners (east Scotland, c.'71 to '83), especially the chemistry-set taste of instant mash, but I have many fond memories of dinner delights so, in fairness, here are ten good things ...

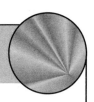

1. Curry, with sultanas. As exotic and unlikely in the early 80s as a date with Yasmin Le Bon.

2. Stewed sausages – skinless links thrown in to drown for hours in gelatinous onion gravy.

3. Sweet chocolate milk drunk through a straw from little boxes.

4. Odd 70s rissole made from pork mince and rice – delicious; was it really called a 'Dutch hamburger'?

5. Biscuity base with thick chocolate fudge on top and a mini-swirl of skooshy cream.

6. Thinly-sliced hot roast beef or pork in mash-mopping gravy. Roast meat was always served 'a l'écossaise' at home, ie roasted then left to go cold and served in thick dollops. Why, why, why?

7. Spam fritters – slabs of processed meat dipped in gooey batter and deep-fried. It shouldn't have worked, but the vestige of War was still in our blood.

8. Glazy jam tart with non-lumpy kitchen-made custard.

9. Biscuity, thick pizza slabs with proper cheddar cheese and tomato.

10. Scotch pies – the one-eyed, sawdust gentleman himself, mutton dressed as mutton, in his little round pastry jacket.

OPPOSITES ATTRACT

Fourteen words which mean the opposite of how they sound

pulchritudinous
should mean: horribly covered in boils
does mean: very beautiful

hagiography
should mean: a biography tearing the subject's character to shreds
does mean: an over-praising biography

persiflage
should mean: a stream of persecutory invective
does mean: playful banter

dilate
should mean: of an aperture, to grow smaller
does mean: to spread out or expand

droll
should mean: sad and humourless
does mean: amusing, laughable

inflammable
should mean: incapable of burning
does mean: easily set alight

disembark
should mean: to leave port, to go on a journey
does mean: to leave a ship

embark
should mean: to enter port, to return from a journey
does mean: to get on a ship

spendthrift
should mean: one who is careful with money
does mean: one who spends freely and wastefully

dirigible
should mean: unmoveable, tied to earth
does mean: navigable, as of an airship

numptious
should mean: unpleasant and arrogant
does mean: delightful and cuddly

cataglottal
should mean: bunged up with phlegm
does mean: pertaining to passionate kissing with tongues

gamesmanship
should mean: sporting behaviour
does mean: deliberately putting off an opponent

wiseacre
should mean: a bright person dripping wit and wisdom
does mean: a naive fool

FAR NORTH
Some fictional Eskimos and Inuits

Nathan Active is an Inupiat state trooper in the detective novels of Alaskan writer Stan Jones such as *White Sky*, *Black Ice* and *Shaman Pass*.

The 1979 LP *Eskimo* by the eccentric US band the Residents consists of a series of six atmospheric sound pieces designed to be played while you read the stories of a group of fictional Eskimos led by the **Angakok**, printed on the record's sleeve.

Published in the late 90s, **Kitaq** *Goes Ice Fishing* is a book for small children by Margaret Nicolai and David Rubin about a boy's first fishing trip in the far North.

The 1933 film *Eskimo* (also known as **Mala the Magnificent**) was the first to have a cast including many Eskimos. It tells of a hunter's troubles after killing a white captain who had wronged him.

'When a man grows old and his balls grow cold …' So begins the infamous pornographic piece of doggerel **Eskimo Nell**. The story has been (very loosely) adapted into two movies, one a 70s British sex comedy, the other a tale of the Australian gold rush.

Clicquot Club was the brand name of a popular ginger ale in the USA from the 20s onwards. The name Clicquot was also given to an Eskimo boy who featured prominently on the bottle's label.

Menie and Monnie are 'The Eskimo Twins' in the eponymous 1914 children's novel by Lucy Fitch Perkins.

Eskimo Bob is a web-based multi-episode cartoon about the adventures of the improbably-named Eskimos **Bob and Alfonzo**.

Another improbable name for an Eskimo is Bob Dylan's pigeon-entrancing, sleep-inducing *The Mighty **Quinn***.

Though **Nanook** was a real person, Robert J Flaherty's pioneering documentary *Nanook of the North* about life on the ice was a fictionalized account using a Westernized Inuk family, in order to recreate the lifestyles of their previous generations.

Julie of the Wolves by Jean Craighead George tells of a 13-year-old Eskimo girl named **Miyax**, also called Julie in English, who runs away and lives with a pack of wolves in the Alaskan wilderness.

MILESTONES

Stephen King's prison novel **The Green Mile** was first published in six monthly parts. It was later made into a highly-rated film starring Tom Hanks. Set on Death Row in a 30s jail, the title refers to the green linoleum on the way to the electric chair. The walk to the chair was also known as the 'last mile' and this was the name of a 1932 movie (remade in the late 50s), also about life on Death Row. This phrase is often used in telecommunications and technology for a problematic late phase in the development of a product or system. A song called 'The Last Mile' was written by Jimmy Page and Andrew Loog Oldham for singer Nico in her pre-Velvet Underground days.

In Rusholme, Manchester, hungry locals on the **Curry Mile** can choose from over 50 low-cost restaurants in what is actually a half-mile stretch. Some of the curry houses have been open since the 70s.

The **Golden Mile** is the name given to the seafront stretch in Blackpool, one of England's most popular traditional holiday resorts, where you will find the amusement arcades, chip shops, bingo stalls and waxworks and where you can see the famous annual show of coloured lights. In Hong Kong, the name is given to the business and nightlife centre of Kowloon, while in Melbourne, Australia, the name is used for the city's heritage trail. There are also Golden Miles in Belfast, Detroit, Montreal, Bournemouth and on the Costa del Sol in Spain. The Golden Mile of Tipperary is an annual competition to find the most beautiful and environmentally laudable stretch of rural road in that part of Ireland.

'Golden Mile' was also a song by John Waite's late 70s rock band the Babys and the title of the 'difficult second album' by late 90s indie-glam group My Life Story. Lastly, the term has also been used for a celebrated annual athletics race held at the Bislett stadium in Oslo.

The **Museum Mile** stretches up Fifth Avenue in Manhattan and contains such attractions as the Metropolitan, the Guggenheim and the Jewish Museum.

The area around the Bank of England in 'the City', London's centre of finance and investment, is sometimes called the **Square Mile**.

The **Miracle Mile** was a shopping area of LA developed in the 20s. The name is also used for various stretches of river where the fishing is good. The phrase is sometimes used for the first sub-four minute mile run by Roger Bannister in Oxford in 1954.

Running down through the centre of the old part of Edinburgh, the **Royal Mile** is one of Scotland's most famous streets. Actually consisting of a few connected streets (and also slightly over a mile), it lies between the Castle and the royal palace of Holyroodhouse. Along the way, you can see St Giles Cathedral, the Heart of Midlothian (marked in the cobbles by the cathedral and spat on for luck), the John Knox House and the Old Tolbooth. Prague also has a Royal Mile which was originally the route taken by the king-to-be on his way to be crowned.

The **Red Mile** in Lexington, Kentucky, is a racetrack famous as one of the main venues for harness racing.

The **Milwaukee Mile** is a major venue for motor racing.

BETWEEN THE COVER VERSIONS

Twelve songs chosen as background music by the BBC's Big Read promotion to represent famous books

1 'I Am The Resurrection' The Stone Roses (*The Lion, The Witch and The Wardrobe*)

2 'Stupid Cupid' Connie Francis (*Emma*)

3 'Love Will Tear Us Apart' Joy Division (*Captain Corelli's Mandolin*)

4 'Money's Too Tight to Mention' Simply Red (*A Christmas Carol*)

5 'Beautiful Ones' Suede (*Brideshead Revisited*)

6 'Bad Girls' Donna Summer (*Tess of the D'Urbervilles*)

7 'Uptown Girl' Billy Joel (*Great Expectations*)

8 'Young Americans' David Bowie (*The Great Gatsby*)

9 'House of Fun' Madness (*Pride and Prejudice*)

10 'The Beautiful People' Marilyn Manson (*Wuthering Heights*)

11 'Oh Happy Day!' Edwin Hawkins Singers (*To Kill a Mockingbird*)

12 'Stuck in The Middle With You' Stealers Wheel (*Catch-22*)

BRAVE TALK
PART ONE

Unusual and charming words and definitions from *The Scots Dialect Dictionary* compiled by Alexander Warrack and first published in 1911

aplochs
corners of cornfields left unmowed for the supposed benefit of the warlocks

arse-cockle
a hot pimple on any part of the body

bagenin
rough, and sometimes indecent, horseplay at harvest time

barla-fummil
a cry for truce by one who has fallen in fighting or wrestling

bawbee-jo
a lover hired to walk with a girl for a shilling or so

bern-windlin
a kiss given in the corner of a barn

bicker-raid
a harvest frolic in which a young man threw down a girl and the other harvesters covered them with their 'bickers' [cups or bowls]

billatory
a restless bull

blind-tam
a bundle of rags made up as a child, carried by beggars

bobantilter
any dangling piece of dress

boucht-curd
sheep droppings that fall into the milk pail

buckalee
a call to negligent herdboys

bumming-duff
a tambourine

chittering-chow
a piece of bread eaten immediately after bathing in the open air

clanter
the noise made by walking in a house with clogs

clinted
used of sheep, caught among cliffs by leaping down to a ledge from which ascent is impossible by leaping back

clobber-hoy
a dirty walker

clugston
an obsolete amusement among farmers

cockertie-hooie
carrying a boy astride the neck

cornief
cats' excrement

cothrochie
to cook in a dirty, disgusting manner

craw-pockies
the eggs of sharks, skate and dogfish

cuddy-wanter
one on the outlook for a donkey

deaf-nit
a woman without money

dirt-flee
the yellow fly that haunts dunghills; a young woman who, after having remained single from pride, at last makes a low marriage

doggindales
clouds of mist clinging to hillsides

drod
a rude candle-holder used in visiting farm offices at night

fag-ma-fuff
a garrulous old woman

faizart
a hermaphrodite of the hen-tribe

feist
a noiseless breaking of wind

flamfoo
a woman fond of dress

foulbeard
a blacksmith's mop for his trough

gaeppie
a large horn spoon, requiring a widely-opened mouth

garwhoungle
the noise of the bittern in rising from the bog

gawlin	a fowl less than a duck, regarded as a prognosticator of fair weather
gin	greedy of meat
girl	to set the teeth on edge
green gown	the loss of virginity in the open air
grimes-dike	a ditch made by magic
haggerdecash	topsy-turvy
hairy-bummler	a name given to certain types of crabs
hammerflush	sparks from an anvil
hinkum	what is tied up into balls
hoometet	covered with a large flannel nightcap
huam	the moan of an owl in the warm days of summer
John Heezlum Peezlum	the man in the moon
jorg	the noise of shoes when full of water
katty-clean-doors	a child's name for snow
keesich	a word used by one entering a room where a person is already seated, and requesting a seat
ken-no	a cheese made to be eaten at a birth by the 'gossips'
kigger	to mess about with soft or semi-liquid foods
kirk-fever	excitement over church affairs
knacks	a disease in the throat of fowls fed on too hot food
knickum	a tricky boy

... continued on p300

227

HIGH FIVES

At last, some severed hand trivia

1

A **Hand of Glory** was a curious device used by burglars as recently as 200 years ago. Made from the dried, severed hand of a hanged man, it was used as a holder for a candle made from a magic recipe including human fat and spices. It was said to open doors and ensure that householders fell into a deep sleep.

2

Around 1900, **W W Jacobs** wrote *The Monkey's Paw* (probably adapting an earlier folk tale) which tells of a cursed, embalmed paw which gives the owner three (dangerous) wishes.

3

A film from **Michael Caine's** quieter years, *The Hand* (1981) tells of an artist who loses his hand in a crash, only to discover it is following him and committing terrible crimes.

4

The third act of Shakespeare's ***Titus Andronicus*** may be the goriest in any play. One of the many difficulties in staging it is producing a realistic spectacle of Titus's hand being lopped off.

5

The cover photo of my own second collection of **poetry** *The Book of Love*, which depicts several entangled hands, had to be in black and white, otherwise the image in colour looked eerily and garishly like a pile of severed hands.

6

Even within the last decade, the embalmed severed hand of **John Kemble** (a Catholic martyr later made a saint) has supposedly been removed from a coffin in Hereford and used to 'cure' priests with terminal illnesses.

7

A creepy but eternally popular children's game is to pass round, in the dark, a 'dead man's eye' (a peeled grape) and a '**dead man's hand**' (a rubber glove filled with water).

8

A similar **glove** is sometimes frozen in the USA at Hallowe'en, the iced 'severed hand' being daubed with fake gore and served with blood-red fruit punch.

9

The Belgian city of **Antwerp** may derive its name from a word meaning 'hand throwing' after the legend of a giant who cut off the hands of those who refused to pay a toll over the river, until a Roman soldier bested him and cut his off, throwing it into the water. A huge fountain in the city depicts the scene.

10

The '**Red Hand of Ulster**' supposedly derives from a race between invaders to claim land. The chief who was losing cut off his hand and threw it ashore, thereby gaining rights on the area. Wouldn't one fingertip have done the trick?

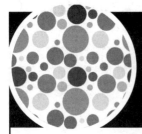

HOPELESS

Twenty things I can't do

1. pick up spiders
2. work showers
3. do handstands
4. understand visual artists when they talk about their work
5. drink Bacardi®
6. click my fingers
7. drive a car
8. get Doonesbury
9. open milk cartons
10. sing or dance in public
11. have a boss, ever
12. stand steady on a chair to change a light bulb
13. finish songs
14. hold hot plates or cups
15. identify cloud types
16. read novels or watch movies
17. follow directions
18. play a musical instrument
19. climb a rope
20. understand women, despite years of kidding myself

VISAGE

1 Gene Hackman described himself as having a face like a mug with handles.

2 Miranda Richardson was said to have a face like an English sky.

3 Charles Bronson compared his own face to 'a rock quarry that someone has dynamited'; it was also said that he had 'a face like a crushed beer can' and looked like 'the death mask of Genghis Khan'.

4 An elderly **W H Auden** claimed his face was like a wedding cake left out in the rain.

5 Abraham Lincoln's face was once fancifully compared to 'a title page of anxiety and distress'.

6 Sylvia Plath wrote that her face was like a dry, chalky mask.

7 Colin Montgomerie – along with several other supposedly surly men, mostly sports stars – has been jocularly described as having a face like a bulldog licking piss off a nettle.

8 Meryl Streep's face was said to look both like a medieval Madonna *and* that sexy blonde at the next table.

9 Richard Harris's description of his own visage was 'a face like five miles of bad country road'.

10 J B Priestley was said to 'have a face like a glowering pudding'.

REST OF THE BESTIARY

Thirteen unusual mammals you probably haven't heard of

baiji long-beaked, nearly blind dolphin found in the Yangtze River, China

binturong shaggy, slothlike creature of Asia with orange eyes

gelada Ethiopian baboon which looks like it has been let loose in a lipstick factory, then blow-dried

monito del monte beady-eyed Chilean tree mouse which lives among bamboo

pacarana rare, sleepy beast of northern South American jungles which stares at its food before eating it

quoll vicious catlike Australian marsupial with a spotty coat

salano Madagascan mongoose which performs acrobatics to throw eggs at stones with its hind legs

serow mysterious and revered grey goat-antelope of south-east Asia which spends most of its life asleep

sewellel small burrowing rodent of north-west USA, the mountain beaver; looks like someone has put batteries in a toy beaver

solenodon long-legged, long-snouted West Indian shrewlike creature, slow-moving and clumsy

teledu short-tailed Indonesian mammal, also known as the stinking badger of Java, whose foul anal secretions were used in perfume-making

uakari South American monkey with shaggy grey hair and odd, naked and crimson humanoid face

yapok cheeky, ratlike swimming marsupial of South and Central America

1970S FEVER

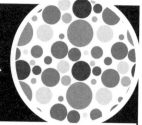

The bestselling singles and albums in the UK in the 70s

1	'Mull of Kintyre'	Wings
2	'Rivers of Babylon'	Boney M
3	'You're the One That I Want'	John Travolta/Olivia Newton John
4	'Mary's Boy Child'	Boney M
5	'Summer Nights'	John Travolta/Olivia Newton John
6	'Bright Eyes'	Art Garfunkel
7	'YMCA'	Village People
8	'Bohemian Rhapsody'	Queen
9	'Heart of Glass'	Blondie
10	'I Love You Love Me Love'	Gary Glitter

1	*Bridge Over Troubled Water*	Simon and Garfunkel
2	*Greatest Hits*	Abba
3	*Tubular Bells*	Mike Oldfield
4	*Greatest Hits*	Simon and Garfunkel
5	*Saturday Night Fever*	soundtrack
6	*The Singles*	The Carpenters
7	*Arrival*	Abba
8	*Dark Side of the Moon*	Pink Floyd
9	*Grease*	soundtrack
10	*40 Greatest Hits*	Elvis Presley

MINDBENDING
Some unusual syndromes

Stendhal syndrome

This is a condition marked by increased heartbeat, dizziness and delusions experienced when the sufferer encounters artworks such as famous paintings or other artistic or architectural masterpieces, especially in the great cities of Europe such as Naples and Paris. It is named after the 19th-century French novelist Stendhal (Henri Marie Beyle), who wrote of experiencing the sensation during a visit to Florence.

Jerusalem syndrome

This is a similar syndrome which can occur when a pious person visits a holy place such as Jerusalem, Mecca or Rome. Symptoms can include a compulsion to preach or convert, self-condemnation, identifying with a religious figure, hallucinations and feelings of helplessness or exhilaration.

Stockholm syndrome

In August 1973, armed robbers led by prison escapee Jan-Erik Olsson burst into a Stockholm branch of the Swedish Kreditbank. A five-and-a-half-day siege ensued, with four bank employees held hostage. The bank workers found that, as time progressed, they felt increasing sympathy with their captors and grew attached to them. This phenomenon is common in hostage situations and is thought to develop from a defence mechanism, fear of violence and the threat posed by a rescue attempt.

Modigliani syndrome

This thyroid problem affects people with particularly long, slender necks. It is named after the Italian artist Amedeo Modigliani (1884–1920) who tended to paint lithe figures in an extended or stretched pose.

Alice in Wonderland syndrome

This is a psychological condition, sometimes occurring in extreme migraine sufferers, where the patient feels that their body is much smaller or much bigger than it is. There may be hallucinations and a skewed sense of perception. There may also be accompanying anxiety and a feeling that your walking is getting nowhere.

Paradise syndrome

This rare condition tends to strike those who have achieved great success and reward in their chosen field, especially comparatively early in life. People such as rich businessmen on early retirement or showbiz celebrities with more money than they'll ever need can feel emptiness and boredom set in when their ambition and drive is replaced with peace, quiet and luxury and this can lead to quite severe depressive problems.

ORANGE RHYME

An age-old quandary – what rhymes with 'orange'? In 2000, La Sierra University (Riverside, California) asked locals at the Orange Blossom Festival to offer suggestions of near rhymes. These included (in order of popularity, with variant spellings thereon):

*… Porridge • Storage • Courage • Sorange
Nothing • Lorange • Burnge • Forge • Floorage
Forage • Sporange • Florange • Stonehenge
Fringe • To rage • Seepage • Gorgeous • Flange
Torrance • Florence • Lorlorn • Arrange
Syringe • Door-hinge • Stone Age • College
Norange • Discourage • Galorange • Strange
Morning • A range • Or Mange • Thorn
Gerund and, um, Orange …*

There are no full rhymes for **orange**. However, for non-dictionary rhymes (though I can't guarantee the pronunciations), we might try these ...

Blorenge (a hill in Wales)

porange (a nonce word describing pinky or purply orange; see also **gorange** etc, various 'pseudo-neologisms' for hybrid colours, juices, etc)

Soranj (a surname)

Lorange (Kirk Lorange, famed slide guitarist)

Gorange (a US fighting robot)

corringe (a variety of rhododendron)

porringe (an old variant of porringer, a soup bowl)

The (originally British) surnames Corringe, Lorringe, Worringe, Morringe, Gorringe (eg Chris Gorringe, leading tennis official), Horringe (eg Sir Thomas Horringe, a Kipling character who 'specializes in tripe') and Torringe all exist and most, I'd imagine, rhyme with orange. The word 'sporange', a botanical word for a spore case, has been suggested as a full rhyme for orange, but this is debatable due to pronunciation.

Many interesting slang words end in -ggy (or -ggie, -gie or -gey)

baggy   of clothes, loose-fitting, giving its name to a style of fashion and indie/dance music prevalent around 1990 and revolving around Manchester bands such as the Stone Roses and Happy Mondays

baggie   a small bag (in north-east Scotland, the suffix *-ie* is added to lots of nouns in speech. Also common in parts of Canada. 'Eh?' is also used at the end of sentences in both areas, probably not by chance

claggy   sticky, dirty, troublesome

craggy   of an elderly male face, lived-in, wrinkled but distinguished

daggy   Australian slang for nerdy; a dag is a piece of clotted, filthy wool around a sheep's tail

draggy   of a woman's clothes, making her look a bit like a drag queen (drag formerly meaning a gathering of homosexuals)

faggy   descriptive of the smell of cigarettes ('there was a faggy stink in the house after the party')

haggy   of a woman, having the tendency to prefer the company of gay men

jaggy   short-tempered, irritable

naggy   tending to find fault with or constantly bother another

raggy   tattered, untidy, especially of hair

saggy   descriptive of a woman's breasts that have failed to defy gravity over time

eggy   of a smell, sulphurous or egglike

leggy   having long legs, especially in the tabloid cliché 'leggy lovely'

THE -GGY FILES

seggy of boots, to be soled with segs, metal tacks which prevent wear

smeggy generally horrid or disgusting; from the Greek for soap, via a medical term (smegma) for a secretion under the foreskin

biggy anything special or noteworthy of its type; a major event

ciggy common British slang for a cigarette

figgy curious or, simply, containing figs (as in 'we all love figgy pudding')

giggy attending lots of popular music concerts, as in 'I'm not as giggy as I used to be'

jiggy US slang for well-dressed, good-looking, keen, sexually attractive

liggy prone to being a 'ligger', ie freeloading or trying to get in free or uninvited to events or parties

piggy greedy; having slightly porcine facial features

wiggy crazed, especially due to LSD

doggy like a dog, as in doggy style (sexual position) and doggy paddle (swimming stroke)

foggy slow-thinking; ambiguous

groggy here's how a French term for 'coarse cloth' (*gros grain*) became a word meaning exhausted or punch-drunk. The cloth was anglicized to grogram and was worn by 18th-century military men such as Admiral Vernon, whose grogram cloak earned him the nickname 'Old Grog'. It was Vernon who decided that the navy's rum rations were too potent and ought to be diluted. This lesser potion was named 'grog' and this term later caught on for booze in general, hence groggy meaning intoxicated and its subsequent current meaning

froggy English slang for French, from the French habit of eating frogs' legs ('I see those froggy farmers are protesting again!')

moggy a cat, especially a non-pedigree specimen

proggy resembling 'progressive rock', the jazz and classical influenced musical style of the early 70s ('this is Yes at their most proggy')

snoggy involving amorous kissing; willing to partake in athletic tonsil hockey

soggy soaked with moisture; inane or insipid

buggy a pushchair for infants

chuggy common UK slang for chewing gum

druggie a drug addict

fuggy of the air in a room, overly warm or smoky

luggy in Scots slang, having big ears, or prone to eavesdropping

puggy in Scots dialect, a monkey (perhaps from pug meaning a flattened nose, as in the dog breed); also, in Scotland and Ireland, slang for any gambling machine ('I've just bunged eight quid in the puggy and I've left a good hold')

spuggy (or spyuggy) a sparrow, especially a young one

tuggy of the hair, knotted or matted

boogie to dance to vigorous music; to leave a location ('this party is total pants, let's boogie')

bogey a malevolent spirit; hardened nasal mucus

dogie US slang for an orphaned calf, sometimes extended to young or herded cattle in general

fogey a person, usually older, who is conservative with old-fashioned beliefs or interests

hoagie a long and large American filled bread roll, also called sub, hero, bomber, poor boy, grinder, torpedo or rocket. It's thought that originally it was hoggie, since only piggy people could eat these outsize sandwiches (slang words for sandwich in the UK include sanger, piece, butty and sarnie).

stogie a thin, long and cheap American cigar originally made in the Pennsylvania town of Conestoga or perhaps named after the 'Conestoga' wagons driven by cigar makers

ROOTS

The real names of 18 reggae DJs from the 60s onwards

Count Machuki	Winston Cooper
King Stitt	Winston Spark
U-Roy	Ewart Beckford
Dennis Alcapone	Dennis Smith
I-Roy	Roy Reid
Scotty	David Scott
Big Youth	Manley Augustus Buchanan
Dillinger	Lester Bullocks
Dr Alimantado	James Winston Thompson
Clint Eastwood	Robert Brammer
Jah Woosh	Neville Beckford
Prince Jazzbo	Linval Carter
Prince Far I	Michael James Williams
Trinity	Wade Brammer
Jah Stitch	Melbourne James
Lone Ranger	Anthony Waldron
Eek A Mouse	Ripton Joseph Hilton
Yellowman	Winston Foster

FORKED TONGUES

Some words in English which are also the names of world languages

Pear (Cambodia)

Mire (Chad)

Song (Thailand)

Anal (India)

Yoke (Indonesia)

Fang (Gabon)

Duke (Solomon Islands)

Puma (Nepal)

Hung (Laos)

Mama (Nigeria)

Vale (Central African Republic)

Bum (Cameroon)

Mum (Papua New Guinea)

Reel (The Sudan)

Bats (Georgia)

Ham (Nigeria)

Male (Ethiopia)

Are (Papua New Guinea)

Boon (Somalia)

Poke (Democratic Republic of Congo)

Noon (Senegal)

Fur (The Sudan)

Mango (Chad)

Label (Papua New Guinea)

Anus (Indonesia)

Day (Chad)

Bile (Nigeria)

Con (Laos)

Moo (Nigeria)

And a few other languages with unusual names

Amis • Enya • Tay Boi • Kola • Grebo • Litzlitz
Mai Brat • Nklapmx • Tenis • Bomboma • Lushootseed
Fum • Quinqui • Zeem • Bateri • Panamint

FELINE FINE

Twenty quotations and proverbs about cats

'What is the victory of a cat on a hot tin roof? … Just staying on it, I guess, as long as she can.' (Tennessee Williams)

'It is easy to understand why the mob dislikes cats. A cat is beautiful, it suggests the idea of luxury, cleanliness, voluptuous pleasures.' (Charles Baudelaire)

A cat in gloves catches no mice. (Proverb)

'When I play with my cat, who knows whether she is not amusing herself with me more than I with her?' (Michel de Montaigne)

'The trouble with a kitten is that/Eventually it becomes a cat.' (Ogden Nash)

'If a fish is the movement of water embodied, given shape, then a cat is a diagram and pattern of subtle air.' (Doris Lessing)

'A kitten is in the animal world what a rosebud is in the garden.' (Robert Southey)

A cat's rage is beautiful, burning with pure cat flame, all its hair standing up and crackling blue sparks, eyes blazing and sputtering. (William S Burroughs)

'Cats, no less liquid than their shadows, offer no angles to the wind. They slip, diminished, neat, through loopholes less than themselves.' (A S J Tessimond)

'Never wear anything that panics the cat.' (P J O'Rourke)

Cats eat what hussies spare. (Proverb)

'Cats are intended to teach us that not everything in nature has a purpose.' (Garrison Keillor)

The cat shuts its eyes while it steals the cream. (Proverb)

'There are two means of refuge from the miseries of life: music and cats.' (Albert Schweitzer)

'Curiosity killed the cat, but for a while I was a suspect.' (Steven Wright)

'Like a one-eyed cat, peepin' in a seafood store.' (lyrics to 'Shake, Rattle and Roll'. See also, from the 19th century, 'as busy as a cat in a tripe shop'.)

'One cat just leads to another.' (Ernest Hemingway)

The cat would eat fish but would not wet her feet. (Proverb)

'Of all God's creatures there is only one that cannot be made slave of the lash, that one is the cat. If man could be crossed with the cat, it would improve man, but it will deteriorate the cat.' (Mark Twain)

All cats are grey in the dark. (Proverb)

I'M THE MAN ...

Some themed nicknames

The Man
Van Morrison, Arnold Palmer, Bear Bryant (American football),
Stan Musial (baseball)

The Man Who Taught America to Sing
Fred Waring (bandleader)

The Man of a Thousand Faces
Lon Chaney (silent horror film actor)

The Man Who Broke the Bank at Monte Carlo
Joseph Jaggers

The Man In Black
Johnny Cash

The Man Who Listens to Horses
Monty Roberts (horse-trainer)

The Man with the Plan
Hugh Gaitskell (UK politician)

The Man in the Iron Mask
unknown

The Man Who Broke the Pound
George Soros (financier)

The Man with No Name
Clint Eastwood (from his Western character)

The Man with the Velvet Voice
Ronald Colman, Nat King Cole

The Man of 1,000 Aces
Goran Ivanisevic (hard-hitting tennis star)

The Man with the Golden Head
Sandor Kocsis (50s football star)

The Man with the Horn
Miles Davis

The Man Who Never Was
Piltdown Man ('ancient' skull hoax)

The Man with the Perfect Profile
Robert Taylor

The Man with a Million Friends
T Texas Tyler (US singer and presenter)

The Man with the Orchid-Lined Voice
Enrico Caruso

The Man of Iron
Lech Walesa (Polish politician)

The Man Who Sold the Milky Way
Bart Bok (astronomer)

The Man Who Murdered Music
Spike Jones (comic musician)

The Man of the People
Abraham Lincoln

The Man Who Colours Stars
David Malin (astronomical photographer)

The Man Who Mistook His Wife for a Hat
unnamed patient of neurologist Dr Oliver Sacks

The Man Who Taught the World to Play the Guitar
Bert Weedon

The Man with the Golden Flute
James Galway

The Man Who Loved Only Numbers
Paul Erdös (mathematician)

The Man with the Golden Trumpet
Eddie Calvert

The Man You Love to Hate
Erich von Stroheim

SWEET AND SOUR SONGS

Seventeen (yes, seventeen!) songs and tunes about pickle

1	'Pickle Barrel'	The Scene is Now
2	'Pickle'	Fun Size
3	'Pickle in the Middle'	Louis Prima
4	'Pickle Head'	Mike Flores
5	'Pickle Bucket'	Post Mortem
6	'The Pickle Song'	Dinosaur Jr
7	'Pickled'	Hooligans
8	'Pickled and Preserved'	Demented Are Go
9	'Pickled Bullhorn'	Universal Congress Of
10	'Pickled Frogs'	Sardina
11	'Pickled Garbage Soup'	The Cows
12	'Pickled Herring'	Chris Bucheit
13	'Pickled Pear'	Pele
14	'A Pickled Poet's Tale'	Ariel
15	'Picklers Leave'	Rachel Portman
16	'Picklehead'	Askold Buk
17	'Pickles'	Allen Toussaint

THE MORNING AFTER

Forty-two supposed hangover cures

gherkins **1**

cabbage water **2**

ginger **3**

red-eye (a name given to various fruit juice and beer or spirit concoctions) **4**

prairie oyster (a concoction of various pungent condiments and raw egg) **5**

Paraxine® (a detox drug) **6**

cysteine (an amino acid) **7**

rabbit droppings **8**

rollmop herrings **9**

Gatorade® **10**

chemotherapy pills **11**

yoghurt with garlic **12**

vitamins B and C **13**

ginkgo **14**

noodle soup **15**

aspirin **16**

junk food **17**

kedgeree **18**

nux vomica **19**

Lucozade® or Irn Bru® **20**

artichoke extract **21**

22 menudo (Mexican tripe soup)

23 toast and sweet tea

24 cola and crisps

25 sleep

26 Bloody Mary

27 bananas and milk

28 cold kebab breakfast

29 pure oxygen

30 milk thistle

31 sex

32 wine-drowned eels and cabbage (ancient Roman tradition)

33 milk shake

34 chicken soup

35 cumin seeds

36 spicy food

37 omelette

38 soot

39 vinegar

40 Lactaid® (a rehydrating solution for sick dogs)

41 pizza

42 breast milk

NO THAIS

Eighteen recent songs the Thai Ministry of Culture reportedly wants to ban for promoting adultery and promiscuity

1. 'I Fear No Sins' ('Bo Yan Bab') by Yinglee Sreechumpol
2. 'I Fear Sin' ('Ai Yan Bab') by Phaithoon Nhunchoke
3. 'Big Flabby Buttocks' ('Tai Aon Yaon') by Phaithoon Nhunchoke
4. 'Secret Lover' ('Choo Tang Jai') by Dhanin Indarathep
5. 'Wrong Way To Love' ('Pid Tang Rak') by Suthep Wongkamhaeng
6. 'Leftovers' ('Suan Kern') by Dowjai Paijit
7. 'One Woman, Two Men' ('Nueng Ying, Song Chai') by Dowjai Paijit
8. 'I Love Her Husband' ('Chan Rak Pua Khao') by Sinjai Plengpanich
9. 'My Wife Had An Affair' ('Mia Pee Mee Choo') by Chai Muangsing
10. 'Tears Of A Lieutenant's Wife' ('Num Ta Mia Nai Roi') by Jintara Poonlab
11. 'Lover' ('Choo Rak') by Why Not Seven
12. 'A Mistress's Ultimatum' ('Kham Khad Mia Noi') by Kanista Thaidachai
13. 'A Step-Husband' ('Pua Boontham') by Samphan Seripab
14. 'Lover' ('Choo') by Lhong Longlai
15. 'Love In Mind' ('Rak Nai Jai') by Winai Panthurak
16. 'The Door Crushes The Hand' ('Pratu Neeb Mue') by Paijit Aksornnarong
17. 'I Know That, But I Still Love You' ('Tang Roo Koh Rak') by Charas Phuang-arom
18. 'Is It Sinful For Us To Love?' ('Bab Nak Rue Ta Rao Ja Rak Kan') by Suthep Wongkamhaeng

The personal pain of songwriters can often make for our personal pleasure. Here are some classic 'break-up' LPs

MY LONELY TEARS

1	Bob Dylan	*Blood On the Tracks*
2	Fleetwood Mac	*Rumours*
3	Ryan Adams	*Heartbreaker*
4	Elvis Costello	*Blood and Chocolate*
5	Virginia Astley	*Hope in a Darkened Heart*
6	Tori Amos	*Boys For Pele*
7	Beck	*Sea Change*
8	Joni Mitchell	*Blue*
9	Marvin Gaye	*Here, My Dear*
10	Blur	*13*
11	Bob Mould	*Workbook*
12	Richard and Linda Thompson	*Shoot Out the Lights*
13	P J Harvey	*Rid of Me*

SPECIFIC HUNGER

Ten particular cravings I get for food and drink far away in time or place

1 Mixed Pakora
(Kebab Mahal, Nicholson Square, Edinburgh)

Pakora are Asian fritters which are sold at kebab houses in Scotland. Since most of these places are run by Pakistanis (as opposed to Turks in England), they sell a mixture of Middle Eastern and Asian fast food. The mixed pakora comprises spicy, bright red chicken wings, chunks of fish in a light spiced batter, deep-fried mushrooms and onion pakoras. Served with a thick red chili sauce, yoghurt sauce and lots of salad.

2 Green Chili
(somewhere in Los Angeles)

The LA equivalents of the British 'greasy spoon' (an inexpensive café) sell home-style Mexican food. Cheap, fast, tasty. You feel like your long lost Aunt Jacinta has cooked you supper. I don't want bubble and squeak or a fry-up with a slice and sugary beans. I want carne verde.

3 Arctic Red
(Western Canada)

This is a beer from the Yukon which is found in good bars in Canada. It's simply delicious, not unlike some of the better US microbrews such as Sierra Nevada. If they had it at my local pub, I'd be even more of a lush.

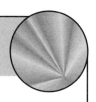

4 Doner Kebab
(Pamuk Kale, Church Street, Stoke Newington, London)

Never has a food had its name(s) (doner, gyros, shawarma, etc) taken so in vain. I love the way the Pamuk Kale (Turkish for 'cotton castle') do theirs. A circle of soft Turkish flatbread, with added lamb or chicken doner or (shivers with excitement) both, slashed from a great wodge on a spit, plied with herby tomato salad, raw onions, hot peppers and lashed with chili and yoghurt sauces. Roll it up. Chew it down. The first time I ever ate a doner (Chalk Farm, 14 April 1981) I wept when it was finished.

5 Chicken in Soy Sauce
(restaurant now demolished, Lauriston Place, Edinburgh)

Chicken done 'lemon chicken' style, ie sliced breast with a very light batter. The sauce was soy based, of course, but rich and delicious. Much missed – and never seen on another menu.

6 Meatball Sandwich
(NYC)

As if I need another reason to love New York! The best one I had was in somewhere on, maybe, 8th Ave, somewhere in the mid 20s to mid 30s. It's no good unless the whole thing collapses and you get messy. Needless to say, the UK has as many good meatball sandwiches as it does bald eagles. Possibly the only good dish containing 'America's Shame', ie its terrible cheese. We have terrible teeth, they have terrible cheese. The other great NYC fast food is those sausages split and cooked under an iron, then served in a soft tortilla with hot tomato sauce.

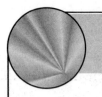

7 Chicken in Batter
(the Italian-run chip shops, Scotland)

Fried chicken, one of the world's most popular and least well-done foods. Scottish chip shops used to do leg portions in the same frothy batter used for fried fish. The trick is getting the cooking time right, so the batter isn't brick-like and the chicken portion cooks through. But they used to be able to do it. Now, it's just the same old KFC-alikes or the bald bits of ex-bird yawning on their hot trays.

8 Pork Curry
(Hung Lam, South Clerk Street, Edinburgh)

Now you can call me Char Sui Boy. But when it comes to the wondrous tan goo that is Chinese curry sauce, I don't want red roast pork. In fact, the man here turned his lip and refused to sell me such a thing many moons ago. Now it's ubiquitous on takeaway menus, while everyday pork (probably the most common meat in real Chinese food) is not to be found. Except here. Gloopy, tangy, satisfying.

9 Stewart's Key Lime Soda®
(San Francisco and elsewhere)

I don't have a sweet tooth, so I don't know why I wake in the night craving this sugary American fizzy drink. It tastes like citrus boiled sweets liquefied. It's oddly comforting and comes in dinky bottles.

10 Pata
(Manila)

I spent a week or two in the Philippines on a literary conference, and Pinoy food is fascinating. The one thing I'd like to taste again is this alternative to spare ribs, actually made from the pig's lower leg. It is boiled up with seasoning and then deep-fried until crispy and served as a snack.

LOAD OF BLEEMING MINCE

A list of 41 minced oaths. With most of these, it's quite clear what word is being minced (God, blood, etc)

1 jings

2 crivvens (these first two are very common in Scotland)

3 gorblimey (God blind me)

4 gosh

5 criminy

6 holy cow (etc)

7 zounds (God's wounds)

8 cor

9 gadzooks (God's hooks, ie Christ's nails; also gadso, odso)

10 gee whizz

11 od's bodikins (God's body)

12 crikey

13 golly

14 darn

15 heck

16 sugar

17 flip

18 jeepers creepers

19 shoot

20 begorra

21 drat

22 goodness

23 strewth (God's truth)

24 frick

25 good grief

26 blinking

27 blinding

28 egad

29 jiminy (perhaps Jesus or Jesu domine)

30 losh

31 bollards

32 dang

33 blooming (itself, along with others, probably a mincing of a minced oath – bloody for 'by our lady')

34 dangnabbit

35 feck

36 bejabers

37 jinks

38 jeez

39 lordy

40 bally

41 fegs

WHEN IN ROME

Forty Latin phrases and what they mean

ab imo pectore	he's all muscles
ab ovo usque ad mala	whisky plus eggs is a bad move
ad literam	to throw rubbish in a park
aliquid haeret	booze rules!
animo non astutia	lively, but a moron
anno domini	government by women named Ann
bona fide	good dog!
corpus delicti	road kill transformed into a tasty meal
de facto	factory-made
deo gratias	free antiperspirant
deus ex machina	in the days before technology
doli capax	to behead Barbie®
ex cathedra	(hanging out) outside church
ex post facto	an excuse involving the words 'lost in the post'
festina lente	a cocktail party held on Shrove Tuesday
fiat lux	a free-to-enter car competition
gloria patri	a dad who has had a sex change
horresco referens	an error in a book of trivia
horribile dictu	doctors' handwriting
ignorantia juris neminem excusat	even a stupid judge won't let you off

inter alia	a fight between Muhammad Ali and Monica Ali
loco citato	the area of any city where the jakies live
locus standi	to freeze and blend in as an insect does on a leaf
modus operandi	a fashion-conscious surgeon
natura abhorret vacuum	an inherent dislike of hoovering
non compos mentis	a mistake made by a conductor
non sequitur	any useless garden tool
nosce teipsum	a runny nose
quis custodiet ipsos custodes?	what sort of custard is this?
poeta nascitur, non fit	to be born a poet is unhealthy
prima facie	a cute face with snub nose and freckles
pro bono publico	willing to admit to owning U2 CDs
servabo fidem	to feed the dog
sub rosa	the cook on a U-boat
tempus fugit	heat rash
terra firma	the rule by fear of the Mafia
veni, vidi, vici	the Matriani triplets of Belmont, West Virginia
vice versa	obscene poetry
virginibus puerisque canto	adolescents like puerile songs
vox populi	any televised singing contest

EXTENDED PLAY

A list of somewhat obscure and very long heavy rock/progressive rock songs. All of these last between 15 and — eek! — 79 minutes

1	Metaphor	'Starfooted in a Garden of Cans'
2	Gandalf	'The River of Permanent Changes'
3	Devil Doll	'The Sacrilege of Fatal Arms'
4	Grobschnitt	'Rockpommels Land'
5	Shadow Gallery	'The Queen of the City of Ice'
6	Priam	'Initiatic Quotient of the Monk'
7	Vulgar Unicorn	'Under the Umbrella'
8	Kalaban	'Eyes of a Seer'
9	Morte Macabre	'Symphonic Holocaust'
10	Black Jester	'Inferno'
11	Gryphon	'Midnight Mushrumps'
12	Frohmader	'Homunculus Part IV'
13	Pulsar	'The Strands of the Future'
14	Manowar	'Achilles, Agony and Ecstasy'
15	Spock's Beard	'The Great Nothing'

... and some tracks over 15 minutes long from better-known artists

1 'Blue Room' (40.00) — The Orb, 1992
2 'A Treatise on Cosmic Fire' (36.00) — Todd Rundgren, 1975*
3 'The Ikon' (30.22) — Utopia, 1974
4 'Dazed and Confused' (live) (26.53) — Led Zeppelin, 1976
5 'Echoes' (23.27) — Pink Floyd, 1971
6 'Sleep' (23.17) — Godspeed You! Black Emperor, 2000
7 'A Plague of Lighthouse Keepers' (23.05) — Van der Graaf Generator, 1971
8 'Supper's Ready' (22.58) — Genesis, 1972
9 'Nine Feet Underground' (22.40) — Caravan, 1971
10 'The Gates of Delirium' (21.55) — Yes, 1974
11 'Ricochet Part 2' (21.05) — Tangerine Dream, 1975
12 'The Remembering – Dance of the Dawn' (20.38) — Yes, 1974
13 'My Father My King' (20.12) — Mogwai, 2001
14 'Healing' (20.00) — Todd Rundgren, 1980
15 'Revelation' (18.57) — Love, 1967
16 'Close to the Edge' (18.50) — Yes, 1972
17 'The Ancient – Giants Under the Sun' (18.34) — Yes, 1974
18 'Halleluhwah' (18.32) — Can, 1971
19 'Singring and the Glass Guitar' (18.24) — Utopia, 1977
20 'Shine On You Crazy Diamond' (17.34) — Pink Floyd, 1974
21 'Aumgn' (17.32) — Can, 1971
22 'Sister Ray' (17.27) — The Velvet Underground, 1967

*This apparently came with the warning that the grooves were pressed so tightly that a worn stylus would ruin the record instantly.

WINGS OF DESIRE

Some excellent butterfly and moth names

Alder Kitten • Small Angle Shades • False Apollo • Bleached Pug
Aquamarine Hairstreak • Beautiful Snout • Pale Brindled Beauty
Ruddy Carpet • Moonlight Jewel • Apricot Sulphur
Setaceous Hebrew Character • Flounced Chestnut
Scarce Chocolate-tip • Raspberry Clearwing • Klug's Xenica
Confused Pellicia • Lemon Pansy • Pretty Pinion • Cynthia Silkmoth
Dew Footman • Dingy Shears • The Drinker
Small-spotted Flasher • Forest Pierrot • Cloudless Giant Sulphur
Great Sooty Satyr • Smoky Wainscot • Pallid Tiger Swallowtail
Heart and Dart • Red Helen • Rannoch Sprawler
Union Rustic • Oslar's Eacles • Black and White Aeroplane
Beautiful Arches • Light Know Grass • Little Glassywing
Hoary Footman • One-eyed Sphinx • Splendid Royal
Double Kidney • Pebble Hook-tip • Chimney Sweeper
Diana Moonbeam • Nut-tree Tussock • Frosted-green Lutestring
Isle of Wight Wave • Lobster Prominent • Ruby Tiger
Neglected Lapland Ringlet • Water Betony • Guatemalan Calico
The Hermit • Lettuce Shark • Rice Looper • Powdered Quaker
Lesser Fiery Copper • Scarce Vapourer • Staff Sergeant
Mexican Sister • Heath Rivulet • Tropical Least Skipper
The Lurcher • Spanish Gatekeeper • Dark Spectacle
Case-making Clothes Moth • Northern Spinach
Straw Underwing • Northern Grizzled Skipper
Zebra Longwing • Pine Processionary
Pale-shouldered Brocade • Cranberry Fritillary

HANDS OUT

Here is some palmistry bunkum which I picked up from a 'palmistry chart' on the reverse of a fortune telling card from a machine in San Francisco's brilliant Musée Méchanique, a wonderful little museum of slot machines

The palm contains lines pertaining to fate, life, the heart, the head and health. These are the areas on the fingers which pertain to certain qualities (first section up to tip):

thumb	love (ball of the thumb), logic, will
index finger	domination, ambition, religion
digitus impudicus	success, recreation, impulse
ring finger	vanity, pessimism, optimism
pinkie	cunning, purpose, oratory

NOMINAL NOTES

Some curious name trivia

Products

Jif cleaning products changed their name to **Cif**®.

Marathon chocolate bar changed its name to **Snickers**®.

Immac hair remover products have been rebranded as **Veet**®.

Opal Fruits sweets meekly became **Starburst**®.

Mr Dog food for small dogs became the regal-sounding **Cesar**®.

Oil of Ulay face cream pushed out the boat and daringly became **Oil of Olay**®.

Gravy and sauce firm Knorr seems to change its name to **Knorr**® (with the K sounded) every few years to fox the public and catch ears during adverts.

Despite years with *Name Change Coming Soon* on the packets, deep-frozen 'canapés' **Crispy Pancakes**® have decided not to bother with the deed poll.

Pseuds

Sometimes pseudonyms cover more than one person. **Ellery Queen**, the detective writer, was actually two cousins, Frederic Dannay and Manfred B Lee. The name **Carolyn Keene** has been used by a number of writers who have penned the adventures of girl detective Nancy Drew over the years. The name **Nicolas Bourbaki** was (and continues to be) used by a group of French mathematicians for publications since the 30s. The mystery novels of **Emma Lathen** are actually written by two friends, Mary J Latsis and Martha Henissart. Similarly, the name of the author **M Barnard Eldershaw**, an Australian novelist and feminist, was a composite of its two inventors, Marjorie Barnard and Flora Eldershaw.

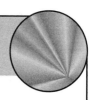

Poets

The Portuguese poet **Fernando Pessoa** (1888–1935) had at least twenty heteronyms (multiple pseudonyms). Some of these were philosophers, prose writers, theorists, pen pals and all were alter egos. These creations would be each other's supporters, critics and influences. Three of Pessoa's heteronyms wrote poetry of high quality – Alberto Caeiro, Ricardo Reis and Álvaro de Campos – each in a different style to the others. Some of Pessoa's alter egos wrote in English (he grew up in South Africa). Other heteronyms included Bernardo Soares (a prose writer), C R Anon, Alexander Search, Dr Panacracio and Jean Seul.

Parrots

The parrot in Disney's *Aladdin* is called **Iago**.

There is a parrot in the Tintin stories also called **Iago**.

The parrot in the cartoon series *Cities of Gold* was **Kukapetl**.

The parrot in Enid Blyton's 'Adventure' books was **Kiki**.

Long John Silver's parrot in *Treasure Island* was **Captain Flint**.

Dr Dolittle's loquacious and over-anxious parrot was **Polynesia**.

Neither Flaubert's Parrot or Monty Python's Norwegian Blue were named.

Stars

Barbara Hershey was known as Barbara Seagull for a period during the mid-70s (though this was not her original name, which was Herzstein). Rumour has it that she made the change after allegedly accidentally killing a seagull.

Samuel Goldwyn's name was Samuel Goldfish (an Anglicized Jewish name).

Cast-Offs

When a director wants to disown a movie he or she has been involved with, it is credited to the name **Alan Smithee**.

Similarly, I have been told (by Chris Meade, head of the organization Booktrust) that the name Chris Meade is sometimes used when an author does not want to use their real name for whatever reason. It is an anagram of Archimedes, which is somehow relevant.

When a British member of parliament wishes to resign, since this is not allowed, he or she applies for the post of Crown Steward and Bailiff of the **Chiltern Hundreds** or the Manor of Northstead. These posts are offices in name only, having no functions or responsibilities, but being appointed to them means that the MP has a 'paid Crown post' and so is instantly removed from their parliamentary duties.

Rainbow People

Ten famous people whose real names were colours:

Gaye Advert (Gaye Black)

Dana (Rosemary Brown)

Helen Hayes (Helen Hayes Brown)

Angie Dickinson (Angeline Brown)

David Ben-Gurion (David Green)

Dennis Price (Dennistoun Rose-Price)

Larry Grayson (William White)

Cilla Black (Priscilla White)

David Jason (David White)

P D James (Phyllis Dorothy White)

SPICE RACK

French Four Spice (Quatre Épices)
white pepper, cloves, nutmeg, ginger or cinnamon

Chinese Five Spice
fennel, star anise, Szechuan pepper, cinnamon, cloves (may sometimes contain cassia, liquorice, aniseed, ginger, nutmeg, etc)

Cajun Five Spice Mix
cumin, oregano, chili, mustard, paprika

Tunisian Five Spice (gâlat dagga)
cloves, cinammon, malaguetta pepper, nutmeg, pepper

Japanese Seven Flavour Spice
(shichimi togarashi)
sancho (Szechuan pepper), white and black sesame seeds, nori (laver seaweed), chili, dried orange or tangerine peel, poppy seeds (may contain rape seeds, pepper leaf, hemp seeds, etc)

Thai Seven Spice
chili, ginger, black pepper, coriander seed, garlic, cumin, lemon peel (occasional alternatives include dried lemongrass, kaffir lime leaves, galangal, cinnamon

VICIOUS AND ROTTEN

Fifty punk rock and New Wave pseudonyms from bands of the 70s and 80s

1   Sid Vicious (The Sex Pistols)

2   Cheetah Chrome (The Dead Boys)

3   Mensi (Angelic Upstarts)

4   Winston Bazoomies (Bad Manners)

5   Penny Rimbaud (Crass)

6   Joe Fungus (!Action Pact!)

7   Beki Bondage (Vice Squad)

8   Jello Biafra (The Dead Kennedys)

9   Monkey (The Adicts)

10   Rat Scabies (The Damned)

11   Poly Styrene (X-Ray Spex)

12   Segovia (UK Decay)

13   Joe Strummer (The Clash)

14   Max Splodge (Splodgenessabounds)

15   Johnny Ha Ha (Alien Sex Fiend)

16   Helen McCookerybook (The Chefs)

17   TV Smith (The Adverts)

18   Buster Bloodvessel (Bad Manners)

19   Stinky Turner (Cockney Rejects)

20   Chuck Wagon (The Dickies)

21   Captain Sensible (The Damned)

22   Johnnie Fingers (Boomtown Rats)

23	Stiv Bators (The Dead Boys)
24	Lester Square (The Monochrome Set)
25	Steve Ignorant (Crass)
26	Budgie (The Slits)
27	Cosey Fanni Tutti (Throbbing Gristle)
28	Lora Logic (Essential Logic)
29	Dru Stix (The Exploited)
30	Siouxsie Sioux (Siouxsie and the Banshees)
31	Dee Dee Ramone (The Ramones)
32	Honey Bane (The Fatal Microbes)
33	Esso (The Lurkers)
34	Gale Warning (The Rezillos)
35	Rudi Protrudi (The Fuzztones)
36	Johnny Goodfornothing (Sham 69)
37	Nicky Tesco (The Members)
38	Genesis P Orridge (Psychic TV)
39	Nick Cash (999)
40	Joy de Vivre (Crass)
41	Jah Wobble (Public Image Limited)
42	Donkey Gut (Splodgenessabounds)
43	Gene October (Chelsea)
44	Wild Planet (Action Pact)
45	Gavin Friday (The Virgin Prunes)
46	Virus (Disorder)
47	Klaus Flouride (The Dead Kennedys)
48	Palmolive (The Slits)
49	Fay Fife (The Rezillos)
50	Johnny Rotten (The Sex Pistols)

The names (old and new) of ailments of horses

NAGGING COUGHS

rain scald
glanders
horse pox
proud flesh
swayback
West Nile virus
poll evil
grease
sweet itch
mallenders
wobbler
 syndrome
thick wind
founder
mud fever
wind-sucking
sidebones
ringbone
grease heel
windpuffs
thoroughpin

monkey mouth
farcy
curbs
jack spavin
stringhalt
heaves
weaving
bog spavin
surra
parrot mouth

moon blindness
fistulous withers
sweeney
cribbing
chink in the
 chine
quittor
gutta serena
osselets
setfast

sand crack
dourine
strangles
grass sickness
broken wind
nasal gleet
headshaking
swamp fever
Cushing's disease
navel ill
glass eye
grogginess
sallenders
roaring
laminitis
Monday
 morning
 disease
tying-up
scours
kissing spine

CURL UP AND DYE

A bunch (oops) of punning hairdressers located in Bristol

A Head of
 Style
Beyond the
 Fringe
Choppers
Clearly Ahead
Clips
Cutting Edge
Hairazors
Hairobics

Hairs &
 Graces
Hairways
Headcases
Headlines
Headmasters
Hotheads
Let's Blow
 Your Top
Look-A-Head

Loose Enz
Making Waves
Permutation
Shampers
Snippitz
Streaks
 Ahead
Talkin' Heads
Top Notch
Upper Cuts

OUT ON THE FLOOR

The taglines of some mobile discos in Bristol

00 Heaven	A Nights Entertainment You'll Always Remember
Atomic	Radiating Great Sounds From The 40s To The Noughties
Astral Disco	Making Your Party Rock!
Bangin' Choons	The Best Sounds from the 50s – Today
Childrens Uptown Disco	Take the Hassle Out Of Your Day
Del Boy's Entertainment	Being Different is Our Business
Discomasters	We Play The Music You Want
Headquake Disco's	Getting Bum's Of Seats & Feet Stepping to the Beat!!
Inspiration	You've Heard the Rest – Now Book the Best
Nite Flite	We Set the Standards Others Follow
Planet Disco	Reliable Cheerful Service – All Era's
Shindig CD Disco	Every Night is Party Night

YOU'LL RUIN YOUR EYES, YOUNG LADY

Britain's ten favourite children's novels (BH*) as voted for in a BBC Waterstone's poll in 1997

1 Roald Dahl *Matilda*
2 Kenneth Grahame *The Wind in the Willows*
3 C S Lewis *The Lion, The Witch and The Wardrobe*
4 A A Milne *Winnie the Pooh*
5 J R R Tolkien *The Hobbit*
6 Roald Dahl *Charlie and the Chocolate Factory*
7 Arthur Ransome *Swallows and Amazons*
8 Roald Dahl *The BFG*
9 Lewis Carroll *Alice in Wonderland*
10 Frances Hodgson Burnett *The Secret Garden*

* Before Harry.

AIEOU

Trying to find words which consist only of vowels is a disappointing business. Most of them are very short (ea, oo, etc). Once you get over three letters, it's a scarce field, unless you include 'y' as a vowel, to which *Vitamin Q* says 'oy, no!' Quite a few words have been coined to be imitative of sounds, such as variations on **aiee** (ouch) and **iaou** (for a cat's mew), or **euoi** (a shout of bacchanalian frenzy). This last one is debatable since, as with the longer **euouae** (a cadence in Gregorian chant music), the 'u' derives from the Greek 'v'. Then there is the **ieie**, a type of Pacific pine tree, but it seems to be more commonly known as just the ie. Also tropical is the **ooaa**, a Hawaiian bird. **louea** is a longer word, however, but is a rather obscure proper noun, a genus of fossil sponges.

BEAUTIFUL GAMES

My ideas for revitalizing certain sports

1 Hurdles to have electric charges

2 Soccer to have two balls at once

3 American football to be a naked sport

4 Ice hockey to be played with bare feet

5 Cricket matches to take place in a twelve-feet-square room

6 Fly fishing to be for nuns (that's *for* nuns, not *by* nuns)

7 Jockeys to carry, rather than ride on, horses

8 Triathlon events to be replaced by macramé, soup making and carving the Bible on a grain of rice

9 Rugby to be played only by teams of five-year-old girls

10 Golf clubs to be replaced by foam mallets

11 The compulsory smiling from synchronized swimming to be extended to tennis

12 Snooker to be played on a round table

THE GREAT
AEGINRST MACHINE

In the world of lists about words, one stands as the top-whack caviar, the Arctic Red, the most unspeakably toothsome. This is 'the great AEGINRST machine', begun in the mid-60s by Dmitri Borgmann, 'the Father of Logology', updated by Jeff Grant a few years back and reproduced in *Making the Alphabet Dance* (Macmillan) by Ross Eckler, the big cheese in the world where words and statistics meet. The list finds 157 transpositions (anagrams) of these eight letters. Some examples ...

'Simple' words
angriest • astringe • gantries • gastrine
genistra • granites • negritas • rangiest
ring-seat • tearings

Place names
Ginestar (Spanish town)
Registan (area of Afghanistan)
Restinga (Moroccan town)
Tiranges (French town)

Surnames
Arnestig • Astering • Astinger • Atsinger
Estringa • Garstein • Gersaint • Graneist
Ingertsa • Sargenti • Serganti • Serignat • Stainger
Staniger • Steingar • Striegan • Tangires

(The list also includes several plurals of surnames, eg Entigar, Reignat, Gantier, as in 'we're off to visit the Gantiers'.)

Oddities

angrites (meteoric stones)

gaitners (those who set up
single sheaves of corn)

ganister (a mineral)

genitras (old word for the testicles)

gratines ('is cooking *au gratin*')

Grisante (another name for St Chrysanthus)

ingestar (an Italian wine measure)

reasting (dialect, becoming rancid)

retangis ('is lamenting again', from a Maori word)

Targesin® (tradename antiseptic)

Tigranes (name of several Armenian kings)

It seems to me that this list could be stretched further than 157 anagrams. The rules run thus: '… any English language dictionary, gazetteer or telephone directory is allowed, including inferred forms (plurals, past tenses etc), multiword phrases and citation form plurals (eg Rigantes = people named Rigante) …' The list allows foreign personal and place names yet doesn't use foreign words per se, so if there is a word *grenista*, say, in Spanish it is not included.

Considering 'inferred forms', we might shift the rules slightly to include words which may not have a citation, but could understandably have one. For a start, I can see another one: angerist, meaning (at least facetiously) someone promoting anger, say, in a primal scream therapy sense. Or, with a capital, a follower or proponent of the director Kenneth Anger.

Further, we might envisage a set of words which are possible transpositions, future anagrams of the eight letters. Given that the set offers the -*s* plural and suffixes such as -*ite*, -*ites*, -*ist*, -*er*, -*an*, -*ian*, we can infer a word such as Reganist, a supporter of someone (eg philosopher, politician) called Regan, or Grestian, a supporter of Gresty, or perhaps even a player for or fan of soccer team Crewe Alexandra, who play at Gresty Road. Any found surname which is an anagram of RGAEN can, with -*ist*, also give a possible transition of AEGINRST. Similarly, the list includes the multiword names of real people (eg Stan Gire), but doesn't infer others (eg Erin Stag, Ian Grest).

I HAVE SEEN THE FUTURE ...

One of the music world's most enduring clichés is to compare a new singer songwriter to Bob Dylan. Here is a list of some of those who were proclaimed 'the new Bob Dylan'

1 Peter Astor
2 John Prine
3 David Bowie
4 Elliott Murphy
5 Melanie
6 Andy White
7 Ryan Adams
8 David Gray
9 Bruce Springsteen
10 Graham Parker
11 Dan Bern
12 Ben Kweller
13 Steve Forbert
14 Beck
15 Elvis Costello
16 Donovan
17 Josh Joplin
18 Willie Nile
19 Conor Oberst
20 John Hartford
21 Loudon Wainwright, III
22 Jewel

SCOTTISH NATIONALIZATION

LESSON 56

Here is this week's vocabulary lesson for those aiming for Scottish citizenship

1   **fit fit fits fit fit?**
    a required saying in Aberdeen, particularly while trying
    on shoes in Saxone* on Union Street, meaning 'which
    shoe fits which foot?'

2   **yawrigh? marigh, mnaepesht, ahwal'is, yonnae
    botes? monnae botes, fer's skipr**
    required in Anstruther and the East Neuk, meaning 'Are
    you all right? I'm fine, I'm not intoxicated, I always walk
    this way. Do you work on the boats? I do, my father is
    a ship's captain.'

3   **he disnae ken whit bucket day it is**
    required in south Edinburgh, meaning that the said
    person is of such low intelligence that he doesn't
    know which day to put his garbage out for collection.

4   **eat up, yer at yer blin' auntie's**
    required in Aberdeenshire, a phrase meaning help
    yourself to more cakes and sandwiches, your aunt is
    blind and won't notice that you are squandering her
    resources.

5   **ah ha'e ha's but ah'll hae tae hae a ha'**
    required in south Fife, as overheard on a Kirkcaldy bus,
    where two elderly women were discussing their
    clothing plans for a forthcoming wedding – 'I hate hats,
    but I will have to have a hat.'

* Saxone, the shoe shop chain, supposedly got its name from a shock
football result many decades ago, when Kilmarnock (of whom
the Scottish founder of the chain, then just one market
stand, was a keen supporter) beat Glasgow Rangers 6–1
(in Scots, 'sax one') The shop name pronunciation has
changed now to 'sax-own'. This, commonly believed to
be a myth, appears to be strange but true.

Rhyming slang is most often associated with working class London, but is used all over Britain, as well as in other countries. Here are some names of people, real and made up, modern and historical, whose names have been used in rhyming slang

Catherine Hayes (days)

Ayrton Senna (tenner)

Charlie Beck (check)

Acker Bilk (milk)

Jack Horner (corner)

Dan O'Leary (weary)

Arthur Ashe (cash)

Eartha Kitt/Brad Pitt (shit)

Jerry McGinn (chin)

Bob Dylan (villain)

Gregory Peck (cheque/neck)

Danny La Rue (clue)

Johnnie Russell (hustle)

Barney Rubble (trouble)

Rosie Lee/Kiki Dee (tea)

Betty Grable (table)

Tom Noddy (body)

Johnnie O'Brien (iron)

Arnold Palmer (farmer)

Nelson Riddle (piddle)

Hank Marvin (starving)

Stirling Moss (toss)

Jack Jones (alone, as in 'stuck here on my Jack Jones')

Lionel Richie (itchy)*

Ruby Murray (curry)

Pete Tong (wrong)

* Two other soul singers appear in similar British slang. A ten pound note (which is brown) is sometimes called a James Brown. The five pound note (which is blue) is occasionally referred to as a Harold Melvin (due to his band the Blue Notes).

THAT'S EASY FOR YOU TO SAY

Fifteen tongue-twisters
translated from their original languages

1 Baker's ginger cake, baker's ginger cake (Estonian)

2 Xi Shi (known as the Helpful Lady of the West) was 44 years old when she passed away (Mandarin)

3 Susan snibbed the chicks' cage (Tagálog)

4 Alli bashed the beaver with a folder (Finnish)

5 A grown-up boxer washes breeches (Norwegian)

6 Put the turschi [a sort of vegetable] in the policeman's pocket (Arabic)

7 The zorilla [a type of polecat] rolled down and ruptured his larynx (Xhosa)*

8 Twenty dwarfs were showing us handstands, ten in the cupboard, ten on the sandy strand (German)

9 Lleshi's hen laid an egg in a woollen basket (Albanian)

10 Robespierre, initiator of the Terror, considered it a terrible mistake to sprinkle verdigris on a rare brown green lizard (Italian)

11 Rain, rain, the frog has no ears (Czech)

12 My aunt gave my uncle pickle in a silver spoon (Punjabi)

13 Watermelon jam competition (Afrikaans)

14 The emperor combed his wife (Polish)

15 The maid cut seven crooked slices of bread (Dutch)

* This (Iqaqa laziqikaqika kwaze kwaqhawaka uqhoqhoqha) is often said to be the hardest to say of all.

THAT LOVING FILLING

Keanu Reeves lists his top sandwiches (from *Empire* magazine, c.1995)

What's your favourite sandwich? 'I have a couple: a toasted baguette with peanut butter and apricot jam with really cold white wine. *Mmmmm.* Philadelphia steak sandwich is really good. Oh, and a really good Italian sausage sandwich. But then you can't beat toasted Swiss cheese and tomato with a little mustard on. *Ooooooh,* or Black Forest ham with German black bread. Oh my God, and coleslaw and Swiss cheese with Russian dressing.'

GAMES OF YESTERYEAR

Here are some playground and park games I recall from my 70s childhood

The Farmer's in His Den

A children's ring game in which the child in the centre has to choose others to be a wife, a dog and then 'a bone', this child being mercilessly patted (ie thumped all over).

In and Out the Dusty Bluebells

A twisting and turning children's dance game accompanied by the song of the same name.

Dead Man's Fall

A piece of mindless boys' genius. Boys take turns to stand at the top of a slope. They are then asked to choose a weapon (eg bazooka, machine gun) by which they will die. The other boys then mime this weapon and the boy has to fall 'to his death' as ostentatiously as possible.

What's the Time, Mr Wolf?

One child turns her back to the rest, answering various times to the question, as they sneak closer across the playing area. When the child shouts, it's dinner time! she can then chase the others.

White Horses

A 'crossing' game similar to the last one. Players rushed across the designated area when the correct signals were given. Compare also the game where kids crossed an area when commanded using various movements, 'baby steps', etc. I can't recall what we called it, but elsewhere it is called Mother May I?, Captain May I?, Crocodile Crocodile, or Follow the Leader. Step styles included baby steps, giant steps, hops, jumps, twirl steps, backwards steps, leaping steps, waddling steps, ballet steps, scissor steps and tiptoe steps.

Kerbie

The lost art of throwing a football at a kerb to try and get it to bounce off and return to you on the opposite pavement. Sounds simple, but it had rules of great complexity. There are still many thirty-something men who long for a game on summer nights.

Join the Crew

A brutal game similar to British Bulldog. Children take turns to try and get past a child in the middle of the playing area. If they fail, they 'join the crew'. If they do get across, all other participants must try to cross to the other side. The game is best remembered for the inevitable 'stripping' of clothes which occurred.

One Touch

Staple game of bored boys, involving a football and a wall against which it had to be kicked, in turns, with just one touch. See other soccer games such as **laneball** (one-to-one in a narrow space), **heady kicks**, **World Cup** (boys choose a country each and the last to score in each free-for-all round is knocked out) and **three-and-in** (three or four boys taking turns to be the single goalkeeper).

Chappie Knockie

This is one name for the ubiquitous game where a child knocks on a door and runs away. Also commonly called Knock Down Ginger, or Knock Up Ginger. Bigger and crueller children got really quite adept at making life a misery for some. Bottles balanced on door handles could be sure to fall and smash when the handle was turned from the other side. A paper bag on fire, when stamped out, would be sure to contain something smelly and nasty.

Chickie Mellie

I've never known this played, but it exists in *Oor Wullie* (basically a 60s/70s Scottish Bart Simpsonesque cartoon strip character.) Wullie plays the game using a string with a tied button, taped above an old lady's window. Hiding nearby, he can manipulate the string, thereby knocking the button on the window pane to repeatedly scare the woman.

Manhunt

Basically, a game of hide-and-seek for older boys, played in two teams, at night, through gardens. No one ever knew the rules, no one ever seemed to win, but boy, was it exciting.

Knifie

Another lost art – I don't recall the complex rules. It was already dying out when I was a child in the 70s. It involved throwing a penknife into grass, and various 'Twister' style contortions to do with moving to where you threw the knife. Played only by wiry tough boys.

Kiss, Cuddle or Torture

Perennial 'learn love the hard way' playground game for 7–11 year olds. Kissing is rare and usually quick, cuddling is for when girl catches girl. Torture is the main dish of the day and involves Chinese burns or dead legs, or, for blushing boys, more kissing.

A CHAIN OF THOUGHT

Mamihlapinatapei is a word from the native language of Tierra del Fuego which means 'a shared glance of longing where both know the meaning but neither is quite willing to make the move', which leads me to …

… the **Philippines**, where, I've been told, a word exists which means 'yes' but connotes the idea of 'no' – the word is used in awkward situations where offence needs to be avoided. So, if a boy asks an unwilling girl to the cinema, she can say 'yes', safe in the knowledge that he knows it means 'no', which leads me to …

… the supposed shortest ever review which was of the album **Yes** by the English prog rock band of the same name. The review simply said 'No'. Later, the review of GTR (a band containing former Yes members) in *Musician Magazine* contained a one-word assessment: 'SHT'. In the *Rolling Stone Complete Guide to Albums*, the eponymously named album *Chase* has a one-word review – 'Flee'. *The Gazette* reviewed *Purpendicular* by Deep Purple with a one word review: 'square' which leads me to …

… the shortest ever teletext letter which appeared on ITV in 2003 from a man in York, who simply suggests '**Tax cyclists**', which leads me to …

… my favourite ever **teletext** letter from a few years back, sent in by an elderly lady who was saying how wonderful it was that the cold, dark nights of winter had returned and she no longer had to listen to the sounds of children playing outside. Don't you just love old people who are unashamedly misanthropic – we can learn a lot from them, ie how NOT to behave when we get wrinkles.

DEFINE WIT

The Chambers Dictionary has always included some witty and humorous definitions. Here are some favourites

abloom
in a blooming state

back-seat driver
someone free of responsibility but full of advice

channel-surf
to switch rapidly between different television channels in a forlorn attempt to find anything of interest

combover
a vain attempt to make the most of one's dwindling resources of hair

devil-dodger
someone who attends churches of various kinds, to be on the safe side

éclair
a cake, long in shape but short in duration, with cream filling and *usu* chocolate icing

fish
to catch or try to catch or obtain fish, or anything that may be likened to a fish (such as seals, sponges, coral, compliments, information or husbands)

he-man
a man of exaggerated or extreme virility, or what some women consider to be virility

jaywalker
a careless pedestrian whom motorists are expected to avoid running down

lady-killer
a man who is, or fancies himself, irresistible to women

lint
small pieces of thread, fluff, etc that cling to
clothes and furniture and accumulate in the filters
of washing machines and driers and in navels

live
a fishmonger's word for very fresh

middle-aged
between youth and old age, variously reckoned to suit the
reckoner

mullet
a hairstyle that is short at the front, long at the back, and
ridiculous all round

old girl
an amicably disrespectful mode of address or reference to
a female of any age or species

petting party
a gathering for the purpose of amorous caressing as an
organized sport

restoration
renovations and reconstruction (sometimes little differing
from destruction) of a building, painting, etc

rock salmon
dogfish or wolffish when being sold as food-fish

Santa Claus
an improbable source of improbable benefits

sea serpent
an enormous marine animal of serpent-like form frequently
seen and described by credulous sailors, imaginative
landsmen and common liars

tracksuit
a loose warm suit intended to be worn by athletes when
warming up or training, but sometimes worn by others in
an error of judgement

tweenager
a child who, although not yet a teenager, has already
developed an interest in fashion, pop music and
exasperating his or her parents

waistline
a line thought of as marking the waist, but
not fixed by anatomy in women's fashions

RECORDINGS

Fifteen tracks which feature the dulcet tones of the recorder

'Stairway to Heaven' (Led Zeppelin) **1**

'Fool on the Hill' (The Beatles) **2**

'Ruby Tuesday' (The Rolling Stones) **3**

'I've Seen All Good People' (Yes) **4**

'Fourth of July' (Bruce Springsteen) **5**

'Mother Goose' (Jethro Tull) **6**

'Comin' Back to Me' (Jefferson Airplane) **7**

'Closer to Fine' (Indigo Girls) **8**

'If 6 was 9' (Jimi Hendrix) **9**

'In Dulce Jubilo' (Mike Oldfield) **10**

'Gently Johnny' (*The Wicker Man* soundtrack) **11**

'Perfect Lovesong' (The Divine Comedy) **12**

'What a Day' (Gemma Hayes) **13**

'Fairy Tales' (Stockholm Monsters) **14**

'Time It's Time' (Talk Talk) **15**

Some interesting street name trivia

In **Manila**, there is a subdivision (housing project) where all the streets are named after beauty queens. **Montreal** is called the City of Saints, as all the early streets were named after saints. The streets of **SoHo** in NYC are named after George Washington's generals. In 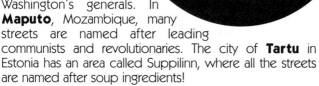 **Maputo**, Mozambique, many streets are named after leading communists and revolutionaries. The city of **Tartu** in Estonia has an area called Suppilinn, where all the streets are named after soup ingredients!

Stratford, New Zealand, has, not surprisingly, streets named after Shakespearean characters. **Hanoi** old town has streets named after produce available at the local market. The Dutch new town of **Almere** has divisions where streets are named after film stars, novelists, seasons, colours, famous parks and dances. **Paris** has a small district nicknamed Europe, since streets there were named for European cities. **Davis**, California, has a Tolkien street name themed subdivision.

On the outskirts of **Nashville**, there is a development named Stonehenge, where all the street names have tangential links to the ancient stone edifice – these include streets named after Abingdon, Salisbury and, erm, Portsmouth and, believe it or not, streets named after the band members from Spinal Tap, who famously had a miniature Stonehenge on stage. In the skiing town of **Banff**, Alberta, most of the streets are named after local wildlife, eg Muskrat Street, Hawk Avenue, Beaver Street.

Strange but true **American** street names include Road to Happiness, None Such Place, Shades of Death Road and Pinchgut Hollow Road while, apparently, in Washington **DC**, there is a set of streets which run alphabetically A Street, B Street, etc, but J is strangely missing. Meanwhile, **Toronto** has both Memory Lane and Milky Way!

In the **British Isles**, there are the following unusual street names

Shoulder of Mutton (Pembroke)

Granny Clark's Wynd (the road which goes on to cross the first and 18th fairways of the famous Old Course at St Andrews)

Land of Green Ginger, **Rotten Herring Street** (both Hull)

Bleeding Heart Yard, **Mincing Lane**, **Poultry** (London)

Mardol, **Dogpole**, **Shoplatch**, **Wyle Cop** and **Murivance** (all Shrewsbury)

Whip Ma Whop Ma Gate, **Bad Bargain Lane**, **Pavement** (all York)

Holy Bones (Leicester)

Split Crow Road (Gateshead)

Gibble Gabble (near Manchester)

Cutlog Vennel, **Needless Road** (both Perth)

Cow Parlour, **Roper's Rest**, **Misery Hill**, **Artichoke Road** (all Dublin)

Air Balloon Road, **Snail Creep Lane**, **There and Back Again Lane**, **Beggar's Bush Lane** (all Bristol)

A NATION AGAIN

Two words the Scots gave the world

1 glamour *

2 galore **

* Originally meaning 'witchcraft'.

** Originally meaning 'too much'.

What are we to make of this?

PRETENTIOUS, MOI?

The twelve episodes of John Cleese and Connie Booth's classic hotel sitcom *Fawlty Towers*

'A Touch of Class'

'The Builders'

'The Wedding Party'

'The Hotel Inspectors'

'Gourmet Night'

'The Germans'

'Communication Problems'

'The Psychiatrist'

'Waldorf Salad'

'The Kipper and the Corpse'

'The Anniversary'

'Basil the Rat'

BIRDSAKES

Ten first names which are also names of birds

1 Colin (the Virginian quail)

2 Jay

3 Lory (a parrot)

4 Martin

5 Mavis (a song thrush)

6 Linnet

7 Rhea (a flightless bird)

8 Robin

9 Roger (a goose)

10 Shirley (a South American bunting)

MEN FROM UNCLE

Some notable uncles

Uncle Tom

Harriet Beecher Stowe's 1852 novel *Uncle Tom's Cabin* was written to try to help bring an end to slavery in the USA. The book traces the lives of two Southern slaves, the pious Christian Tom (based partly on a man named Josiah Henson) and the daring and beautiful Eliza. Abraham Lincoln claimed that the book helped him win power. Later, the phrase 'Uncle Tom' was appropriated and became a derogatory term used against each other by African-Americans, meaning one whose co-operative attitude to white people is thought to be disloyal to black people.

Uncle Mac

The early BBC radio presenter for youngsters and writer of children's books Derek McCulloch adopted this nickname in the 30s. Much later, in the 70s, the phrase became ironic rhyming slang for heroin (mac/smack).

Uncle Sam

The original Uncle Sam is popularly believed to be one Samuel Wilson, a meat company owner and inspector of provisions who reportedly stamped his shipments to the army (during the War of 1812) with the letters 'US'. Soldiers supposedly began to say this stood for 'Uncle Sam'. Later, the cartoonist Thomas Nast developed a character called Uncle Sam with a white beard, tall hat and star-spangled outfit. During World War I, this figure appeared on a famous recruiting poster with the slogan 'I WANT YOU'.

Uncle Ben

The original Uncle Ben was an African-American rice grower from Texas. He was said to produce such a high quality yield that the standard became rice that was 'as good as Uncle Ben's'. When Gordon L Harwell founded a commercial company to extend his rice business, he picked the name Uncle Ben's and used the logo of an avuncular black man, still to be seen on the packets.

Uncle John
'Uncle' has long been a euphemism for a pawnbroker. 'Go and sell this to your Uncle John', people would say. This phrasing is thought to come from a time long ago when pawnbrokers used to use a hook (*uncus* in Latin) to handle the goods offered to them by customers.

Uncle Buck
A 1989 movie from the heyday of director John Hughes. It stars John Candy as a slobbish and unreliable uncle with woman problems who has to baby-sit for his brother due to a family emergency. The children (including Macaulay Culkin) eventually come round to his unorthodox housekeeping style.

Uncle Tupelo
This early 90s band from Illinois were one of the first groups to fuse alternative rock and punk sounds with country music, perfecting a sound somewhere between Hank Williams and Hüsker Dü. Songwriters Jay Farrar and Jeff Tweedy fell out after only a few years and a handful of records, but the band was influential on many country rock bands throughout the next decade. (Uncle is a surprisingly common element in band names with many examples such as Uncle Bonsai, Uncle Sid, Uncle Mudfish and Uncle X.)

Uncle Joe
During World War II, President Franklin D Roosevelt faced a problem in persuading the American public to accept his pact with Joseph Stalin, the Russian leader. However, the propaganda machine soon scratched its head and came up with the epithet 'Uncle Joe', to make Stalin seem a little more cuddly. Stalin ('man of steel') was not his real name, which was the rather harder to pronounce Iosif Vissarionovich Dzhugashvili.

Uncle Scrooge
Donald Duck's tight-fisted millionaire uncle Scrooge McDuck first appeared in the cartoon story *Christmas on Bear Mountain* in 1947, but not on screen for another 20 years. He is best known from the 80s series *Duck Tales*, which included

many stories about him dealing with the antics of the mischievous ducklings Huey, Dewey and Louie. His servants have included Miss Quackfaster, Bettina Beakley and Duckworth the butler. His strong accent (voiced by Alan Young) helps to reinforce the unfortunate cliché about Scottish meanness.

Uncle Tungsten

The noted neurologist and science writer Oliver Sacks wrote a memoir of this name about his love of science when a boy in the 40s. His Uncle Dave manufactured light bulbs and shared with him a fascination for physics and chemistry. Sacks nicknamed him Uncle Tungsten.

Uncle Remus

In the early 1800s, Joel Chandler Harris began to publish a series of books of songs, sayings and tales recounted by Uncle Remus, a fictional elderly former slave. These were based on stories he recalled hearing from slaves during his Georgia childhood. Many of them were animal fables about Brer Rabbit and Brer Fox. He also published Remus's poems and sayings, and stories drawn from this old man's life.

Uncle Meat

A 1969 double album by Frank Zappa and the Mothers of Invention. It was originally intended as the soundtrack to a film and is largely instrumental. Zappa claimed that the sparse lyrics were based on band in-jokes. The music is a wild mixture of styles. Among the 31 tracks are the wonderfully named 'Ian Underwood Whips It Out', 'Cruisin' for Burgers', 'Electric Aunt Jemima', 'Dog Breath, in the Year of the Plague', 'Sleeping in a Jar' and 'The Voice of Cheese'.

Uncle Oswald

As well as being one of the most famous writers for children, and renowned for his 'tales of the unexpected', Roald Dahl had another string to his bow, writing rather ripe, erotic fiction such as the stories in *Switch Bitch*. *My Uncle Oswald*, one of his only adult novels, is the tale of 'the greatest fornicator of all time' and how, with the help of Yasmin Howcomely, he cons 'sperm donations' from the rich and famous.

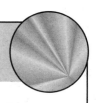

Uncle Fester
The Addams Family's loveable, bald rogue was played by Jackie Coogan in the TV series and later by Christopher Lloyd in the film version. The character arose as part of Charles Addams' macabre cartoons in *The New Yorker* from the 30s onwards.

Uncle Vanya
This Chekhov drama deals with a professor's return, complete with new, young second wife, to his family home where he has to deal with his deceased first wife's family, not least the modest Vanya who falls in love with the new wife. The play deals with the family ties and sexual tension which eventually lead to Vanya attempting to kill the professor.

Uncle Albert
As played by Buster Merryfield in the UK sitcom *Only Fools and Horses*. White-bearded Albert came to live with chancer brothers Del and Rodney when their grandad died. He was prone to telling rambling yarns from wartime and his disastrous maritime career.

Uncle Jumbo
Grover Cleveland, whose first given-name was Stephen, was the second heaviest man to hold the office of president of the USA (only Taft, who weighed over 300 pounds, was bigger). His nicknames included 'Big Steve' and 'Uncle Jumbo'.

Uncle Bob
In 1881, A J Balfour was appointed Chief Secretary for Ireland, having already served as Secretary for Scotland and as President of the Local Government Board. In all three of these positions, he was appointed by Lord Salisbury, the Prime Minister who was known as Bob and who happened to be Balfour's uncle. From this came the still current phrase 'Bob's your uncle', used when something has happened easily. Balfour continued to rise and later emulated his relative by also becoming Prime Minister.

MARY/MARIE

Common Mistakes No. 376

The *Mary Celeste* – a half-brig which was found adrift off the Azores in late 1872. Ten people are thought to have drowned after setting off in a small boat after abandoning the MC, wrongly convinced it was sinking.

The *Marie Celeste* – the name of the boat in an early story by Sir Arthur Conan Doyle, which elaborated and embroidered the above facts. Also, a ballad of the same name which popularized the myth of the still hot cups of tea, possible mutiny and so on.

Ten famous people who were originally named Smith or Jones

Smith
P J Proby **1**
Wolfman Jack **2**
Mary Pickford **3**
Sugar Ray Robinson **4**
Jay Silverheels **5**
Kim Wilde (and Dad Marty) **6**

Jones
Sir Edward German **7**
Mark Lamarr **8**
David Bowie **9**
Edith Wharton **10**

ALIAS SMITH AND JONES

POP GOES TO HOLLYWOOD

Seventeen song titles name-checking film stars

1	'John Wayne Is Big Leggy'	Haysi Fantayzee
2	'Frances Farmer Will Have Her Revenge On Seattle'	Nirvana
3	'Robert De Niro's Waiting'	Bananarama
4	'Bette Davis Eyes'	Jackie DeShannon
5	'Clint Eastwood'	The Upsetters
6	'Bela Lugosi's Dead'	Bauhaus
7	'Michael Caine'	Madness
8	'Cary Grant's Wedding'	The Fall
9	'Clint Eastwood'	Gorillaz
10	'Monty Got a Raw Deal'	REM
11	'Winona'	Drop Nineteens
12	'Charlton Heston'	Stump
13	'Fred Astaire'	Donna Summer
14	'Brando'	Dory Previn
15	'James Dean'	The Eagles
16	'Chaplin in New Shoes'	Chet Atkins
17	'Laurel and Hardy'	The Equals

STINK TANK

Forty things which people have claimed to be responsible for 'the worst smell'

mercaptoacetic acid or methyl mercaptan (a chemical said to be repulsive) **1**

skunk spray **2**

hot tar **3**

fermented chicken feed **4**

brothy armpits **5**

hockey goalies **6**

Bigfoot **7**

mildew and related moulds **8**

the teledu (the Indonesian 'stinking badger') **9**

paper mills **10**

boiled cabbage **11**

the durian (the fruit that 'tastes like Heaven but smells like Hell') **12**

unchanged bandages **13**

baby sick **14**

the hoatzin (an Amazonian bird with a pungent odour) **15**

soft dog food **16**

Staten Island **17**

high oysters **18**

Shasta daisies (which smell like sweaty feet) **19**

boiled urine **20**

well-used trainers **21**

poultry farms **22**

radiator water **23**

bad breath **24**

burnt hair **25**

the waste products of
maggots **26**

dirty toilets **27**

brussels sprouts **28**

'bottom burps' (especially a dog's) **29**

egg sandwiches **30**

dead rats and other rotting rodents **31**

vomit **32**

ammonia **33**

rotten fish **34**

burning human flesh **35**

burnt popcorn **36**

lime chutney **37**

navel fluff **38**

tanning hides **39**

wet dog **40**

The government is on to all this, of course, with UK and US governments having recently developed two chemical smells planned to dispel mobs, though they are not yet legal. US Government Standard Bathroom Malodour is said to be an overpowering smell of human faeces, but highly concentrated, while 'Who Me?' is a sulphur-based aroma, based on the smells from rotting carcases and decaying food. The Los Angeles County Sheriff's department have started to use a substance called SkunkShot® to keep squatters out of vacant buildings. This petroleum gel spray has a nauseating stench which lasts for weeks.

TARTAN FIRSTS

Twenty-four things the Scots supposedly invented

1   the fax machine

2   the kaleidoscope

3   the iron plough

4   hollow pipe drainage

5   the reaping machine

6   the reflecting telescope

7   Bovril®

8   the blackboard

9   the bicycle

10   the breech loading rifle

11   the threshing machine

12   the decimal point

13   coal gas lighting

14   the percussion cap

15   the telephone

16   the thumbscrew

17   the hot blast oven

18   marmalade

19   the vacuum flask

20   the adhesive postage stamp

21   the television

22   the steamboat engine

23   the pneumatic tyre

24   suspenders

SPANGLE MAKERS

The Cocteau Twins, one of the most celebrated British 'alternative' bands of the 80s and 90s, were prone to using unusual names for their songs. Here are ten of their strangest song titles

1 'Mizake the Mizan'
2 'It's All But an Ark-Lark'
3 'The Itchy Glowbo Blow'
4 'Great Spangled Fritillary'
5 'Ella Megablast Burls Forever'
6 'Calfskin-Smack'
7 'Frou-Frou Foxes in Midsummer Fires'
8 'Spooning Good Singing Gum'
9 'Sultitan Itan'
10 'The High-Monkey Monk'

CLOTH CAPS
An A–Z of materials

1 armozine
2 beaverteen
3 cubica
4 dornick
5 everlasting
6 fitchew
7 grogram
8 homespun
9 indienne
10 jaconet
11 kersey
12 lustring
13 marquisette
14 nainsook
15 organza
16 petersham
17 qiviut
18 rawhide
19 seersucker
20 tammy
21 union
22 Viyella®
23 winceyette
24 Xydar®
25 yuft
26 zibeline

Some of the many, many sausages and sausage dishes from around the world

bockwurst a pale and fat German sausage made with white meat, eggs, milk and green herbs such as parsley and chives.

boerewors a sweet and spicy South African beef or lamb sausage with cloves, allspice and wine.

boudin blanc a peppery, light-coloured white meat sausage often containing pork fat, milk, eggs and rice flour, common in French and Cajun cooking; **boudin noir** is a darker sausage flavoured with pig's blood.

bumbar (or mumbar) a Middle Eastern or Turkish sausage made from mutton, rice and spices, and eaten sliced and fried.

cassoulet a classic rich French bean stew containing various meats, including herby Toulouse sausages, goose fat and bacon.

cervellata a sausage from the Milan area of Italy, made from pork with veal fat and flavoured with nutmeg, parmesan cheese and saffron. The name suggests it was originally made with pig's brains. This sausage, through time, gave its name to the humble **saveloy**, the red-skinned porky banger served in English chip shops and which is related to the **red pudding** served in Ireland and Scotland.

WITH A BANG

chaurice a strong, smoked chorizo-style sausage from Cajun cuisine. It is often used in New Orleans favourites such as the nippy soup-stew gumbo and the rice and meat feast jambalaya. A similar, herby sausage is the

andouille, not to be confused with the potent French **andouilette**, which is made from pork intestines and is an acquired taste.

Chicago red hot
a speciality hot dog comprising a hot sausage in a bun swamped with side helpings of pickle, mustard, onions, hot peppers and tomatoes.

chorizo
a hard, air-cured or smoked Spanish pork sausage highly flavoured (and coloured) with paprika and Aleppo pepper.

corn dog
a Southern US delicacy, originally Texan, this sausage on a stick is dipped in corn batter, fried and served with sweet mustard.

dirty rice
an American dish made by cooking crumbled sausages or other meat and spring (green) onions with cooked rice.

feijoada
this celebrated Brazilian stew contains sausages and other meat with hot peppers, parsley and coriander, served with rice, oranges and black beans.

Freetown sausage
a speciality from Sierra Leone in Africa, these are thick Frankfurters made from chicken meat and served with a thick, piquant sauce.

hopple popple
a mishmash potato dish made from eggs, cheese, vegetables, Italian herbs and spicy sausage.

kishke
a hefty Jewish sausage made from beef intestines and flavoured with onions, matzo and suet.

klobasa
a Slovakian lean pork sausage, highly flavoured with garlic and marjoram and eaten with sauerkraut.

lap cheong
these sweet, fatty Chinese sausages are similar to pepperoni and are often steamed on top of cooking rice.

linguica

a fat, dark red, spicy Portuguese sausage flavoured with vinegar and sometimes sherry. The short and fat Filipino **longanisa** is a similar sausage.

Lorne sausage

also known as sliced sausage. This is a Scottish sausage patty, like a beef and pork burger, often eaten as part of a breakfast fry-up and popular with workmen on bread rolls with vinegary brown sauce for lunch.

loukanika

a rich, thin Greek sausage made with pork, lamb, wine, orange zest and herbs. A similar, coarser sausage is **horiatika**.

merguez

a delicious hot North African lamb sausage spiced with paprika, garlic and coriander.

Milwaukee brat

a German-style Bratwurst hot dog made from pork and beef and served in a bun with sauerkraut and hot sauce.

mortadella

a fat, steamed Italian sausage for slicing, it is made with pork and pork fat and often containing peppercorns and pistachio nuts.

nam kao tod

a Thai starter made of puffed rice and garlic sausage, flavoured with peanuts, lime and chillies.

pique macho

this filling Bolivian dish consists of steak and spiced sausages, peppers and onions served on top of fried potato chips and garnished with hard boiled eggs.

piyozli kasi

a sausage made with horse meat and onions which was a speciality of Uzbekistan.

pølseret

a Swedish hash dish made from potatoes, milk, onions and slices of hot sausage.

ring bologna

an old-fashioned but still popular Italian beef and pork ring sausage, tied together at the ends, coarse and quite highly spiced.

rúllupylsa | an Icelandic sausage made using trussed and pressed meat scraps, traditionally flavoured with saltpetre.

salamina mista | an Italian salami sausage from Lombardy, now made from pork or beef but often in the past made from working animals such as oxen, horses or donkeys.

Salem sausage stew | an African-American 'soulfood' dish containing hot sausage, various beans and a piquant sauce flavoured with brown sugar and Worcester sauce.

scrapple | an Eastern US speciality made from sausage meat and cornmeal, fried in thick slabs and eaten for breakfast with grits or eggs.

smacafam | a tart from the far north-east of Italy, made with a polenta-like paste, spicy sausages and Portobello mushrooms.

stampot van boerenkool met worst | a hearty Dutch stew made with cabbage, potatoes and smoked sausage, such as Polish **kabanos** or **kielbasa**.

sweet Italian sausage | the unmistakable smell of this pork sausage lingers in Italian streets and Italian neighbourhoods across the world; it is flavoured with fennel seeds and parsley.

toad in the hole | a traditional English dish with sausages covered in egg batter and baked in a tray in the oven.

tunnbrödsrulle | a fast food dish from Sweden, a speciality of city hot dog kiosks. It consists of boiled hot dogs and a helping of mashed potato, wrapped inside a layer of flat bread.

BRAVE TALK
PART TWO

More unusual and charming words and definitions from *The Scots Dialect Dictionary* compiled by Alexander Warrack and first published in 1911

labichrie	a long story about nothing
lanland	all the stories of a house
lassie-days	girlhood
layan	the curing of a rickety child in a smithy, by bathing it in a tub of water heated by plunging hot irons into it
leirichie-larachie	to whisper together
loofie-lair	proficiency in fisticuffs
lunchock	the angle made by the thighs and belly
mushlin	one who is fond of dainty food eaten secretly
nose-feast	a storm
nurgling	a person of catlike disposition
oaf	an animal whose face is so covered with hair that it can scarcely see
paddle-doo	a frog formerly kept in a cream jar for luck
partan-cartie	an empty crab shell used as a toy cart
paysyad	a woman with nothing new to wear at Easter
pen	an old, saucy man with a sharp nose
pinkie-winkie	a barbarous pastime against birds among young children

proggles	the spines of a hedgehog
quee-beck	the cry of a startled grouse
querny	of honey, abounding in granules
rabbit's-kiss	a penalty in the game of forfeits, in which a man and a woman have each to nibble an end of the same piece of straw until their lips meet
rangunshock	to roar incessantly
rattan-houkit	dug by rats
roug-a-rug	a fishwife's cry
rummle-de-thump	mashed potatoes
rumple-thyke	the itch when it has got a full hold
saut-water-fowk	visitors to the seaside
scafferie	the contents of a larder
scargivenet	a girl from 12 to 14 years of age
scraighton	a person fond of screaming
scran-pock	a beggar's wallet for scraps
scuffle	to use a Dutch hoe
shoggle	a large piece of ice floating down a river when a thaw comes
slivver	to give wet kisses
smeerikin	a stolen kiss
sneerag	a child's toy, made of the larger bone of a pig's foot and two worsted strings, and worked so as to give a snoring sound
sniggert	one chargeable with wilful malversation

sole-ale	ale given at the finishing of the windowsills
spauly	having too much leg for beauty
spyle	to sample cheese with a scoop
stoog	the central matter in a boil
strib	to drain the last drops from a cow's udder
sweig	a very bad homemade candle
taisch	the voice of a person about to die
tornbelly	a herring having its belly torn open
useless	the crab's claw or lady's thumb
warlock-fecket	a magic jacket woven from the skins of water snakes
wheezan	the noise carriage wheels make when moving fast
whisky-tacket	a pimple supposed to be caused by intemperance
Willie Cossar	a large brass pin; an expression of bigness applied to a turnip, animal or woman
wimplefeyst	a sulky humour
windy-wallets	one given to fibbing, exaggeration or breaking wind behind
woman-house	a laundry
wowfness	the condition of being somewhat deranged
yaw	a child's name for an eel
yeery	afraid of goblins
yoornt	of a postman, going his round easily, because seasoned

IT CAME FROM THE NORTH

Twenty-six entertainers who you may not know are (or were) actually Canadian

1	Pamela Anderson
2	Paul Anka
3	Dan Aykroyd
4	Raymond Burr
5	John Candy
6	Jim Carrey
7	Kid Creole
8	Yvonne De Carlo
9	Michael J Fox
10	Brendan Fraser
11	Margot Kidder
12	Lois Maxwell
13	Rick Moranis
14	Alanis Morissette
15	Mike Myers
16	Leslie Nielsen
17	Matthew Perry
18	Christopher Plummer
19	Jason Priestley
20	Keanu Reeves
21	Robbie Robertson
22	William Shatner
23	Homer Simpson
24	Donald Sutherland
25	Meg Tilly
26	Shania Twain

BODY IN TROUBLE

Some phrases for bodily flaws

cockeyes
knock-knees
cauliflower ear
pigeon chest
widow's peak
flat-feet
inverted nipples
hammer-toes
thunder thighs
bingo wings
snub nose
redeye
beer belly

stubby fingers
barrel chest
bow legs
glass chin
banana breasts
turkey neck
withered arm
hare-lip
monobrow
club foot
pigeon toes
love handles
crow's-feet

A list of the correct Elizabethan verbs for the serving and carving of meats and poultry, taken

from *The Accomplisht Cook* by 17th-century food writer Robert May

Lift that Swan
Rear that Goose
Dismember that Hern
Unbrace that Mallard

Unlace that Coney
Allay that Pheasant
Wing that Partridge
Display that Quail
Unjoynt that Bittern
Unlatch that Curlew
Break that Egript
Thigh that Woodcock

First names that are (or have previously been) used for both boys and girls

Alex	Kerry
Ali	Kim
Angel	Laurie/Lori
Aubrey	Lee
Bernie	Leslie/Lesley
Beverley	Lindsay
Billy/Billie	Lorne
Cameron	Lou
Carol	Lyn/Lynn
Cary/Carrie	Mandy
Charlie	Marion
Chris	Marty/Marti
Courtney	Mel
Dale	Meredith
Dana	Morgan
Darcy	Nat
Dee	Nicky/Nicki
Drew	Noel
Eddi, Eddie	Pat
Esmé	Perry
Francis/Frances	Ray/Rae
Gene/Jean	Robin/Robyn
Gerry	Sam
Glen/Glenn	Sandy
Gus	Sasha
Hayden	Sharon
Hilary	Shirley
Hyacinth	Sid/Cyd
Jan	Taylor
Jo	Tony/Toni
Jocelyn	Tracy
Jordan	Valentine
Jules	Vivian
Kelly	Winifred
Kelsey	

BOTH SIDES NOW

HEY GOOD LOOKIN'

A baker's dozen of beauty standards

1 Familiarity Looks – those which set off that pleasant sensation derived from perusing an old friend or colleague of whom, however unattractive or unconventional, one has grown fond.

2 Super Looks – bland, perfectly symmetrical, mathematically provable good looks which are instantly forgettable. See: any clothes model.

3 Beholder Looks – having one of those features (snub nose, eagle nose, jutting chin) or looks (china doll, fop, tomboy, goth) which do it for 5% of us but not for the rest.

4 Teller Looks – mild but unthreatening good looks, a few degrees above 'plain', of the sort required by law in order for you to work in a bank.

5 Ooh! Oh! Looks – remarkable first impressions which fade fast. 'Ooh, he's good looking! Oh, actually, now I look closer, eurgh!'

6 Blind Looks – those which seem only to appeal to a loved one. The way a mother in denial feels about a child with an especially interesting physiognomy.

7 Character Looks – otherwise known as 'jolie laide', ie pretty/ugly. Unusual looks which are somehow at once both attractive and unattractive.

8 Fleeting Looks – those which are purely down to age and sadly won't last.

9 Fox Looks – having 'fox looks' means to be basically conventionally unattractive, but still to cause sensations of lust in the majority of onlookers.

10 Kind Looks – those belonging to someone who, though short of sexual charisma, you instantly want to befriend and settle down with.

11 Transplant Looks – applied to people who are physically unattractive, but have other things going for them such as fame or money. Think inbred heiresses, fat comedians and gangsta rappers.

12 Glow-in-the-Dark Looks – some people's faces just *change* in the darkness during intimacy, making them radiantly beautiful (even if they aren't to begin with), as if lit from within. There's no telling who will have this capacity and who won't. It seems to be like tongue-rolling or finger-clicking – you can do it or you just can't.

13 Side-on Looks – that phenomenon by which someone can be very handsome in profile but somewhat frightening face-on. Side-on looks are often encountered on train journeys, when you realize that the apparently dishy character you have been sneaking looks at across the aisle is not all they seem.

SPIN NO MORE

Twenty-five unlikely numbers on the list of 'lyrically questionable' (ie temporarily banned) songs allegedly made by radio station giant Clear Channel following terrorist attacks in the USA

1	Bangles	'Walk Like an Egyptian'
2	Nena	'99 Red Balloons'
3	The Beatles	'Obla Di, Obla Da'
4	Jimi Hendrix	'Hey Joe'
5	Jackson Browne	'Doctor My Eyes'
6	U2	'Sunday Bloody Sunday'
7	Queen	'Killer Queen'
8	Pink Floyd	'Mother'
9	John Parr	'St Elmo's Fire'
10	Steam	'Na Na Na Na Hey Hey'
11	The Drifters	'On Broadway'
12	Peter and Gordon	'I Go To Pieces'
13	The Zombies	'She's Not There'
14	Elton John	'Rocket Man'
15	Louis Armstrong	'What A Wonderful World'
16	Peter Paul and Mary	'Blowin' in the Wind'
17	The Rolling Stones	'Ruby Tuesday'
18	Three Degrees	'When Will I See You Again'
19	Martha and the Vandellas	'Dancing in the Street'
20	The Hollies	'He Ain't Heavy, He's My Brother'
21	Don McLean	'American Pie'
22	Buddy Holly and the Crickets	'That'll Be the Day'
23	Bobby Darin	'Mack the Knife'
24	Creedence Clearwater Revival	'Travelin' Band'
25	Chi-Lites	'Have You Seen Her'

BACK OF BEYOND

Most languages and cultures have sayings for the back of beyond. In Australia, they sometimes say someone lives **way out Woop Woop**, or **beyond the black stump** (referring to a burnt tree trunk in deepest Queensland once supposedly used as a marker by surveyors and mappers); they also refer to **beyond the back blocks** and **beyond the wallaby**.

Even the Bible indulged in this suspicion of the faraway, with Cain being banished to the scary-sounding **land of Nod on the East of Eden**. In Scotland, sometimes **Inversneck** is used (an occasional nickname for Inverness or any distant rural town of the north.) **Boondocks**, used by Americans, was a term US soldiers picked up in the Philippines, from the local word for mountains.

In the fine book *Your Mother's Tongue*, which is all about swearing and slang in European languages, Stephen Burgen collects some more of these, some of which were new to me: the French say **en plein bled** (in the open desert), or **Tripatouille-les-Oies**, a mock town name which means 'the place where they tamper with geese'. Germans say 'where the fox and hare say goodnight to each other' or just 'where the foxes bid one another goodnight'. The Hispanics tend to be as religious and surreal on this as on everything. In Spain, they talk of 'where Christ dropped his lighter'. In Portugal, it is 'where Judas lost his boots' while in Cuba, curiously, they talk of the back of beyond as 'where God painted St Peter and didn't get round to the bicycle'.

IF MARVIN HAD LIVED

How Mr Gaye might have altered his repertoire for the older generation

I Heard It Through The Grapevine …
Mrs Jones had a hysterectomy.

What's Going On …
with all those beeping noises on the bus?

Sexual Healing …
when are they going to sort my prostate out?

Let's Get It On …
World Championship Bowls on BBC2

Mercy, Mercy Me …
the price of peppermints these days!

Wherever I Lay My Hat …
I always forget where I put it.

TWO KNOTWORDS

hellspawn – are you a pawn of Hell or the spawn of Hell?

cowslip – are you the lip of a cow or a slip for a cow?

HAPPY FAMILIES

The tradesmen whose families appear in the children's card game (they have varied over time, but these seem to be the most common)

Mr **Sole** the FISHMONGER
Mr **Bun** the BAKER
Mr **Stamp** the POSTMAN
Mr **Bud** the FLORIST
Mr **Field** the FARMER
Mr **Bacon** the BUTCHER
Mr **Constable** the POLICEMAN
Mr **Green** the GROCER
Mr **Chalk** the TEACHER

ELFIN CREED

The five varieties of the fairy family in Cornwall*

The Small People
The Spriggans
Piskies or Pigseys
The Buccas, Bockles or Knockers
The Browneys

* According to *Popular Romances of the West of England* by Robert Hunt (3rd ed., 1903)

A list of rules for square dancing from c.1875

1 Admittance 50 cents, refreshments included.

2 The music is to consist of a fiddle, a pip or tabor, a hurdy gurdy. No chorus is to be sung until after dancing is over.

3 No lady to dance in black stockings – nor must she have her elbows bare.

4 Every lady to come with a clean handkerchief with her name marked.

5 To prevent spitting, no gentleman to chew tobacco or smoke.

6 No gentleman to dance in a great coat unless his under one torn.

7 No lady to dress her hair in tallow candle, nor must she have a bunch of hair sticking up, top of her head.

8 Leather small clothes except newly washed are forbidden, as they might soil the ladies gowns – and to prevent the tearing of the planking, no gentleman to dance in nailed shoes or boots.

9 No whispering to be allowed – if anyone shall be found to make insidious remarks about anyone's dancing, he or she shall be put out of the room.

10 No scissors or gimlets are to be brought either by ladies or gentlemen unless their pockets are whole.

11 No gentleman to appear with a cravat that has been worn more than a week or a fortnight.

12 Long beards are forbidden, as they would be very disagreeable, if a gentleman should happen to put his cheek beside a lady's.

13 Those ladies who have not white stockings and black morocco shoes will not be admitted under any pretence whatever. Two old ladies will be provided to examine all who enter.

14 No lady must appear with a veil on even if it be turned aside, as the gentlemen will not have an opportunity of looking at their faces distinct.

15 No gentleman must squeeze his partner's hand, nor look earnestly upon her; and furthermore he must not pick up her handkerchief, provided it were to fall. The first denotes he loves her, the second he wishes to kiss her and the last that she makes a sigh for both.

16 For distinction sake, the master of ceremonies is to wear a red coat, buff small clothes, black stockings, green shoes and a furtout. The word of command is, tumble up ladies.

BUT ELIZABETH!

The ten most 'sensual' girls' names

Hope **4**
Beth **5**
6 Charlotte
7 Kitty
Colleen **3**
8 Ceri
Erin **2**
9 Melanie
Madeleine **1**
10 Samantha

SEEING DOUBLE
Thirteen famous people with a lesser-known twin

1. Kiefer Sutherland
2. Kim Deal
3. Jerry Hall
4. St Benedict
5. Jim Thorpe
6. Alanis Morissette
7. Kofi Annan
8. Montgomery Clift
9. Mario Andretti
10. Curtis Strange
11. Henry Cooper
12. Joseph Fiennes
13. Isabella Rossellini

The ten most dangerous places to be a journalist in 2003

5 Chechnya
4 Afghanistan
3 Vietnam
2 Cuba
1 Iraq

HACK ATTACK

6 The West Bank and Gaza
7 Eritrea
8 Togo
9 Colombia
10 Belarus

ARE YOU DANCIN'?

Fad dances and dance crazes since the 50s

The Twist

After Chubby Checker recorded Hank Ballard's song 'The Twist' in 1959, the fad went into overdrive. The arm-swinging, hip-shaking dance was fast and sexy (leading it to be banned in Buffalo, NY, and at some religious universities.) It originated in the South as an African-American dance band boogie, but was popularized in the clubs of Philadelphia after Checker's hit. It particularly took off in London, with celebrities and even royalty taking to the dance floors of the capital's nightspots and shaking their things.

Boogaloo

A jerky mamba-based dance popular in the early 60s, with improvised, fast movements from the hips. Favoured by the fast-stepping Godfather of Soul James Brown, probably its finest exponent.

The Frug

A slow twist developed from a dance called **the Chicken**. Mainly consists of side-to-side hip shaking. It was the stepping stone between The Twist and the many, similar line dances (sometimes just the arm movements changed) of the early 60s dance craze such as The Grunt, The Mashed Potato, The Swim, The Madison, The Pony, The Hully Gully (a medley of several other dances shouted by a caller), The Monkey, The Dog, Walking the Dog, The Watusi, The Jerk, The Wabble, The Mess Around, The Bird, The Hitchhike, The Stroll, The Monster Mash, The Surf and The Locomotion. These dances were often made up to sell records of the same name. Teen magazines enthusiastically printed the steps to new dances and they were featured on the hugely popular television show *American Bandstand*. The teenagers who regularly danced on shows became celebrities in their own right.

The Freddie

Freddie Garrity, lead singer of Freddie and the Dreamers, had a novel way of dancing. He kicked each leg up outwards and backwards in turn, the result being somewhat comical. This was the heyday of the fad dance as well as the post-Beatles 'British Invasion' and he was persuaded to add vocals to a novelty record called 'Do The Freddie'. Chubby Checker recorded a song of the same name which suggested duck wing flapping was the proper accompaniment to the back-kicking.

The Hustle

A mixture of swing and Latin dance, this term (originally a late 60s line dance) was eventually settled on for the main couples' dance of the disco era. Partners would make extravagant mirror or counter moves while circling their partner and moving to a constant beat. Van McCoy's ecstatic 1975 hit 'The Hustle' was the standard number. The dance was made even more popular by the film *Saturday Night Fever*.

Headbanging

A dance of sorts originating in the late 60s and popular throughout the 70s and 80s with long-haired young men with a penchant for loud rock music. The head is dipped forward and jerked up and down to the song's beat. The hair is tossed over and back. The dance is often enhanced by the addition of an 'air guitar'.

The Funky Chicken

Rufus Thomas had already 'walked the dog' and in 1969 he recorded 'Do The Funky Chicken', a dance track with silly moves which became popular with children and adults and is still commonly performed at weddings and parties. It consists of various chicken style movements (bobbing, flapping, kicking the feet). For a while, American football players took to dancing like this when they scored a touchdown.

Northern Soul style

In 70s England there was a craze for rare soul cuts from 60s America. This was soon dubbed 'northern soul' since it was especially prevalent in northern England, and the major venues were the Twisted Wheel in Manchester, the Golden Torch in Stoke and the famed Wigan Casino. The musical movement was all about athletic dancing, vigorous spinning and highkicks, with pep pills ensuring dancers could keep at it all night 'out on the floor'.

Pogoing

Hardly a dance, more a cathartic fit of jumping up and down and head-butting the air. It became the standard dance at punk rock gigs (and school discos) in the mid-to-late 70s.

Breakdance

The origins of breakdancing are said to be in gang rituals of the 70s Bronx. Gang leaders would square up to one another and perform a cross between dance and martial arts. This was as influenced by the Brazilian martial art of capoeira as by James Brown's boogaloo. They would sometimes carry a stick or knife, but the two would never touch and disagreements could therefore be solved without violence. The winner was the one who could pull the most audacious moves. The acrobatic moves were perfected in the early 80s by crews of hip-hop loving 'b-boys' who would lay out mats and perform spins, twists and body-slams. **Body-popping** was the mime-like offshoot fad from breakdance, where dancers would move rhythmically or mechanically as if they were robots or puppets.

The Moonwalk

At the show to celebrate Motown's 25th anniversary, Michael Jackson pulled off this glitzy and impressive disco step during a rendition of his classic late disco number 'Billie Jean'. It is an illusion and needs to be obsessively practised. The dancer appears to be walking backwards without lifting his feet.

Shambling

A moody and short-lived British dance craze associated with 80s indie rock music. Dancers (usually pale young men) would rock slowly from foot to foot, first extending one way in front of the other, then pulling it as far back as possible. If possible, the hair was shaken around a little. The music would be supplied by bands such as The Jesus and Mary Chain and The Wedding Present.

Vogue

Originating in France, this minimalist dance became a craze in New York, particularly in gay clubs, in 1990. The dancers start and stop, throwing poses similar to those used by catwalk models. It was popularized by Madonna's hit song 'Vogue' and its accompanying video.

Lambada

A merengue-style Brazilian dance which became a club fad in 1989. Intimate and sensual, the dancers writhe up and down with their bodies very close. The dance was partly spread by a catchy song of the same name by French group Kaoma which was a hit all over Europe. The craze spread to America, where a 1990 Joel Silberg film called *Lambada* failed to propel the dance beyond anything more than a craze.

Moshing

The 'moshpit' is the area nearest the stage at a punk rock or heavy metal concert. Young men perform this ritual dance of sorts by body-slamming, stumbling and tumbling over each other. Not generally popular with girls or anyone over 25.

Macarena

'Macarena' was a poppy flamenco hit for Spanish duo Los Del Rio, first released in 1993. It tells of a hedonistic girl who entertains her boyfriend's mates while he is off joining up with the army. The accompanying dance became a craze all over the world. It is basically a hand jive with some rump-shaking and clapping. Other post-60s hits which have had popular dance moves include the Gap Band's 'Oops Upside Your Head' (dancers sitting and pretending to row a boat), 'Saturday Night' by Whigfield (hand jive and hopping) and the Village People's 'YMCA' (throwing shapes like the letters).

Freak Dancing

A bump and grind rhythmic style of dancing which appeared in 2001, popularized by rap and R&B music videos. It consists of a mixture between the West Indian limbo-like skanking and bogling and aspects of erotic dancing. Dancers go low and shake their bottoms in a titillating manner. They grind up and down, sometimes against each other. American schools started banning it the same way they banned The Twist over 40 years before.

Clown Dancing

A dance craze from LA, clowning sees children and teenagers, mainly from African-American and Hispanic communties, paint themselves with clown make-up and compete, breakdancing style, with rival gangs. Many of the participants take part to escape from the pressures of teen gang warfare. The dances are a cross between hip-hop styles, bump and grind and African tribal dances. A faster, more boisterous, performance based version is known as krumping.

10,000 MANIA

Ten facts about the number 10,000

1 The 10,000th prime number is **104,279**.

2 The band 10,000 Maniacs adapted their name from the B-movie *Two Thousand Maniacs!*. Their best album is *The Wishing Chair*, though *In My Tribe* is good too. And *Blind Man's Zoo* contains 'Headstrong', perhaps their best song.

3 10,000 is the name of both a card game and a dice game.

4 Alaska contains the volcanic area known as the Valley of 10,000 Smokes while, down South, Florida has the 10,000 Islands, mangrove islets in the Everglades region.

5 'One picture is worth ten thousand words' wrote mathematician Frederick Barnard in the 20s (paraphrasing a Chinese proverb – the Chinese are keen on images including the number 10,000). The exchange rate of this expression has decreased by 90% over time.

6 The Italian film *10,000 Dollars Blood Money* is set in America. The American film *Ten Thousand Bedrooms* is set in Italy.

7 £10,000 is often quoted as the average student debt of a British graduate.

8 In 'A Hard Rain's A-Gonna Fall', **Bob Dylan** 'saw ten thousand talkers whose tongues were all broken' and much later he recorded a song called '10,000 Men'. It is a popular number with songwriters: there are also songs called 'Ten Thousand Cattle' (Slim Critchlow), 'Ten Thousand Sheep' (Sorma), '10,000 Dogs' (Jacques) and '10,000 Horses' (Candlebox). French noodleurs Air made a record called *10,000 Hz Legend*.

9 Basketball star Kobe Bryant, at the age of 24 years and 193 days, became the youngest player to reach 10,000 career points in March 2003.

10 The Danish scientist and philosopher **Piet Hein**, known for many inventions and theories, also wrote about 10,000 short, pithy poems, which he called 'grooks'.

Those teenage Potter sagas, coming soon

1 *Harry Potter and the Rumbles of Puberty*

2 *Harry Potter and the Popbabe Poster*

3 *Harry Potter and the Faceful of Pimples*

4 *Harry Potter and the Screech of Nu-metal*

5 *Harry Potter and the Slamming of Doors*

6 *Harry Potter and the Fat Stash of Porn*

7 *Harry Potter and the Purchase of Contact Lenses*

8 *Harry Potter and the Sneer of Disdain*

9 *Harry Potter and the Litre of Cider*

10 *Harry Potter and the Diary of Angst*

HARRY POTTER — THE WONDER YEARS

A list of homosexual similes — some of these are superbly inventive, while others appear to make little sense

as gay as cheese
as gay as the day is long
as gay as an arrow
as gay as Popeye
as gay as a pair of white shorts
as gay as a pink hairnet
as gay as peacocks
as gay as a daisy
as gay as pink ink
as gay as a goose
as gay as a house
as gay as crêpe paper
as gay as a window (or windmill?)
as gay as a seal (France)
as gay as a little dog
as gay as a daffodil
as gay as a Care Bear
as gay as birthday cakes
as gay as the Queen of Scots
as gay as a taffeta chandelier
as gay as a lame pigeon (Spain)
as gay as a red squirrel
as camp as knickers
as camp as a row of tents
as camp as a two bob clock
as camp as Christmas (or a Christmas stocking/Number One/Island)
as camp as Kylie
as camp as Dale Winton at a Village People convention
as camp as a drag queen's wardrobe
as camp as the Liberty Bell
as camp as Butlins®
as camp as solid gold bath taps
as camp as brunch
as camp as a tent factory
as camp as tinned ham
as camp as a pair of tights
as camp as a row of mauve Vespas®
as camp as a cakestand
as camp as a fondant fancy
as camp as a bottle of coffee and chicory essence
as camp as a vicar's bicycle
as camp as a case of Babycham®

CARRY ON CAMPING

A SPELL ON YOU

On Walter, Chicago and Britney ...

There are over 70 variants of the spelling of the surname of the Elizabethan adventurer Sir Walter Raleigh, including Rawleyghe, Raylygh, Rawley, Wrawly and so on. It seems to have been pronounced to rhyme with Dolly rather than Sally. Walter himself generally used Ralegh, which historians are latterly coming round to using. In legend, if not in truth, he is also said to have given his name, indirectly, to the uncommon term 'switter-swatter' meaning hanky-panky. It is said that the knight was pleasuring a young lady against a tree when, in her rising passion, she began to repeat the words 'Sweet Sir Walter!' with increasing speed until they became 'switter-swatter, switter-swatter'.

When it comes to the spelling of the place name Chicago, there may be over a hundred early variants (everything from Checagou to Stktschagko). Because the name was based on a hard-to-pronounce Algonquin word meaning 'place of onions', there were many French and English attempts at phonetic spelling, leading to all those unusual variants.

One of the most misspelled names of recent years is that of Miss Britney Spears. A list compiled by the search engine Google® shows the many versions – almost 600 – of the vedette's first name typed in by at least two searchers over a period of just three months in 2001. The most common mistakes were to spell her first name as Brittany, Brittney or Britany, but butterfingers got as far away as Prietny, Brither and Bruteny. Presumably with the added mistaken versions of her surname, the permutations of errors are close to endless.

SET OUT YOUR STALL

Some fruit- and veg-related sayings

1. cool as a cucumber
2. to not have a bean
3. couch potato (also now 'mouse potato')
4. to dangle a carrot
5. like peas in a pod
6. cauliflower ear (a sports injury)
7. to know your onions
8. face as red as a beetroot
9. knitting lentils (aka 'knitting yoghurt', living an 'alternative' lifestyle)
10. mushroom cloud
11. to be a total cabbage (to do nothing, aka 'to veg out')
12. pea-souper (a thick fog)

1. to not give a fig
2. go nuts
3. play gooseberry (to be an unwelcome third party)
4. to cherry pick (to select the best bits)
5. to (talk) rhubarb (to pretend to talk in the background of a film or play)
6. plum position
7. to blow a raspberry (aka 'Bronx cheer')
8. sour grapes
9. to play second banana (to be a sidekick or deputy)
10. the apple of one's eye
11. to be a lemon (a disappointment or sham)
12. peaches and cream (a certain complexion)

A list of boys' nicknames I remember from c.1981 in my home town of St Andrews. Nicknames were perhaps particularly prevalent in Scotland due to the overuse of simple biblical boys' names (John, David, Mark, etc).

BOYS WILL BE ... ?

False Arms	Bunny
Specs	Snappo
Flash	Lugs
Lumpy	Flea
Toad	Dobird
Prince	Gnome
Sparry	Tento
Monkey	Beans
Baffies	Plum
Slim	Dozy
Worzel	Tosh
Sticky	Dochick
Chuff	Noz
Pea	Bummer
Froggy	Tank
Log	Dinger
Bun	Craw
Werts	Tooly
Rabbit	

FIZZ PUFF

Twelve slogans for Coca-Cola®

1 The Great National Temperance Beverage

2 The Only Thing Like Coca-Cola Is Coca-Cola Itself

3 Thirst Knows No Season

4 The Pause That Refreshes

5 Ice Cold Sunshine

6 Things Go Better With Coke

7 It's The Real Thing

8 Whoever You Are, Whatever You Do, Wherever You May Be, When You Think of Refreshment Think of Ice Cold Coca-Cola

9 Where There's Coke There's Hospitality

10 Coke Adds Life

11 Have A Coke And A Smile

12 Coke Is It!

Perhaps the most famous Coke 'slogan' of all, 'I'd Like To Buy The World A Coke', wasn't actually an official slogan at all. It was an advert, part of the 'It's the Real Thing' promotional campaign, but it proved so popular that Coke bosses now consider it to be an honorary slogan.

FOR THOSE ABOUT TO RALPH, WE SALUTE YOU

live salamanders	**1**
crayons	**2**
raw eggs	**3**
5g piece of limestone	**4**
cat food	**5**
roast guinea pigs	**6**
peppermint schnapps	**7**
kimchi	**8**
tobacco juice	**9**
shaving cream	**10**
celery	**11**
bongwater	**12**
raw calf's fry	**13**
kangaroo on a stick	**14**
chocolate liver sushi	**15**
shit sandwich	**16**
octopus	**17**
pig brains	**18**
cobra's blood	**19**
lentils	**20**
pheasant sweat	**21**

Twenty-one answers from heavy rock fans to 'the worst thing I ever tasted'

327

THE PEOPLE SPEAK

The letter pages of teletext are a breeding ground for hangers, floggers, transport bores and political extremists. It's a good place to go looking for tired and abused language. Here is a collection of buzz phrases and hollow clichés gathered during only two visits to these text pages

1. truly remarkable
2. millions like him
3. mortgaging our children's future
4. the ramblings of hypocrites
5. carry on the good work
6. the sudden realization
7. I was horrified recently
8. willing to proclaim
9. the majority of the people
10. costing the taxpayer money
11. British legal history
12. rightly concerned
13. stop this nonsense now
14. in jeopardy
15. and all her ilk
16. here we go again
17. solve this once and for all
18. so-called do-gooders
19. we don't need reminding
20. utterly sick and tired
21. wreak havoc
22. the _____ brigade
23. blood price
24. let us not forget
25. people of my age
26. whose only crime was to
27. bleeding heart liberals
28. hands up all those who

GOOD EVENING MISS MOONLUST

The literal translations
of some Finnish surnames

Alkio	Mrs Embryo
Autiosaari	Mr Deserted Island
Eväs	Mr Picnic Lunch
Haveri	Mr Shipwreck
Hiekkalinna	Mr Sandcastle
Ihanaranta	Mr Lovely Beach
Inha	Mr Disgusting
Kanala	Mrs Hen House
Kurasto	Mr Mud Collection
Lastuvuori	Mr Chip Mountain
Lehtiö	Ms Note-pad
Leini	Mr Fibrositis
Liete	Mrs Liquid Manure
Loukko	Mr Hellhole
Purkantie	Ms Bubblegum's Road
Raaste	Mrs Grated Vegetable
Rantatulkkila	Mr Beach Interpreter
Rinta-Runsala	Mrs Breast-Ample
Rokka	Mr Pea Soup
Teini	Ms Teenager
Tikkari	Mr Lollipop
Vahalinna	Mr Wax Castle
Valtimo	Mrs Artery

COLIN ROCKS

Sixteen bands which made it despite having a member named Colin

The Zombies **1**

Black **2**

Gillan **3**

Mull Historical Society **4**

Camel **5**

Manfred Mann **6**

Men at Work **7**

Idlewild **8**

9 Magnum

10 Wire

11 Honeybus

12 XTC

13 The Foundations

14 Mungo Jerry

15 Radiohead

16 The Bee Gees (their early drummer)

BAGPUSS AND BENN

A favourite programme for small children, **Bagpuss** was made by Oliver Postgate and Peter Firmin in 1974. A girl named Emily kept a shop for fixing lost objects in the hope of returning them to their owners. When a new object appeared, a spell would bring to life the saggy cloth cat and his puppet friends including Madeleine the rag doll, Professor Yaffle the woodpecker bookend, Gabriel the musical toad and the mice on their mouse-organ. Adventures would ensue. Only 13 episodes of **Bagpuss** were ever made. They were ...

'Ship in a Bottle'	'The Mouse Mill'
'The Owls of Athens'	'The Giant'
'The Frog Princess'	'Old Man's Beard'
'The Ballet Shoe'	'The Fiddle'
'The Hamish'	'Flying'
'The Wise Man'	'Uncle Feedle'
'The Elephant'	

Three years earlier, David McKee helped turn his **Mr Benn** story-book creation into another set of often-repeated 13 episodes. Mr Benn was a mild-mannered everyman who had a penchant for fancy dress. He would visit the costume shop where the mysterious shopkeeper would help him choose an outfit. A magic door in the changing room would lead him into a world of adventure linked with his clothing. The costumes selected by the magic shopkeeper for Mr Benn were ...

1	Red Knight	**12**	balloonist
2	clown	**13**	magic carpet rider
3	caveman	**14**	convict (this original book plot was thought unfit for kids' TV)
4	hunter		
5	wizard		
6	cowboy	**15**	gladiator (this in a much later book-only adventure)
7	spaceman		
8	diver		
9	cook		
10	zoo keeper		
11	pirate		

LUCKY LUCKY

Seven things that have stopped a bullet

A book that wasn't the Bible: during an assault on Montauban during World War I, a British sergeant reported that 'two bullets had gone through my metal shaving mirror, through my pocket book case, and had nosed their way into a book I was carrying.'

Breast implants: in 2002 it was reported that a Brazilian woman caught in crossfire during a police drugs operation was shot in the chest, but was saved when the bullet was slowed down by the silicone implant in her breast.

A mobile phone: three men were transporting the takings from a supermarket in Nagoya to a safe when they were robbed by an elderly Korean man, who fired shots when they gave chase. Apparently, one of the men was saved when the bullet went through a pad in his pocket and was stopped by his mobile phone.

A policeman's badge: apparently, a motorcycle cop in Santiago, Chile, was shot in the chest while chasing jewel thieves. Thankfully, the bullet hit his metal badge, and though the force knocked him over, he suffered only bruising.

Body fat: also in Santiago, a 33-year-old bus driver was reportedly shot while attempting to stop a man who was robbing some passengers. The driver managed to climb on top of the robber and subdue him, but not before he had been shot. However, the driver was so overweight that the bullet lodged in his body fat and did little lasting damage.

A diary: Solon Blaisdell received a gunshot wound during a battle in the American Civil War. A diary in his coat pocket saved him. Thereafter, he still used the diary, carefully writing round the hole left by the bullet.

A bra: a woman in Michigan City, Indiana, supposedly went to hospital after some shots were fired into her home from a car. It transpired that her bra elastic had saved her from more serious injury after it stopped a bullet fragment piercing her side.

The only ten post-World War II Scottish Cup football finals without an appearance from either of the dominant forces of the two 'Old Firm' Glasgow teams, Celtic or Rangers

OLD FIRM OFF DAYS

1947
Aberdeen beat Hibs

1952
Motherwell beat Dundee

1957
Falkirk beat Kilmarnock

1958
Clyde beat Hibs

1959
St Mirren beat Aberdeen

1968
Dunfermline beat Hearts

1986
Aberdeen beat Hearts

1987
St Mirren beat Dundee United

1991
Motherwell beat Dundee United

1997
Kilmarnock beat Falkirk

REMEMBER REMEMBER

Twelve common mnemonics

1 Every Good Boy Deserves Favour/Fun (lines on a treble clef; the spaces are remembered as FACE)

2 She Makes Harry Eat Onions (for remembering the Great Lakes)

3 Tall Girls Can Flirt And Other Queer Things Can Do (Mohs' scale of hardness of minerals from talc to diamond)

4 Mites Grow Up, Tights Come Down (difference between stalagmites and stalactites)

5 Spring Forward, Fall Back (clocks change by one hour at beginning and end of summertime)

6 My Very Easy Method – Just Set Up Nine Planets (nine planets in order from the Sun)

7 Lucky Cows Drink Milk (larger Roman numerals in ascending order)

8 Richard Of York Gave Battle In Vain (colours of a rainbow in order)

9 Some Old Hippie Caught Another Hippie Tripping On Acid (for remembering trigonometry equations)

10 Divorced, Beheaded, Died, Divorced, Beheaded, Survived (six wives of Henry VIII)

11 Kings Play Cards On Fat Girls' Stomachs (kingdom, phylum, class, order, family, genus, species)

12 Beer before wine, everything fine, wine before beer, everything queer (debatable drinking rule)

I FOR AN EYE

Some versions of the Cockney alphabet, aka the taxi driver's alphabet. This comic list works on howling soundalike puns — A for 'orses = hay for horses, and so on

A for 'orses/Gardner
B for mutton/you go/slive in Canada
C for miles/yourself
D for dumb/payment
E for brick/knocks you out/either
F for vescent/ready
G for goodness sake/Indian
H for a scratch/a ride
I for an eye/the Engine
J for screepers/oranges
K for Sutherland/teria
L for leather/pixie
M for sis/a mock chop at the Deep Sea
N for Hoxha/a penny/ness
O for the wings of a dove/the rainbow
P for a whistle/relief
Q for the pictures/playing snooker with
R for Ashe/bitter
S for Rantzen/you
T for two/sharp
U for me/got to come
V for Las Vegas/pitch
W for a quid
X for breakfast
Y for heaven's sake/mistress
Z for the doctor

FRUIT SHOP

Some unusual fruit variety names

apple
American Mother
Peasgood's Nonsuch
Suntan
Cathead
Norfolk Beefing
Bess Pool
Foxwhelp
Brown Jersey
Sheep's Nose
Fillbarrel

blackcurrant
Malling Jet
Boskoop Giant
Ben Sarek
Wellington XXX

cherry
Stella
Van
Early Frogmore
Sweetheart
Bing
Staccato

gooseberry
Careless
Whitesmith
Leveller
Invicta
Hinnonmaki Red

grapefruit
Genetic Dwarf
Henderson Ruby
Brown Marsh
Rex Union

lemon
Frost Thornless Eureka
Dr Strong Lisbon
Pomona Sweet
Yen Ben

lime
Millsweet Sweet
Mary Ellen Sweet
Giant Key
Bearss
Miranda Mexican

melon
Collective Farm Woman
Amish
Hearts of Gold
Minnesota Midget
Cream of Saskatchewan
Georgia Rattlesnake
Sugar Baby

orange

Skaggs Bonanza
  Navel
Cutter Valencia
Rotuma Island
  Sweet
Madam Vinous
  Sweet
Cluster Navel
Moro Blood
Bouquet de Fleurs
  Sour

pear

Beth
Clapp's Favourite
Ovid
Vicar of Winkfield
Hendre Huffcap
Green Horse

plum

Czar
Oullin's Gage
Pershore Egg
Ontario
Warwickshire
  Drooper
Quetsche

raspberry

Zeva
Allgold
Leo
Lloyd George
Cascade Delight

redcurrant

Red Lake
Rovada
Junifer

rhubarb

Cawood Castle
Timperley Early
Hawke's
  Champagne
Egyptian Queen
Tottle's Improved

strawberry

Pantagruella
Sophie
Seascape
Hampshire Maid
Cambridge Vigour
Red Gauntlet
Sweet Charlie
Ovation

LET'S HEAR IT AGAIN FOR ...

Some famous stammerers

1	Moses	**17**	Vyacheslav Molotov
2	Aristotle	**18**	Samuel L Jackson
3	Demosthenes	**19**	Theodore Roosevelt
4	Virgil	**20**	Margaret Drabble
5	Aesop	**21**	Aneurin Bevan
6	Emperor Claudius	**22**	Marilyn Monroe
7	Sir Isaac Newton	**23**	Bruce Willis
8	Charles Lamb	**24**	James Earl Jones
9	W Somerset Maugham	**25**	Rowan Atkinson
10	Charles Darwin	**26**	Philip Larkin
11	Lewis Carroll	**27**	Gareth Gates
12	King Charles I	**28**	Porky Pig
13	King George VI	**29**	John Updike
14	Sir Winston Churchill	**30**	Carly Simon
15	Henry James	**31**	Tom Paulin
16	Vladimir Ilyich Lenin		

IRISH HEAVYWEIGHT RHYMING

The Irish poets Ciaran Carson and Paul Muldoon are both renowned for their very inventive use of rhyme. Here are some examples from each of them

Rhymes from *Opera Et Cetera* (Bloodaxe Books) by Ciaran Carson

1 AWOL/narwhal
2 syllabub/Beelzebub
3 La Cucuracha/Appalachia
4 boomeranged/meringue
5 low-key/synedoche
6 barricade/orangeade
7 Sherlock/Bartok
8 buttonhole/Charles de Gaulle
9 fingerbowl/rigmarole
10 kazoo/Belfast Zoo
11 Lima beans/hashasheens
12 herringbone/Twilight Zone

Rhymes from *Hay* (Faber & Faber) by Paul Muldoon

1 razzle-dazzle/Yggdrasill
2 clapiers/coolibars
3 Fionnuala/vanilla
4 psoriasis/Xerxes
5 Tuaregs/wether-tegs
6 Canada geese/trouser crease
7 Volvo/alfalfa
8 mittens/frost-bitten
9 cardboard box/Ultravox
10 Citadel/Dettol
11 cloudier/pig-gelder
12 Consulate/consolette

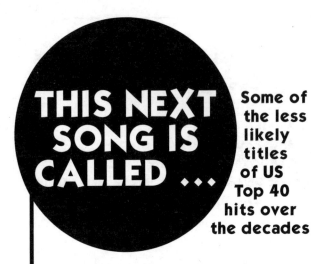

THIS NEXT SONG IS CALLED ... Some of the less likely titles of US Top 40 hits over the decades

'**1432 Franklin Pike Circle Hero**' (Bobby Russell, 1968)

'**Alvin's Harmonica**' (The Chipmunks, 1959)

'**Bobby Sox to Stockings**' (Frankie Avalon, 1959)

'**Calling Occupants of Interplanetary Craft (The Recognized Anthem of World Contact Day)**' (Carpenters, 1977)

'**Cheeseburger in Paradise**' (Jimmy Buffett, 1978)

'**The Days of Sand and Shovels**' (Bobby Vinton, 1969)

'**Don't Go Out Into the Rain (You're Going to Melt)**' (Herman's Hermits, 1967)

'**Don't Let the Rain Come Down (Crooked Little Man)**' (Serendipity Singers, 1964)

'**Dreams of the Everyday Housewife**' (Glen Campbell, 1968)

'**Epistle to Dippy**' (Donovan, 1967)

'**Fa All Y'All**' (Da Brat, 1994)

'**Glycerine**' (Bush, 1996)

'**Groovy Grubworm**' (Harlow Wilcox, 1969)

'**Hey, Bobba Needle**' (Chubby Checker, 1964)

'**Hey Little Cobra**' (The Rip Chords, 1964)

'**Hot Diggity (Dog Ziggity Boom)**' (Perry Como, 1956)

'**Jeremiah Peabody's Poly Unsaturated Quick Dissolving Fast Acting Pleasant Tasting Green and Purple Pills**' (Ray Stevens, 1961)

'**Like, Long Hair**' (Paul Revere & The Raiders, 1961)

'**Muskrat Love**' (Captain & Tennille, 1976)

'**New York Mining Disaster 1941**' (Bee Gees, 1967)

'**Pandora's Golden Heebie Jeebies**' (The Association, 1966)

'**Popeye the Hitchhiker**' (Chubby Checker, 1962)

'**She's a Bad Mama Jama (She's Built, She's Stacked)**' (Carl Carlton, 1981)

'**Sister Mary Elephant (Shudd-Up!)**' (Cheech & Chong, 1973)

'**Sweet Cream Ladies, Forward March**' (The Box Tops, 1969)

'**Thank You (Falettinme Be Mice Elf Agin)**' (Sly & the Family Stone, 1970)

'**(The System of) Doctor Tarr and Professor Fether**' (Alan Parsons Project, 1976)

'**thuggish ruggish-Bone**' (Bone Thugs-N-Harmony, 1994)

'**Velcro Fly**' (ZZ Top, 1986)

'**You Can't Roller Skate in a Buffalo Herd**' (Roger Miller, 1967)

'**Your Bulldog Drinks Champagne**' (Jim Stafford, 1975)

EINSTEIN'S ARTICHOKES

Ten real book titles name-dropping philosophers

1
Foucault's Pendulum

2
Voltaire's Coconuts

3
Voltaire's Bastards

4
Schopenhauer's Porcupines

5
Kant and the Platypus

6
Nietzsche and the Vicious Circle

7
Heidegger, Habermas and the Mobile Phone

8
Wittgenstein's Poker

9
Descartes's Ballet

10
Hegel's God

THEMATIC INDEX

THEMATIC INDEX

347

NAMES

351

352

354

Vitamin

Twenty words and phrases for good-bye
1. adieu
2. cheerio
3. in a bit
4. chin-chin
5. byee
6. later
7. mind how you go
8. hasta la vista
9. catch you later
10. ciao
11. toodle-pip
12. TTFN
13. baked potater
14. toodleloo
15. ta-ta
16. have a nice day
17. so long
18. take it easy
19. auf wiedersehen
20. farewell